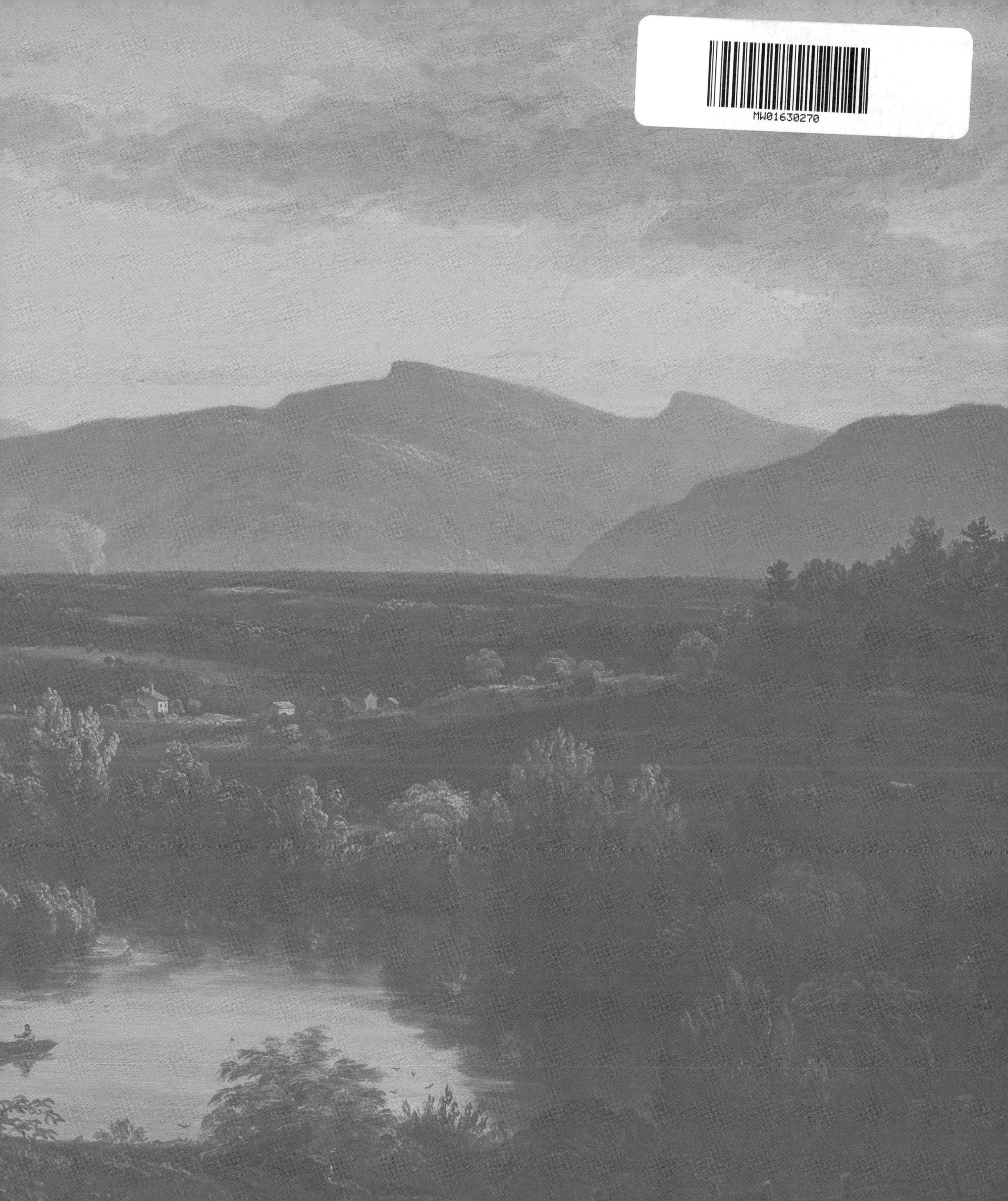

MW01630270

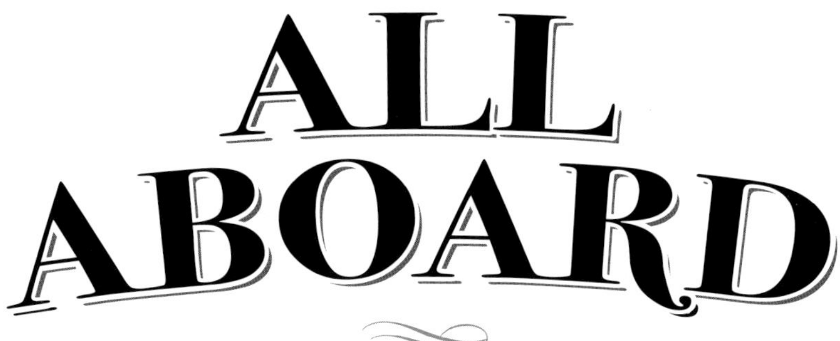

ALL ABOARD

THE RAILROAD IN AMERICAN ART 1840–1955

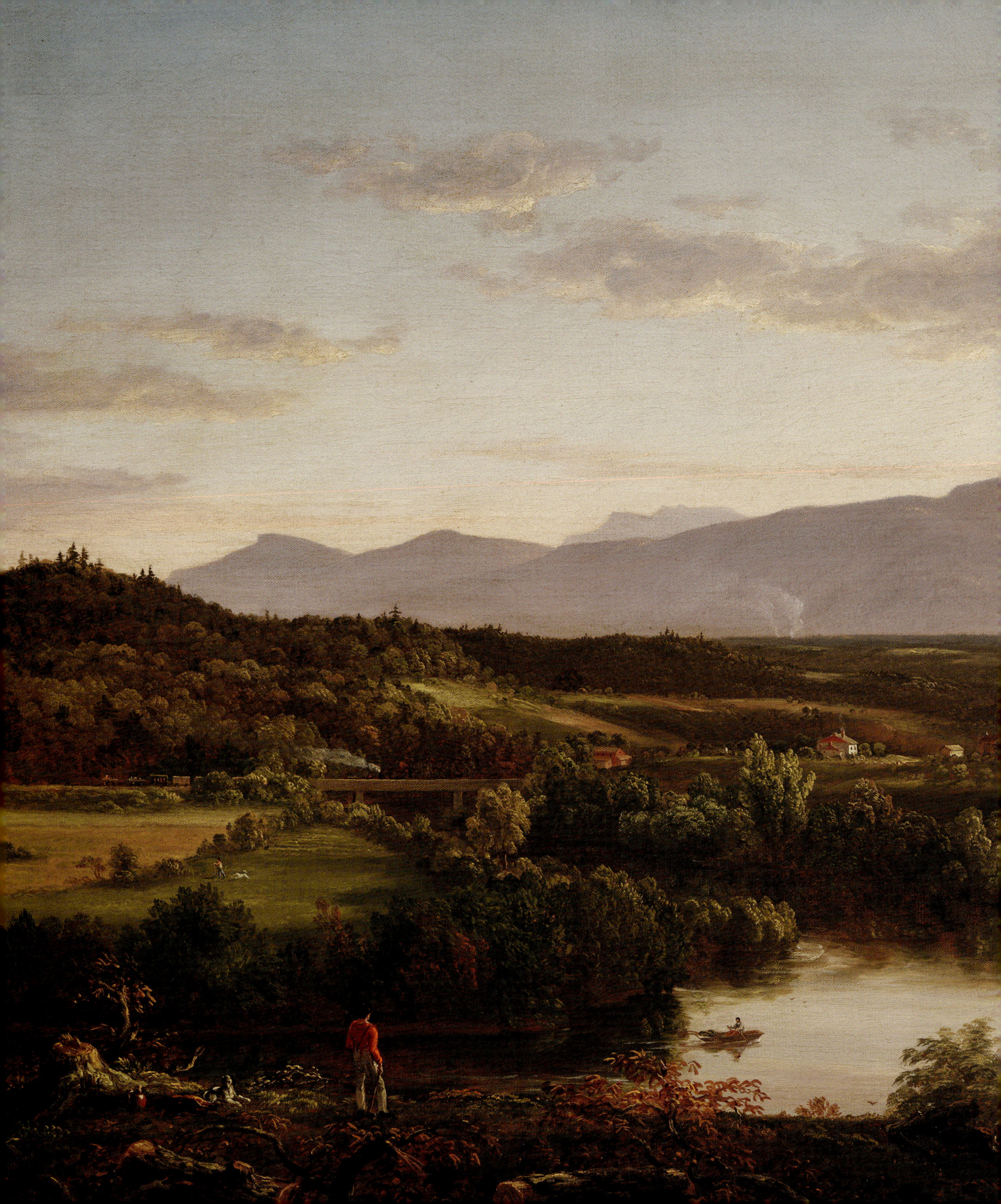

ALL ABOARD

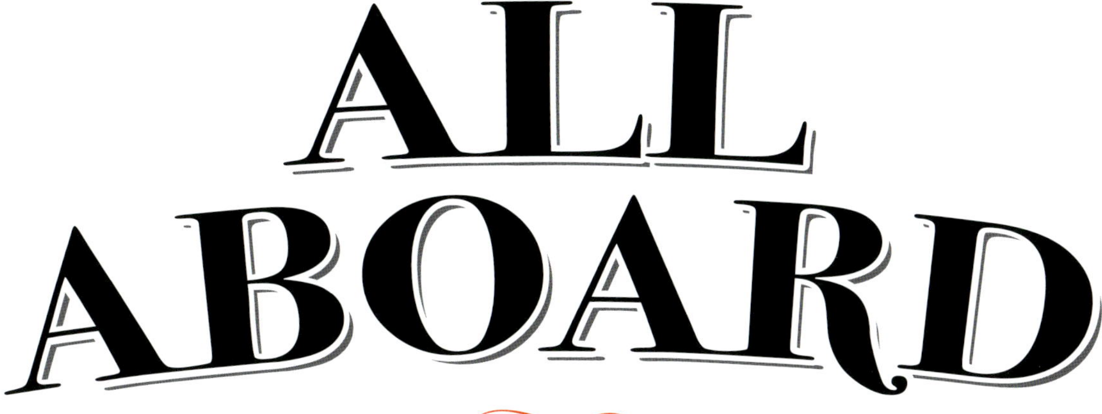

THE RAILROAD IN AMERICAN ART 1840-1955

Edited by Julie Pierotti

Contributions by Thomas Busciglio-Ritter, Ellen Daugherty, Thomas Denenberg, Julie Pierotti, and Kevin Sharp

Dixon Gallery and Gardens, Memphis
in association with D Giles Limited

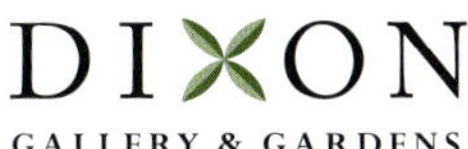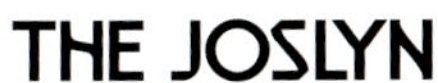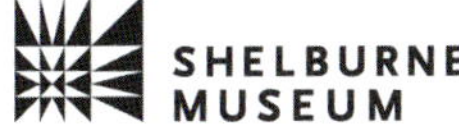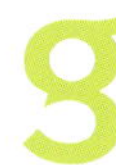

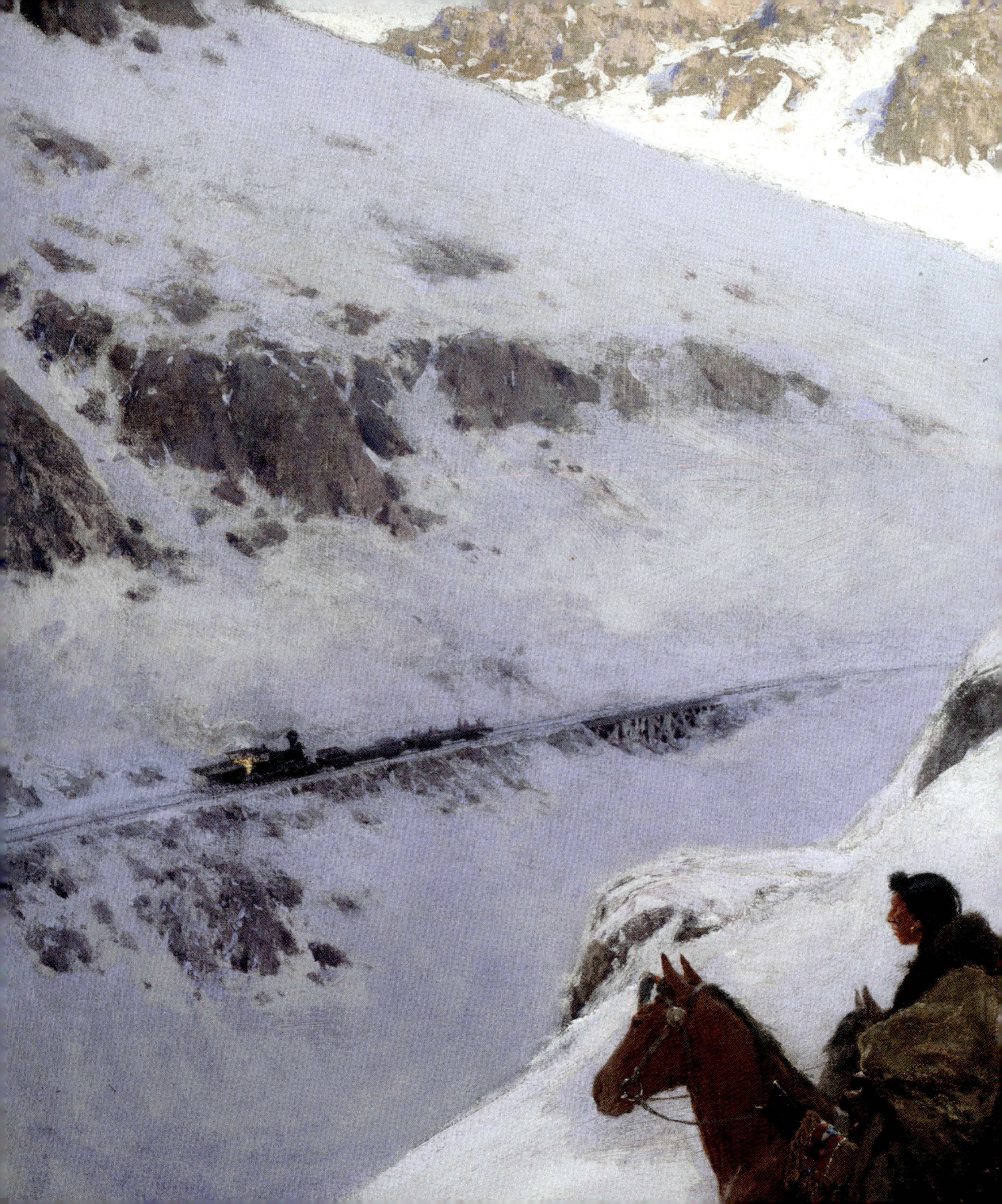

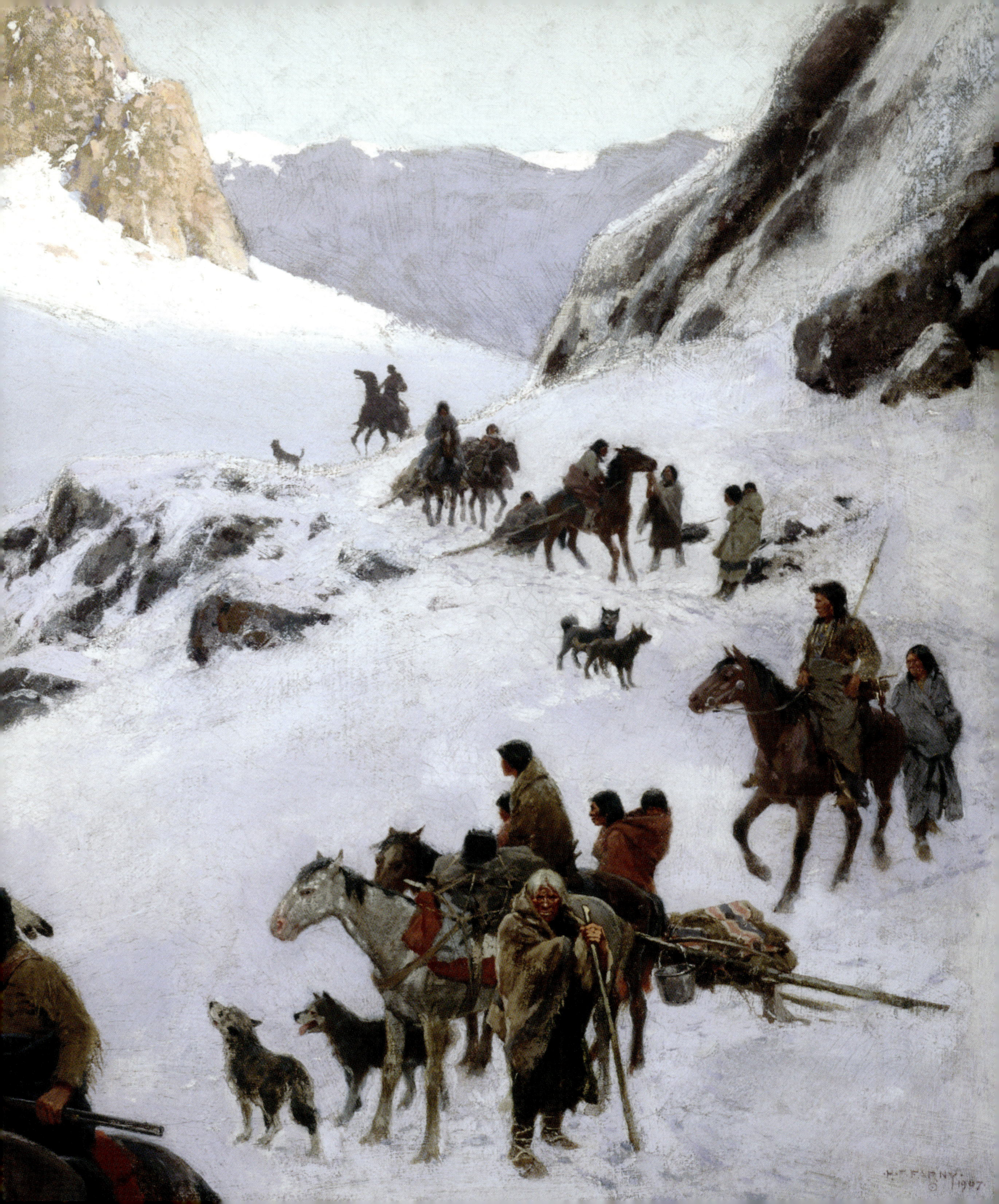

This publication was produced in conjunction with the exhibition *All Aboard: The Railroad in American Art, 1840-1955*, on view at Shelburne Museum, Vermont, from June 21, 2024, to October 20, 2024; Dixon Gallery and Gardens, Memphis, from November 2, 2024, to January 24, 2025; and Joslyn Art Museum, Omaha, from February 15, 2025, to May 4, 2025.

Dixon Gallery and Gardens
4339 Park Avenue
Memphis, Tennessee 38117
(901) 761-5250
www.dixon.org

Library of Congress Control Number: 2023921476

First published in 2024 by GILES
An imprint of D Giles Limited
66 High Street,
Lewes, BN7 1XG, UK
gilesltd.com

ISBN: 978-1-913875-60-2

For D Giles Limited:
Copy-edited and proofread by Jodi Simpson
Designed by Matthew Wilson
Produced by GILES, an imprint of D Giles Limited
Printed and bound in Europe

All measurements are in inches

Front cover: Cat. 22, p. 87: Thomas Hart Benton, *New Mexico (Landscape)* (detail), 1926; Denver Art Museum; © T.H. and R.P. Benton Trusts / Licensed by Artists Rights Society (ARS), New York

Back cover: Cat. 32: Walter Pach, *The Subway*, 1919; Saint Louis Art Museum

Frontispiece: Cat. 1: Thomas Cole, *River in the Catskills* (detail), 1843; Museum of Fine Arts, Boston

pp 4-5: Cat. 3: Henry Farny, *Morning of a New Day* (detail), 1907; National Cowboy & Western Heritage Museum, Oklahoma City

pp 16-17: Cat. 2: Charles Louis Heyde, *Steam Train in North Williston, Vermont* (detail), 1850; Shelburne Museum

pp 42-3: Cat. 11: John Sloan, *Six O'Clock, Winter* (detail), 1912; The Phillips Collection, Washington, DC

pp 74-5: Cat. 20: John Marin, *Grain Elevator* (detail), ca. 1910-15; Promised Gift to Crystal Bridges Museum of American Art, Bentonville, Arkansas

pp 108-9: Cat. 31: Samuel J. Woolf, *The Under World* (detail), ca. 1909-10; Virginia Museum of Fine Arts

CONTENTS

FOREWORD AND ACKNOWLEDGMENTS

THE RAILROAD TRANSFORMED MODERN EXISTENCE IN nineteenth-century America (and around the world) in much the same way that the digital age dramatically altered life just before and probably long after the turn of the last millennium. Not unlike the capacity of email, the Internet, social media, and smartphones to instantly move and receive information of almost any kind, there was simply nothing like the power of railroads for transporting people and products between growing metropolitan centers in the eastern United States and ever westward across the continent. By the 1850s, American railways had effectively stitched together a still relatively new nation in a manner its citizens could scarcely have imagined just thirty years earlier as they watched steamboats on the Hudson and Ohio Rivers or canal boats towed by mules. Just as the digital revolution has in the present day, the railroad largely reinvented the American experiment in the nineteenth century.

The history of the railroads in the United States is also the history of many other things. The unfettered rise of this extraordinary technology ushered in a second Industrial Revolution, facilitated restless western expansionism, gave rise to the flawed ideology of Manifest Destiny, sparked the first spectacular wealth creation in America and the inequality that accompanied it, and contributed to the steady destruction of Indigenous ways of life. By the dawn of the Gilded Age, railroads had fundamentally transformed any number of related industries, from coal mining to steel production, and introduced innovations never before seen in banking, finance, modern warfare, farming and ranching, tourism, urban planning, and, unmistakably, if inadvertently, in the fine art of oil painting.

Cat. 18: Carl Frederick Gaertner, *Swamp Spur* (detail), 1944; The John and Susan Horseman Collection, Courtesy of the Horseman Foundation

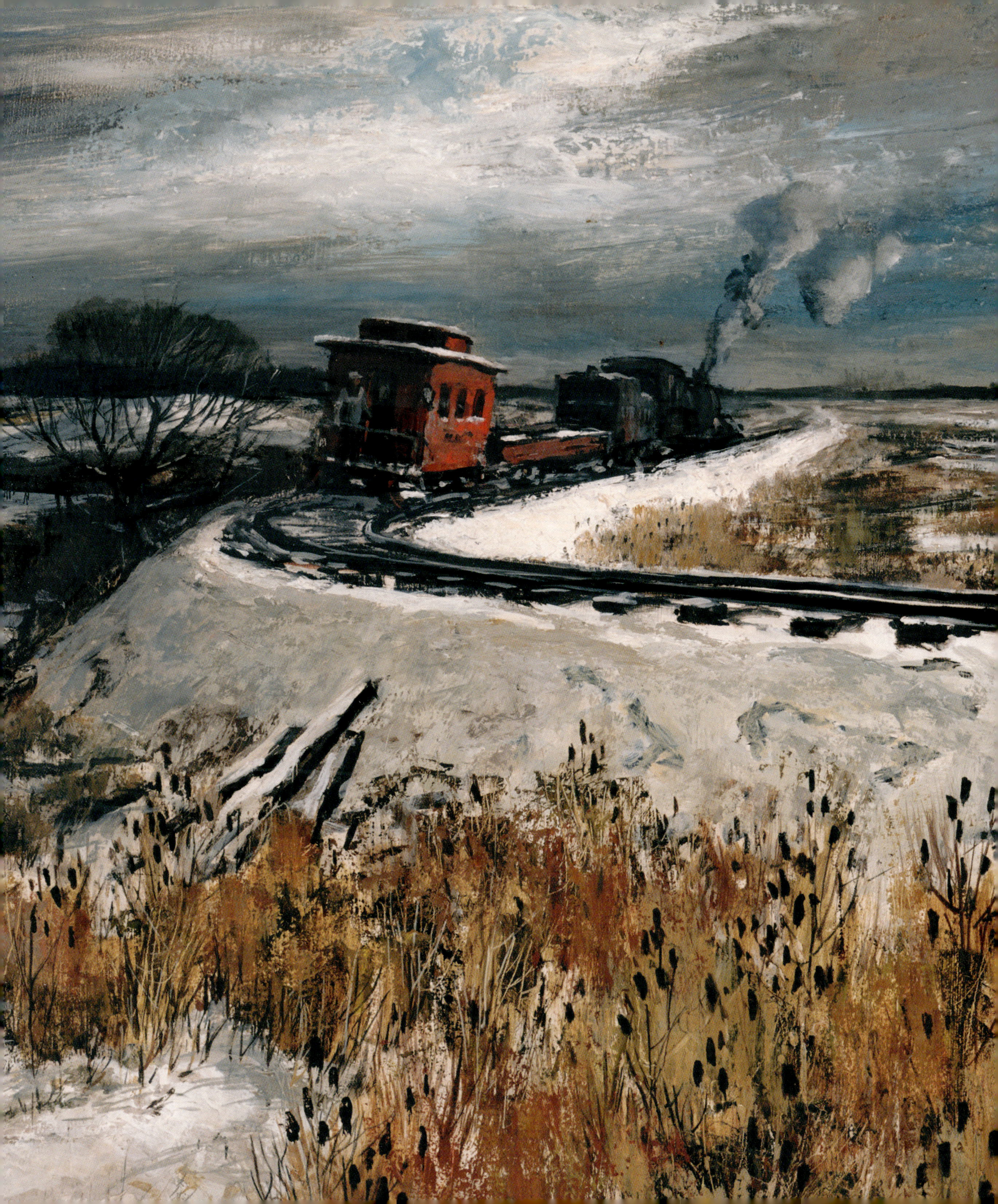

A generation later, at the turn of the twentieth century, the railroad was scarcely a novelty anymore and its era of disruptive innovation was by then well behind it. It was no longer "that devilish Iron Horse," as Henry David Thoreau had described the Boston to Fitchburg line in 1854,[1] and less the sole province of robber barons and corrupt politicians as it had seemed to be (and was) during the period of Reconstruction. By 1900, steam and steel rails had been effectively normalized into the American consciousness, and for the artists who came of age at that particular time, train whistles and the clickety-clack of iron wheels had simply always been there. Those particular artists were not the first generation to be born into the age of boxcars and rail travel, but they were the first that could fully take the presence of those forms for granted.

By the end of World War I, the railroad as an industry had largely been tamed—or at least defanged. Fifteen years of trust busting, followed by the nationalization of the rails during the war years, had seen to it. The age of robber barons, land grabbing, and union busting may not have been entirely over, but it was much less evident (even if only better disguised) in the second, third, and fourth decades of the twentieth century than it had been in the railroad's days of industrial dominance during the last three decades of the nineteenth. To Americans in the 1920s and 1930s, railroads and those who operated them were about as menacing to an honest citizenry as any other public utility, which is to say, on the surface of things, not at all. For most Americans, some of whom would see their first airplanes and own their first automobiles in the 1920s or 1930s, railroads slipped in the

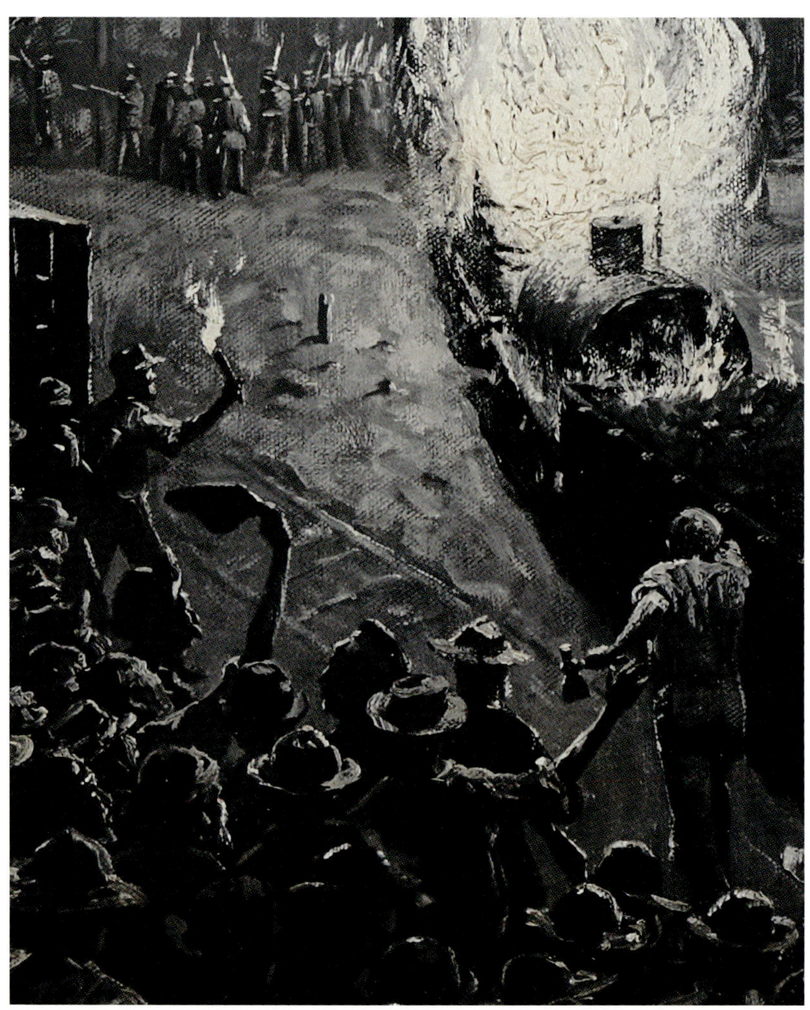

Cat. 6: William Robinson Leigh, *The Attempt to Fire the Pennsylvania Railroad Roundhouse in Pittsburgh, at Daybreak on Sunday, July 22, 1877* (detail), 1895; Carnegie Museum of Art

Cat. 7: Colin Campbell Cooper,
Pittsburgh, PA (detail), ca. 1905;
The Westmoreland Museum of
American Art

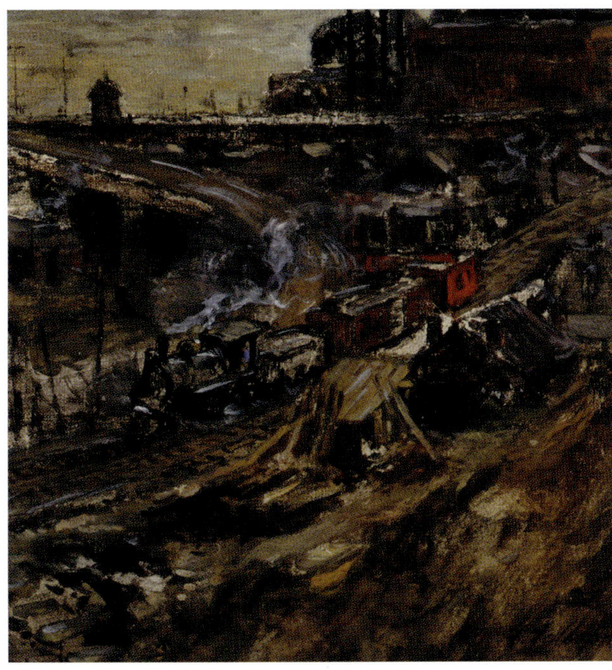

collective consciousness from a place of industrial might to a pageant of expressive metaphor and even quaint nostalgia.

— ✕ —

All Aboard: The Railroad in American Art, 1840-1955 examines the often symbiotic relationship between painters in the United States and the passenger and freight trains that populated cities, towns, and countrysides across the nation. The exhibition and the publication that accompanies it are divided into four broad sections. The first examines the almost simultaneous emergence of the American railroad and a school of landscape painting that marked the growing maturity of both industry and aesthetics in the United States. Whether painters despised the intrusion of railways into otherwise pristine wildernesses or celebrated its arrival, they could not ignore its presence and they did not. Northern railways helped win the Civil War and restore the Union, and railroad men and politicians parlayed the positive public perception of American rail traffic into a vast expansion of the national network and even larger financial windfalls. As Thomas Busciglio-Ritter, the Joslyn Art Museum's Richard and Mary Holland Assistant Curator of American Western Art, observes in his essay, the American railroad industry attempted to slake an almost unquenchable thirst for wealth, and for the first fifty years of its history it succeeded, but only at enormous cost to native people and to the rail's own labor forces.

Section two focuses on American artists' representations of the railroad, starting in the Gilded Age and moving through the Progressive Era. During this roughly fifty-year period, American railroads experienced an extraordinary expansion in the number of miles of track laid, in profitability, and in the sheer number of people employed. But with unparalleled growth came unavoidable travails, including increasingly volatile relations between management and labor, devastating strikes, and broad public suspicion of railroad industry leaders. Julie Pierotti, the Dixon Gallery and Gardens's Martha R. Robinson Curator, notes in her essay that the pervasiveness of railway lines themselves and the almost daily discussion in the popular press of the business affairs of the largest companies is reflected in the frequency with which American artists painted railroad subjects and the public interaction with it.

When President Wilson brought the American railways under federal control in 1917, as the United States entered World War I, most Americans were finally beginning to see railroads in something of a gentler and more sympathetic light. Section three explores the sentimentalization of the railroad in the early twentieth century and the interesting shift that occurs in the way painters tended to represent railroads in the 1910s, 1920s, and 1930s. Whereas in the nineteenth century the American railroad was largely perceived as a builder of connections, beginning in the second and third decade of the twentieth century, as American life became more fractured and mobile, the railroad was often portrayed by artists as a vehicle of separation, migration, loss, and especially loneliness. Kevin Sharp, the Dixon's Linda W. and S. Herbert Rhea Director, writes that while the 1920s were for many people the machine age, the Jazz Age, the Harlem Renaissance, Art Deco, and the flapper era—unmistakably dynamic forces—they were also a period in which American mobility led almost inevitably to separation and a pervasive sense of loneliness. That displacement and isolation was expressed repeatedly in the way American artists perceived and portrayed the railway.

In section four, Thomas Denenberg, the Shelburne Museum's John Wilmerding Director, contributes an essay on people of the rail. While in the nineteenth century representations of railroad workers were largely limited to rail executives and owners, often in grand-manner portraits that emphasized their wealth and power, in the twentieth century it was those who labored in section yards, who mended track, who conducted and engineered, and who toiled for pay that garnered artists' attention most. These working people increasingly dominated both artists' portrayals of the industry and the popular imagination of what the railroads meant to the American psyche.

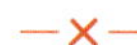

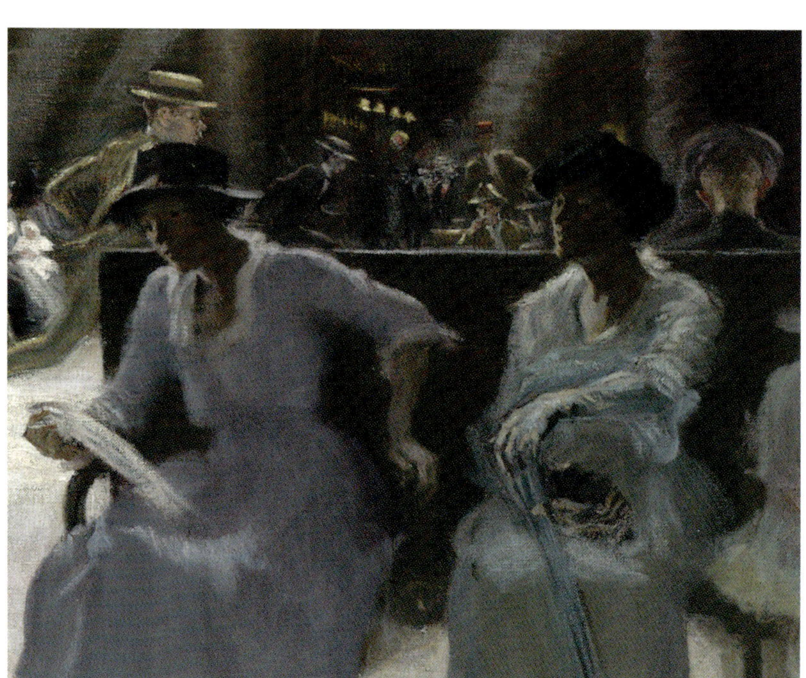

Cat. 33: Edmund Charles Tarbell, *In the Station Waiting Room, Boston* (detail), ca. 1915; Crocker Art Museum

The organization of *All Aboard* has been a collaborative effort between the dedicated staffs of the Shelburne Museum in Vermont, the Dixon Gallery and Gardens in Memphis, and the Joslyn Art Museum in Omaha. It is not the first time these institutions have worked together on a thematic exhibition of broad popular interest. In 2016-17, the three museums (along with the Amon Carter Museum of American Art in Fort Worth) conceived and developed *Wild Spaces, Open Seasons: Hunting and Fishing in American Art*, an exhibition and catalogue focused on artists' representations of the sporting life and sustenance hunting and fishing between the 1830s and the 1940s. Certainly, that collaboration, its success and many satisfactions, led to the work we are pleased to be presenting now. Of course, the staffs of the three museums are responsible for bringing this project together and we would like to take this opportunity to thank them now.

At the Shelburne Museum, we are grateful for the excellent work of Bill Bessette, Catherine Camp, Margaret Cicchetti, Lily Cote, Devon Davis, Shaina Driscoll, Giancarlo Filippi, Louis Godin, Sue Hale, Allison Harig, Alex Kikutis, Katie Wood Kirchhoff, Benjamin Krevolin, Deana LaFleche, Arin Lustberg, Justin Mayo, Erin Moore, Reed Nye, Kate Owen, Chris Patterson, Nancie Ravenel, John Rogers, Kory Rogers, Stephen Sperry, Chip Stulen, Sara Turner, Brian Verville, Jason Vrooman, Jackson Walsh, Ron Wannamaker, Lee Wheeler, Sara Wolfson, and Leslie Wright.

At the Dixon Gallery and Gardens, we would like to thank Miguel Alcantar, Christian Allen, Melvin Avendano, Kori van der Bijl, Juliana Bjorklund, Jacob Blair, Melissa Bosdorf, Marlin Burnwatt, Sarah Catmur, Ellen Daugherty, Jenny Duggan, Chris Emanus, Jordan Fisher, Erika Fuller, Wanda Gaines, Jeff Goggans, Braden Hixson, Anna Hood, Gail Hopper, Mitzi Igleharte, Stuart Janssen, Susan Johnson, Hope Jones, Robert Jones, Shawn Jones, Kristen Kimberling, LaArie King, Sarah Lorenz, Kyle McLane, Norma Montesi, Glenn Overall, Lorenzo Perez, Julie Pierotti, Kristen Rambo, Angela Robinson, Christine Ruby, Kim Rucker, Margarita Sandino, Corkey Sinks, Dale Skaggs, Karen Strachan, James Valentine, Stephanie Valentine, Charlene Williams, Cameron Waters, and Jessie Wiley. We would be remiss if we did not also thank the following supporters of the Dixon, who made the presentation of *All Aboard* possible in Memphis. We are particularly grateful to Karen and Preston Dorsett, Andrea and Doug Edwards, Amanda and Nick Goetze, Rose M. Johnston, Anne and Mike Keeney, Nell R. Levy, Nancy and Steve Morrow, Gwen and Penn Owen, Chris and Dan Richards, Susan Adler Thorp, and Adele Wellford. The Theodore W. and Betty J. Eckels Foundation, The First Horizon Foundation, Opus East Memphis, the Joe Orgill Family Fund for Exhibitions, the Mary and Jeff Simpson Charitable Trust, and Wilson, Arkansas, all made significant contributions to this project in Memphis and we are most grateful.

Our colleagues at the Joslyn Art Museum contributed to the success of *All Aboard*, and we offer them our most heartfelt thanks. Among them are Taylor J. Acosta, Candace Berger, Amanda Bulger, Thomas Busciglio-Ritter, Kristy Durkin, Erin Foley, Jennifer Gleason Gillen, Sarah Haines, Katie Herring, Amy Himes, Rebecca Manning, Elizabeth Powell, Nancy Round, Amy Rummel, Kevin Salzman, and Luke Severson.

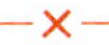

The success of every loan exhibition is entirely dependent upon the tremendous collegiality and support of outstanding museum professionals from coast to coast. The art museum project and its place as a producer of ongoing and meaningful exhibitions benefits from the spirit of cooperation so often found within the walls of these noble institutions. In various projects over the years, one or more of us have thanked these same colleagues again and again for their service to our exhibitions. At times, the lists of names and institutions that appear in the acknowledgments of exhibition catalogues can seem like nothing more than a mere tally of debt. But when you have been organizing exhibitions for as long as the three of us have been, it is absolutely beyond certainty that the obligation is real and the thanks are beyond sincere.

At this time, we would like to thank Alex Gregory and Kim Mahan from the Amarillo Museum of Art; Tobi Bruce and Shelley Falconer from the Art Gallery of Hamilton; Leah Rosovsky from the Boston Athenaeum; Eric Crosby and Marie-Stéphanie Delamaire from the Carnegie Museum of Art, Pittsburgh; Lial Jones and Scott Shields from the Crocker Art Museum, Sacramento; Austen Barron Bailly and Rod Bigelow from Crystal Bridges Museum of American Art, Bentonville, Arkansas; Christoph Heinrich and JR Henneman from the Denver Art Museum; Elizabeth Dunbar from the Everson Museum of Art, Syracuse, New York; Emma Acker and Thomas P. Campbell from the Fine Arts Museums of San Francisco; Tracee Glab and Sarah Kohn from the Flint Institute of Arts; Stephanie Heydt and Rand Suffolk from the High Museum of Art, Atlanta; Nandini Makrandi Jestice and Virginia Anne Sharber from the Hunter Museum of American Art, Chattanooga; Ann Burroughs and Kristen Hayashi from the Japanese American National Museum, Los Angeles; Sabine Eckmann from the Mildred Lane Kemper Art Museum, St. Louis; Patricia Lee Daigle and Zoe Kahr from the Memphis Brooks Museum of Art; Keasha Dumas-Heath from the Museum of African American Art, Los Angeles; Ethan Lasser, Matthew Teitelbaum, and Christina Yu Yu from the Museum of Fine Arts, Boston; Pat Fitzgerald from the National Cowboy and Western Heritage Museum, Oklahoma City; Kaywin Feldman and Franklin Kelly from the National Gallery of Art, Washington, DC; Brett Abbott from the New Britain Museum of American Art; Catherine Evans and Linda C. Harrison from the Newark Museum of Art; Mark White from the New Mexico Museum of Art, Santa Fe; Erin Coe and Adam M. Thomas from the Palmer Museum of Art, State College, Pennsylvania; Jonathan Binstock from The Phillips Collection, Washington, DC; Min Jung Kim and Melissa Wolfe from the Saint Louis Art Museum; John N. Hoover and Julie Dunn-Morton from the St. Louis Mercantile Library; Susan Longhenry from the Sheldon Museum of Art, Lincoln, Nebraska; Randall Griffey and Stephanie Stebich from the Smithsonian American Art Museum, Washington, DC; Leo Mazow and Alex Nyerges from the Virginia Museum of Fine Arts, Richmond; Diane Mullin and Alejandra Peña-Gutiérrez from the Frederick R. Weisman Art Museum, Minneapolis; Douglas W. Evans, Jeremiah William McCarthy, and Suzanne Wright from the Westmoreland Museum of American Art, Greensburg, Pennsylvania; Scott Rothkopf and Adam Weinberg from the Whitney Museum of American Art, New York; and Tera Hedrick and Anne Kraybill from the Wichita Art Museum.

We are especially grateful to the generous private collectors who were willing to part with treasured works of art for the relatively long interval of a traveling exhibition. We offer our sincerest thanks to Jennifer Ballentine, Susan and John Horseman, and other private collectors who wish to remain anonymous.

At this time, the organizers would like to gratefully acknowledge the patience and support of Amber Degn, Lester Katz, Ronald Pierotti, and Erin Riordan for their ongoing service to this exhibition and to countless other projects as well.

Finally, we extend our best thanks to the team at D Giles Limited, the United Kingdom–based publisher of the book you now hold. We are grateful to Dan Giles, Liz Japes, Susan Kelly, Allison McCormick, and Louise Ramsay for their attention to detail, their patience, and their outstanding experience and advice in bringing *All Aboard: The Railroad in American Art* to completion. We hope you enjoy it.

Thomas Denenberg
John Wilmerding Director and CEO
Shelburne Museum

Kevin Sharp
Linda W. and S. Herbert Rhea Director
Dixon Gallery and Gardens

Jack F. Becker
Executive Director and CEO
Joslyn Art Museum

Endnote

1   Henry David Thoreau, *Walden; or, Life in the Woods* (Boston: Ticknor & Fields, 1854), 13, https://archive.org/details/waldenorlifeinwo1854thor.

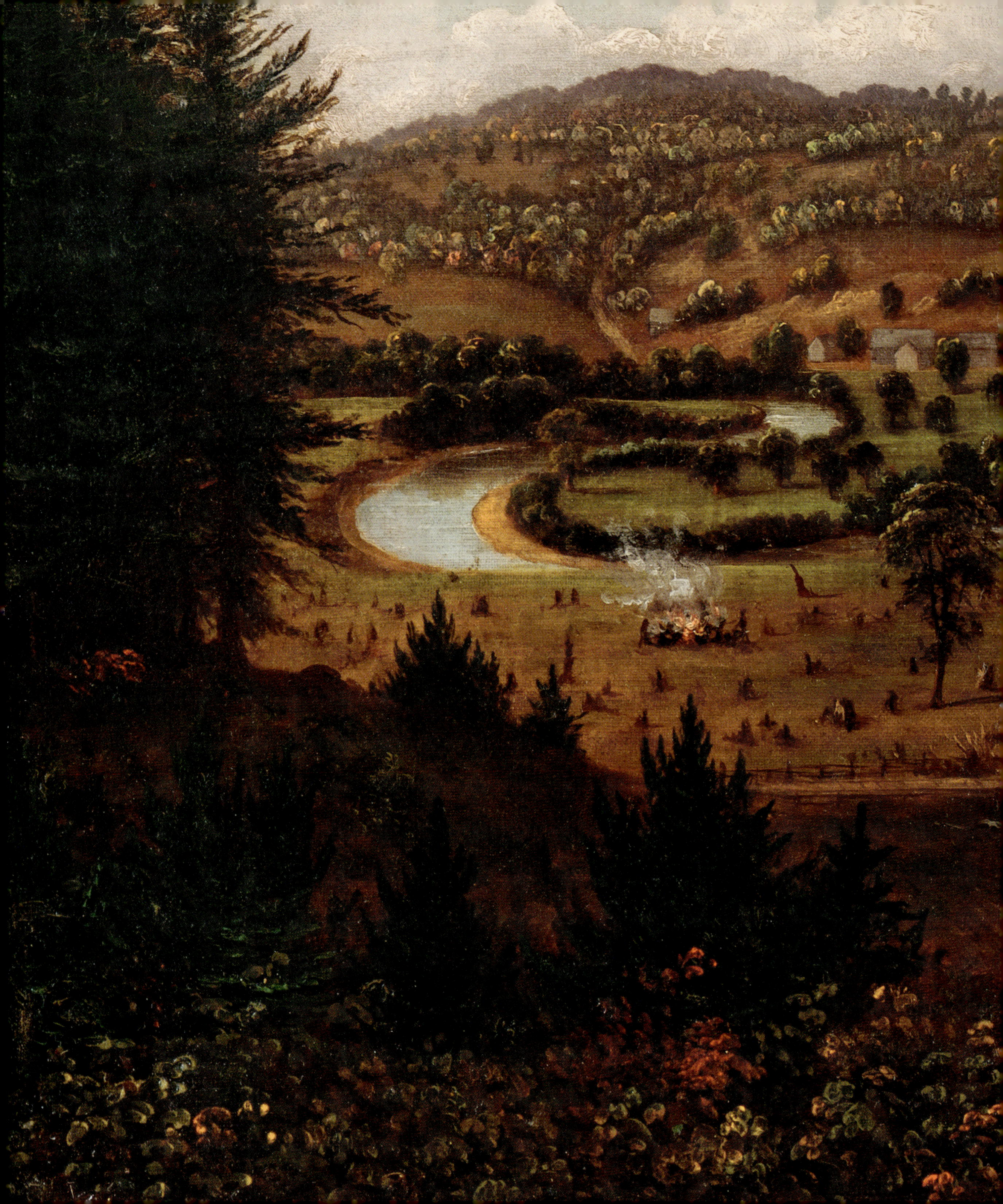

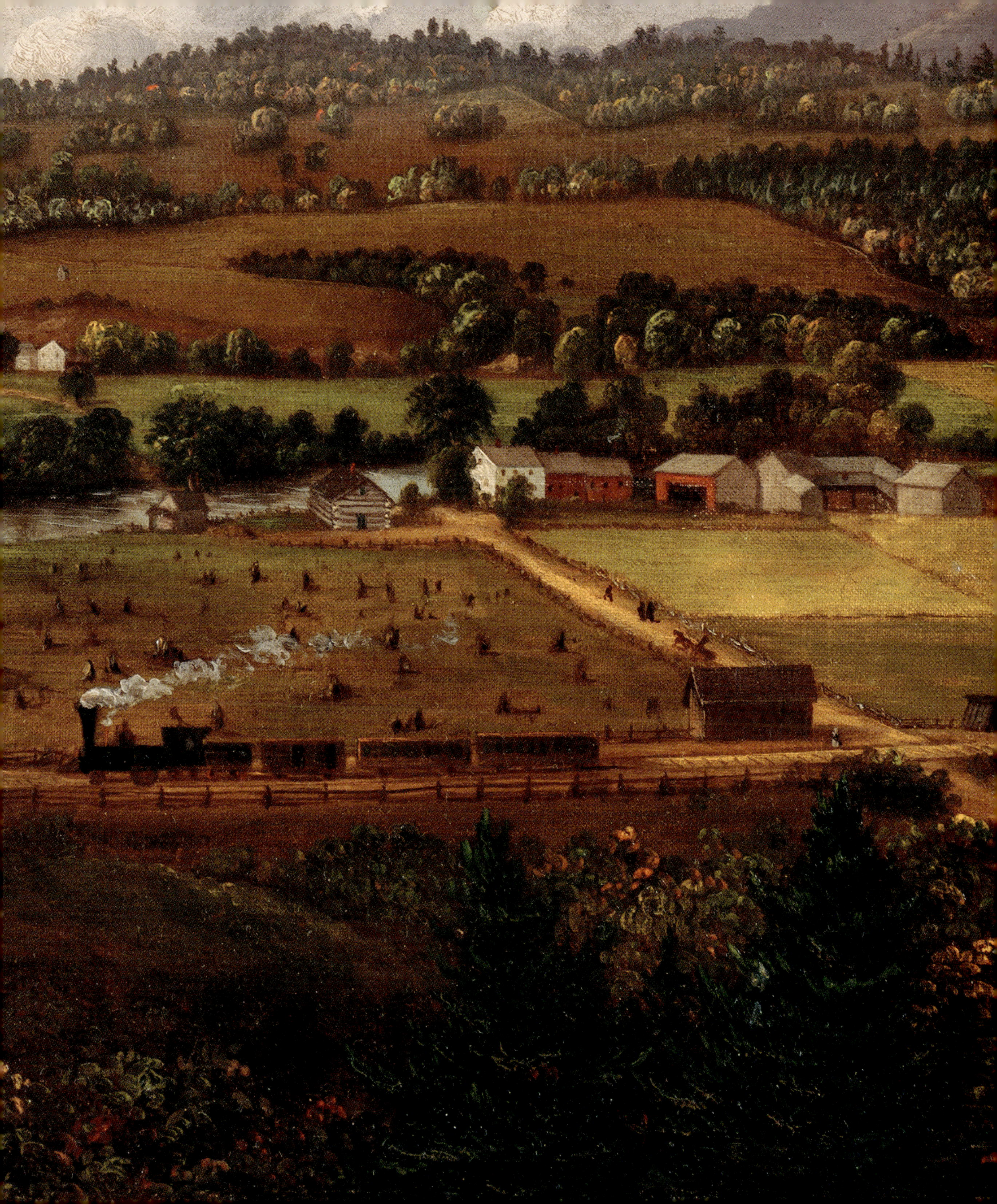

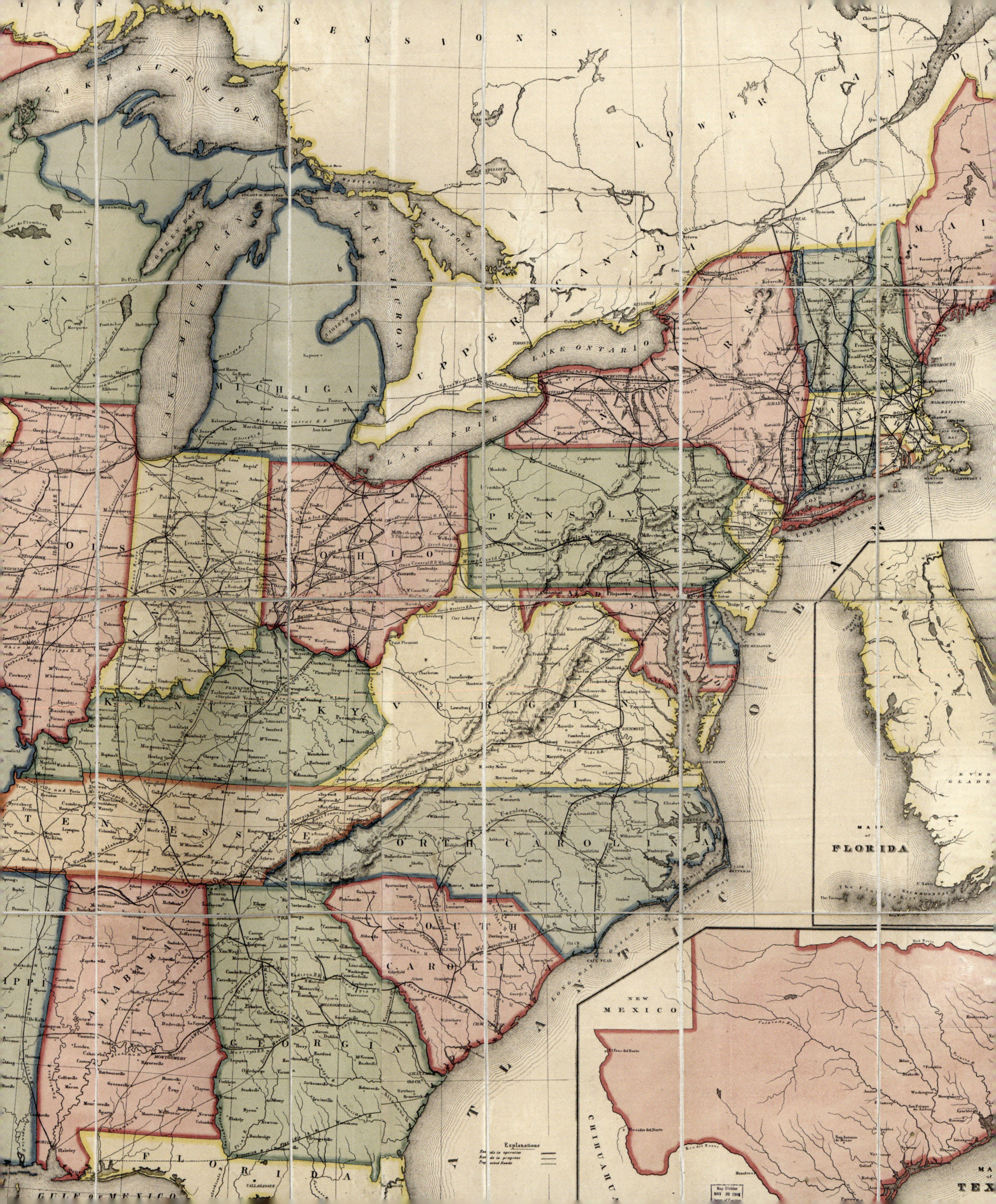

1

SMOKE IN THE WILDERNESS

American Landscape Painting and the Railroad, 1840-1900

Thomas Busciglio-Ritter

ON JUNE 1, 1858, A TRAIN DEPARTED BALTIMORE'S Camden Station with an unusual group of passengers. Headed for Wheeling, in present-day West Virginia, the convoy included writers, journalists, and artists invited by the Baltimore & Ohio Railroad to partake in an excursion on its longest line to date.[1] With their line completed in 1852, Baltimore & Ohio continued to face strong competition from Pennsylvania-based railroads. In an effort to increase ridership, Baltimore & Ohio executives experimented with new strategies, including the promotion of tourism throughout previously impenetrable terrains. To document the remarkable scenery, the firm engaged landscape artists, including prominent figures later associated with the Hudson River school. The traveling party sent to Wheeling included the painters Asher Brown Durand, John Frederick Kensett, Thomas Prichard Rossiter, Louis Rémy Mignot, James Augustus Suydam, and John R. Johnston. Their sketches were intended to complement the views taken on the way by five photographers hired by the company. As fellow excursionist David Hunter Strother recounted in an article for *Harper's New Monthly Magazine*:

> Latterly, steam and the fine arts have scraped acquaintance. The real and the ideal have smoked pipes together. The iron horse and Pegasus have trotted side by side in double harness, puffing in unison, like a well-trained pair. What will be the result of this conjunction Heaven knows. We believe that it marks the commencement of a new era in human progress; and it is meet, therefore, that some record of the event should be given to the world.[2]

One of the great artistic products of the trip was Thomas Rossiter's *Opening of the Wilderness* (1858-59; fig. 1), a dramatic scene of smoking trains ready to leave their roundhouse to carry goods and people across the land. Inspired in part by the storage infrastructure of the Baltimore & Ohio Railroad in Wheeling, the composition sends a clear message:

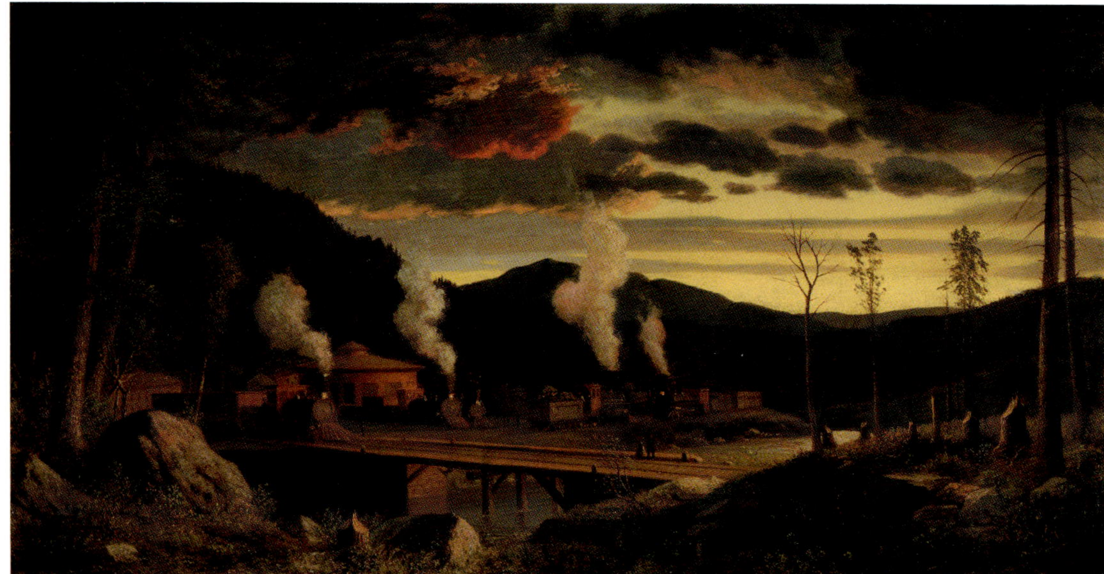

Fig. 1

**Thomas Prichard Rossiter
(American, 1818–1871)**
Opening of the Wilderness, ca. 1857–59

oil on canvas
17½ × 32½ in.

Museum of Fine Arts, Boston

Bequest of Martha C. Karolik for the
M. and M. Karolik Collection of
American Paintings, 1815–1865, 48.471

the once-inaccessible wilderness has been split open by the rail and nature has been subjected to the designs of man.[3] Cleared in preparation, the surrounding forest, now a mere alignment of tree stumps, allows tracks to run through. Romanticizing the railroad, Rossiter's view effectively served the interests of a booming industry, and the painter's trip on the Baltimore–Wheeling line would become one of the many expressions of the close relationship between rail technology and the visual arts at the time.

American artists were not unique in their fascination with railway technology and its effects. The subject was notably taken up by the British painter Joseph Mallord William Turner in his *Rain, Steam, and Speed—The Great Western Railway* (fig. 2), completed in 1844.[4] Railroads were promoted as symbols of faster and more effective transportation, promising greater mobility and economic development. They would also be used by several European countries to help tighten their control over colonized spaces overseas, making them a powerful tool of commercial imperialism.[5] Nineteenth-century America, however, differed in that regard, as evidenced in pictures like Rossiter's. In the United States, the railroad always underlay environmental, economic, and racial

preoccupations that were a direct extension of a national project over a continental space not yet incorporated but already thought of as belonging to the nation. Images featuring railroads became projections of the country's future in the making for (white) immigrants. They constituted an art of prophecy, or the vision of a self-fulfilling ideal of domination. Yet artworks also exposed the complexities and limitations of two idiosyncratic discourses: Manifest Destiny and the myth of the wilderness. Depictions of railroads in mid- to late-nineteenth-century US paintings may be read as manifestations of a contested settler-colonial project affecting the actual landscape and its people, with lasting impacts that may be detected behind the veneer of fine art.

Landscape Painting and the "Railroad Sublime"

In 1964, historian Leo Marx published the landmark volume *The Machine in the Garden: Technology and the Pastoral Ideal in America*. In it, he examined the construction of US identity as once defined by the pastoral ideal of a land cultivated by free citizens.[6] For Marx, the emergence of "machine imagery" in the early nineteenth century challenged pastoral peace by introducing tension and noise into the landscape.[7] Factories, mills, and railroads disrupted

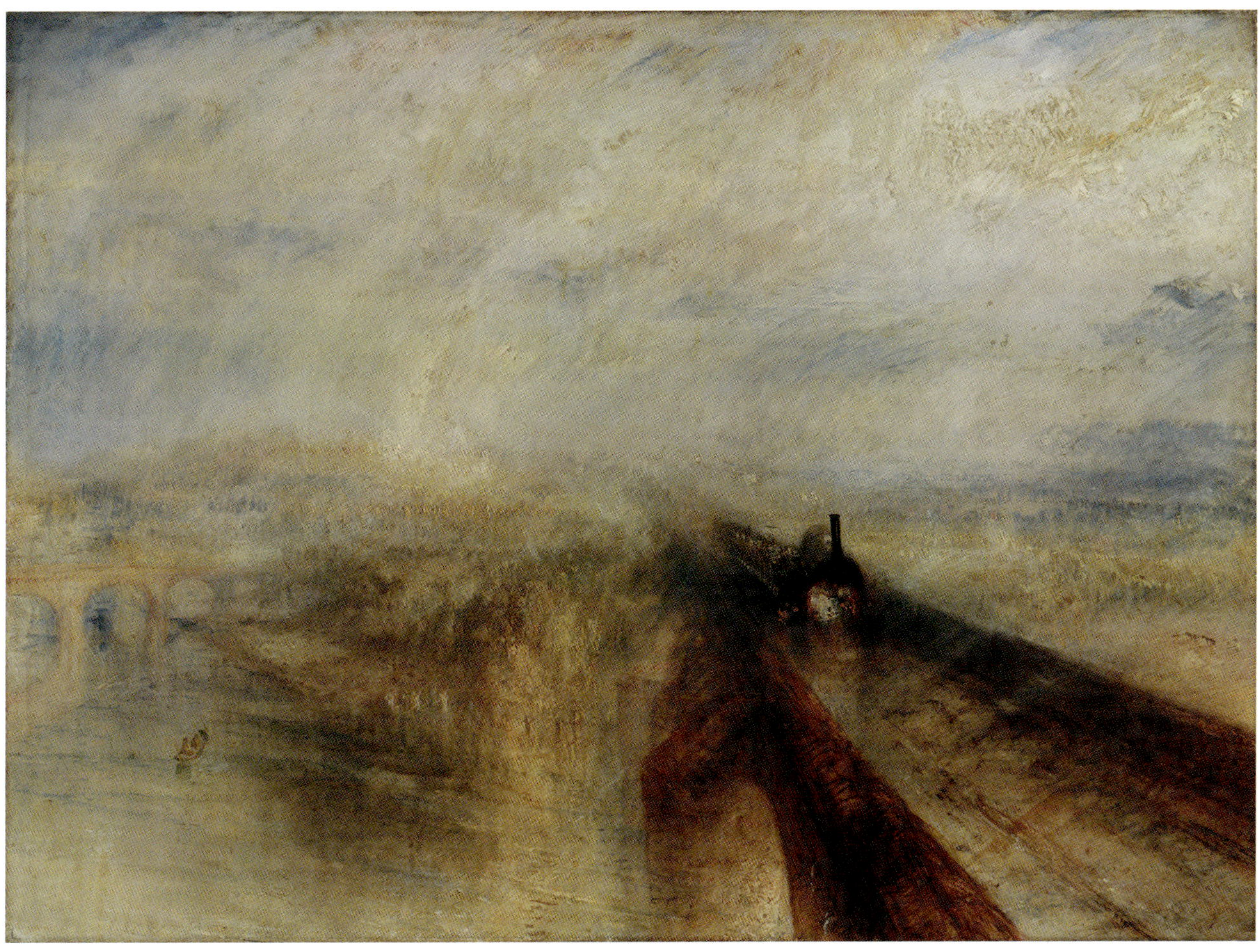

Fig. 2

**Joseph Mallord William Turner
(British, 1775–1851)**
*Rain, Steam, and Speed–
The Great Western Railway*, 1844

oil on canvas
36 × 48 in.

The National Gallery, London

Turner Bequest, 1856, NG538

the "pastoral design" and the unspoiled landscape of America, increasingly invaded by civilization.[8] However, these dramatic changes to the landscape were not immediately viewed by all as incongruent with the preservation of its supposed pristine quality. The illusion of a harmony between nature and artifice permeated the technological American consciousness, and artists, in particular, picked up on this trend.

To an entire generation of landscape painters, the advent of the railroad and its encroachment on landscapes regarded as untouched posed a conundrum. In the Northeast, followers of Thomas Cole and the informal association of artists who would later be called the Hudson River school perceived the new infrastructure as a challenge to the idea of wilderness on which the tenets of the American spirit were based. Cole's first picture featuring a train,

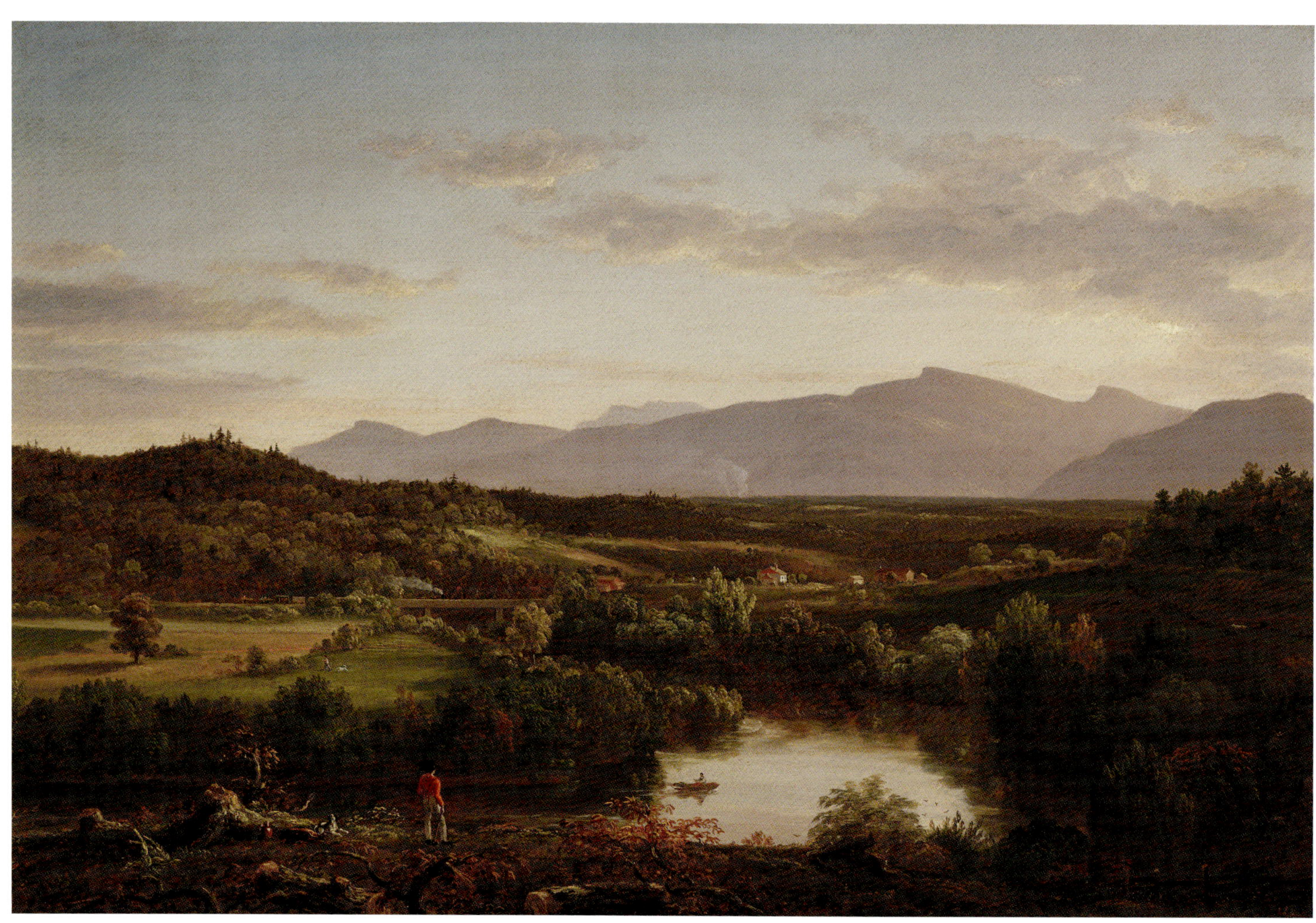

Cat. 1

Thomas Cole (American, 1801-1848)
River in the Catskills, 1843

oil on canvas
27½ × 40⅜ in.

Museum of Fine Arts, Boston

Gift of Martha C. Karolik for the
M. and M. Karolik Collection of American
Paintings, 1815-1865, 47.1201

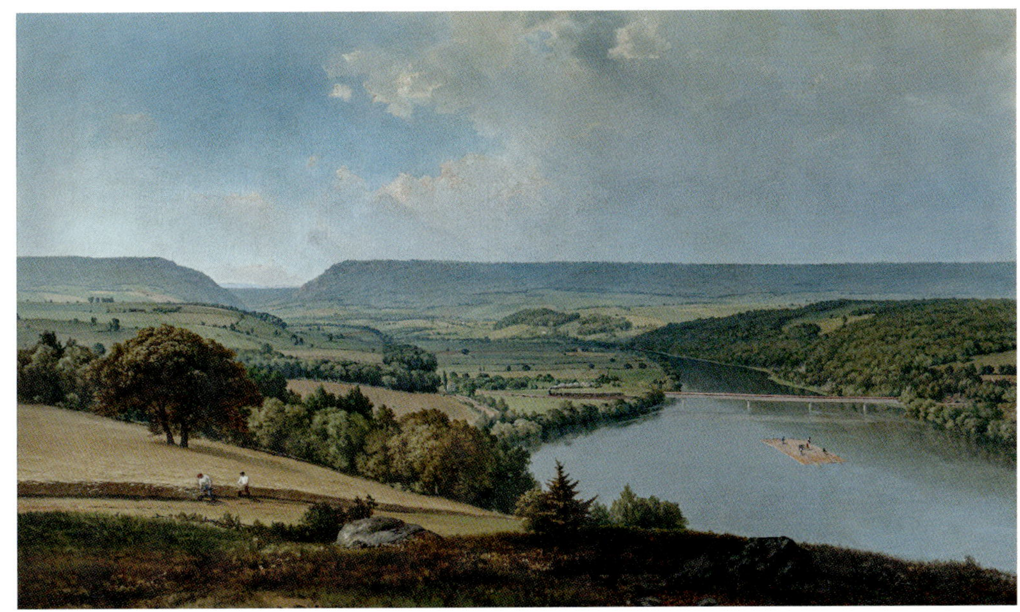

Fig. 3

George Inness Sr.
(American, 1825–1894)
Delaware Water Gap, 1857

oil on canvas
32 × 52 in.

Private collection

River in the Catskills (1843; cat. 1), treads cautiously. Relegated to the background, the steam-powered engine is still overwhelmed by the surrounding natural beauty of the Catskill Mountains of New York. The composition questions the place of the railroad within the grand scheme of nature, offering an antipastoral vision of the landscape.[9] Images of agrarian rurality in the antebellum United States functioned as metaphors of goodness, independence, republican ideals, and familial harmony. In contrast, by enabling material comfort and an expansion of commerce, trains threatened the admirable values of restraint supposedly embodied in the raw wilderness and expressed in the American spirit.

Landscape art of the 1850s and 1860s would continue to grapple with the ambiguities of pastoralism and technology as perceived in the eastern United States. George Inness's 1857 view of the Delaware Water Gap (fig. 3)—one of many he painted—juxtaposes the speed of the railroad in the background with the manual labor of two quaint-looking harvesters in a field of golden, ripe wheat. For its part, the format and composition of Martin Johnson Heade's *Lynn Meadows* (1863; fig. 4)

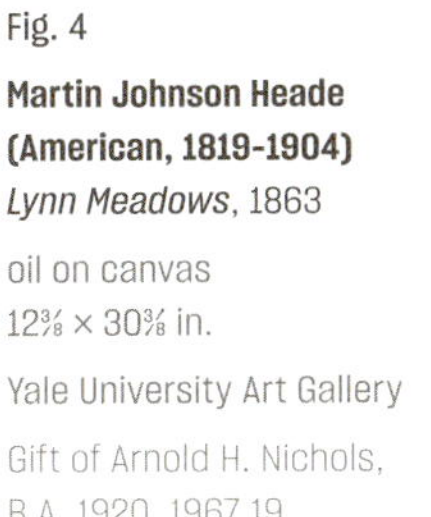

Fig. 4

Martin Johnson Heade
(American, 1819–1904)
Lynn Meadows, 1863

oil on canvas
12⅜ × 30⅜ in.

Yale University Art Gallery

Gift of Arnold H. Nichols,
B.A. 1920, 1967.19

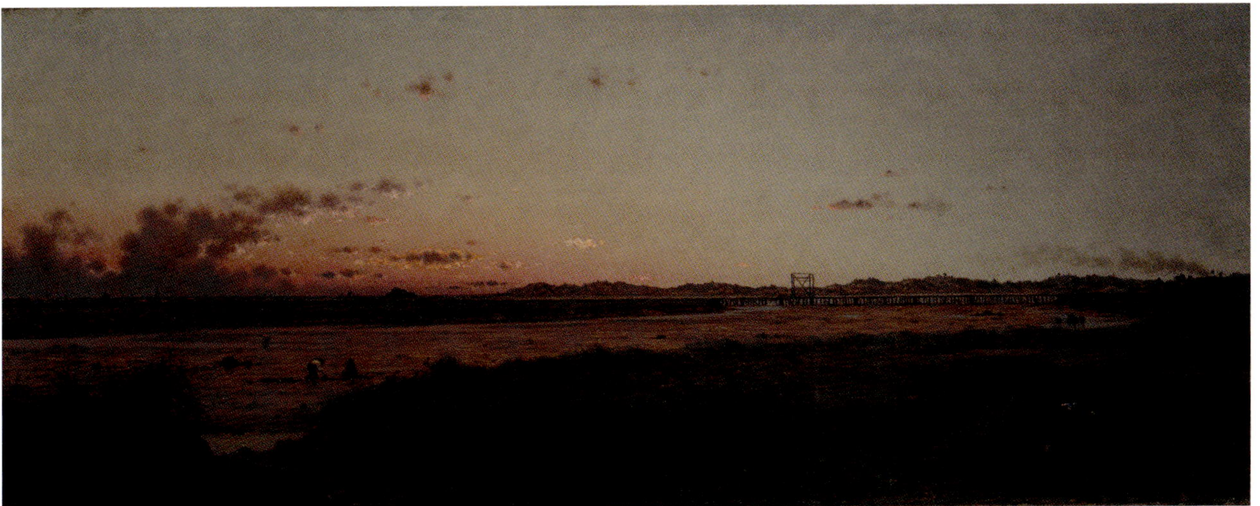

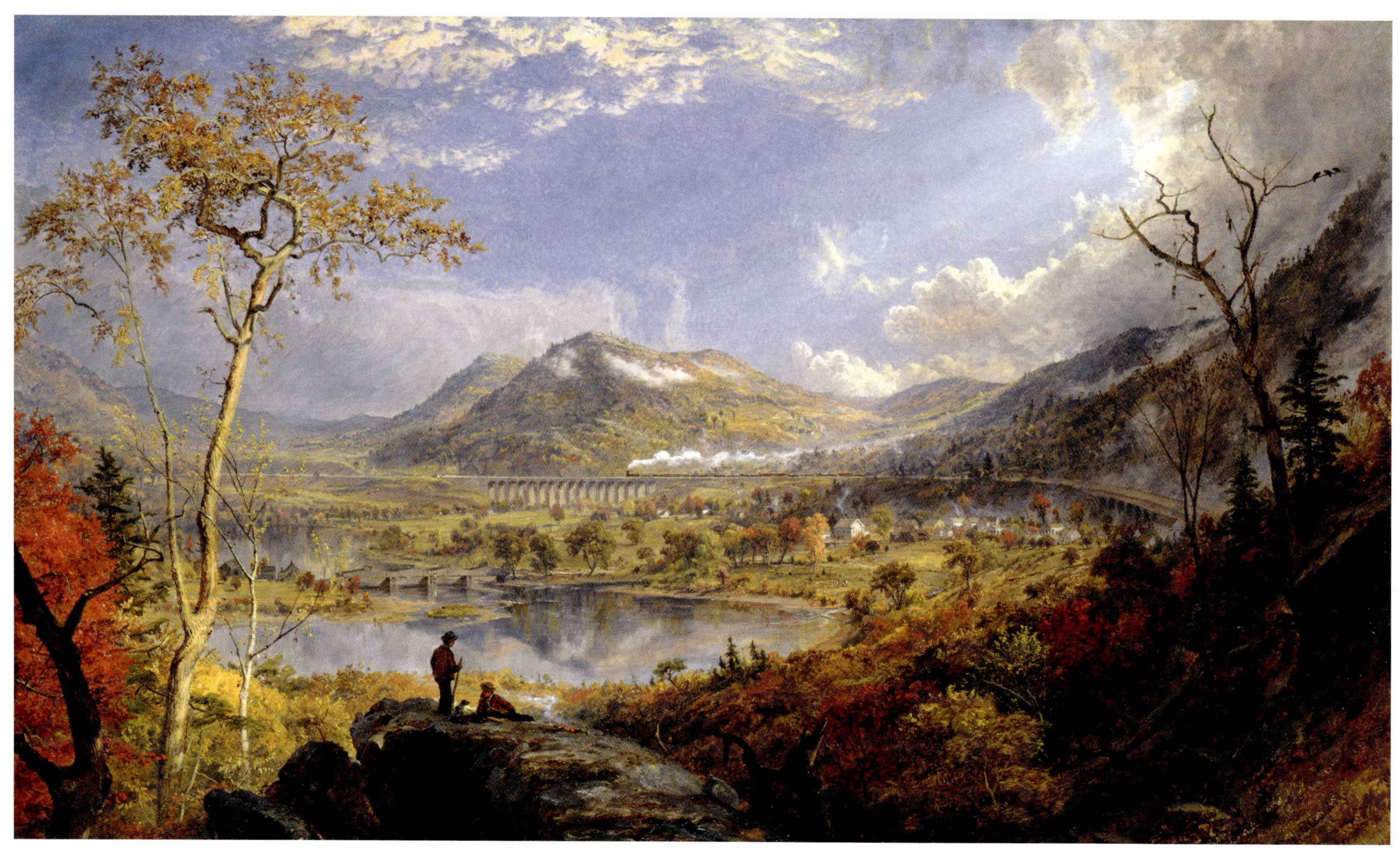

Fig. 5

Jasper Francis Cropsey (American, 1823-1900)
Starrucca Viaduct, Pennsylvania, 1865

oil on canvas
22⅜ × 36⅜ in.

Toledo Museum of Art

Purchased with funds from the Florence
Scott Libbey Bequest in Memory of her
Father, Maurice A. Scott, 1947.58

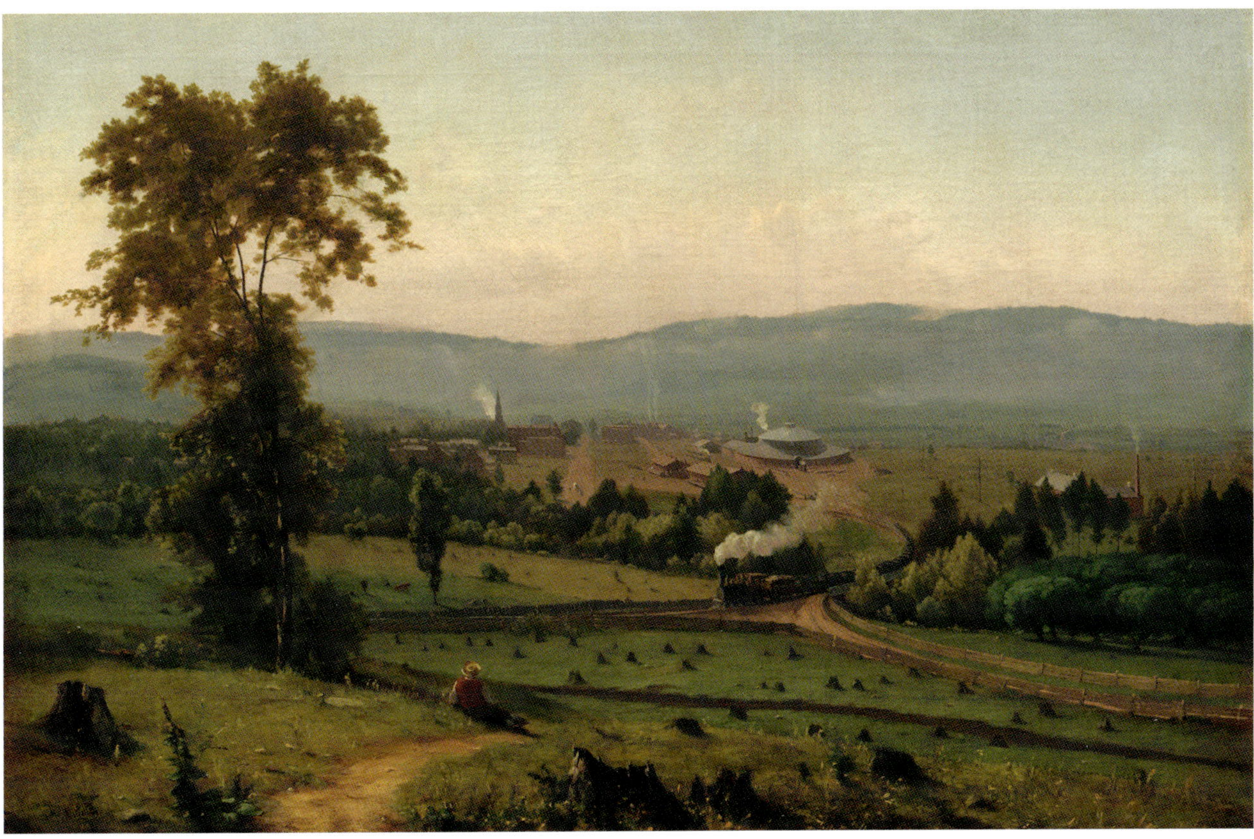

invite viewers to read it horizontally as an unfolding narrative.[10] To the right, a smoking locomotive rushes out of view, proceeding ever forward. Behind it, a handful of figures are digging for clams in the mud of a marsh after the recess of the tide. Their static appearance is in direct contrast with the dynamism of the quickly passing train. Read from left to right, the picture offers a progression from past to present and, by extension, future. New technology implies broader horizons for American trade, and the smaller world of localized labor cannot compete with the velocity and power of mechanization.

In opposition to these melancholic or contemplative views, however, some landscape artists had already embraced a "technological sublime." After the 1840s, a number of painters endeavored to integrate trains into their compositions while still promoting picturesque scenery. In an attempt to improve the aesthetic and spatial upheavals brought by this new infrastructure, they made the machine an object of awe on par with nature itself. Historian David E. Nye has dated the emergence of this approach back to the laying of the cornerstone of the Baltimore & Ohio Railroad on July 4, 1828, thirty years before the company organized its strategic artists' trip.[11] Among those promoting the beauty and power of the machine itself, making it the focus of their compositions, was Jasper Cropsey. In his 1865 *Starrucca Viaduct, Pennsylvania* (fig. 5), for instance, human infrastructure is glorified alongside the scenery, not in opposition to it.[12] Railroad tracks and a smoking train share the space with an idyllic forest displaying fiery autumnal colors. Nestled between a lake, the mountains, and the eponymous viaduct, a rural community still embodies the ideal of American independence and enterprise, now strengthened by the advent of technology.

Similarly, in *The Lackawanna Valley* (ca. 1856; fig. 6), Inness himself had exposed a scarred landscape of tree stumps in a painting actually

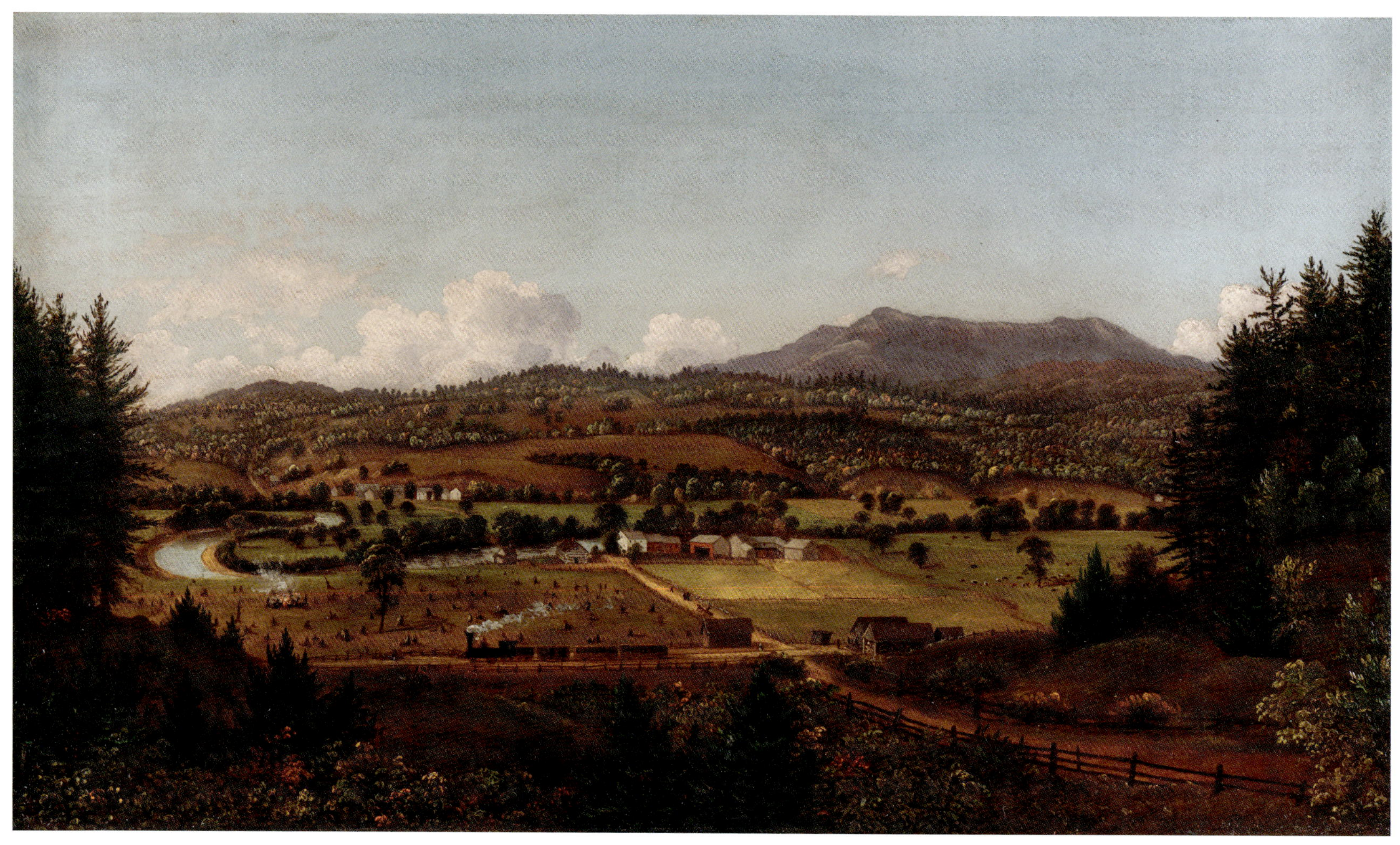

Cat. 2

Charles Louis Heyde
(American, 1822-1892)
Steam Train in North Williston,
Vermont, 1850

oil on canvas
20⁹⁄₁₆ × 35³⁄₁₆ in.

Shelburne Museum

Gift of Edith Hopkins Walker, 1959-49.1

commissioned by a railway company, the Delaware, Lackawanna & Western Railroad. Focused on the city of Scranton, Pennsylvania, the picture presents a vision of an industrialized age and the consequent and irreversible environmental changes. One of the most famous artworks to depict railroads before the Civil War, Inness's view stands at the crossroads of praise and discomfort, as, in Barbara Novak's estimation, "one of the most puzzling pictures in American art."[13] Beheld by a lonesome figure lying down near a dirt path in the foreground, the dramatically beautiful scene recenters its appreciation on the machine itself. Though some scholars have interpreted Inness's intent as proto-environmentalist, his view rather points to a shift in the discourses of American landscape painting, from a celebration of nature to a celebration of conquered nature. This narrative is also palpable in the landscapes of Vermont painter Charles Louis Heyde, including *Steam Train in North Williston* (1850; cat. 2), whose field of cut-down trees becomes the befitting cradle of an industrial civilization. Similar ideas would soon be applied to the wider space of the so-called American West, responding to the complex ideology of Manifest Destiny.[14]

Manifest Destiny, or Railroad Imagery in the American West

The technological sublime became increasingly complex in the decades following the Civil War, as railroads emerged as a potent agent of US expansion westward. The introduction of trains over that vast territory had devastating effects on Indigenous communities, especially in the Plains and Rockies. Moreover, these developments helped support an ideology and rhetoric that relegated Native Americans to a bygone past, their traditions to be inevitably replaced by a machine-driven Euro-American society, shorthanded as the myth of the "vanishing Indian." Historian Manu Karuka has emphasized the role of such rhetoric in attempts to delegitimize Indigenous societies and their land claims.[15] The myth was espoused by all strata of the US government to promote the idea of an inevitable retreat of Indigenous cultures in the face of Euro-American civilization.[16] Respected as noble and brave, Native Americans were nonetheless destined to sacrifice their freedoms for the making of the United States and the expansion toward the Pacific Ocean. In public discourse, stereotypical representations of Indigenous nations would be used jointly with the concept of Manifest Destiny, a phrase coined in 1845 by journalist John Louis O'Sullivan.[17] According to this belief, divinely commanded to settle and dominate the entire continent, white Americans were bound to shape it into the image of an ideal pastoral society already projected in the East.

Visual artists took up these themes in the 1850s with a flurry of images propagating a vision of Native cultures on the wane as Euro-American society fulfilled its God-given right to occupy and use their lands. The railroad, in that context, was seen as one of many instruments of Native erasure. Asher B. Durand, an heir to Thomas Cole's stylistic approach, staged this compellingly in his monumental *Progress (The Advance of Civilization)* (1853; fig. 7), a work that laid out a true civilization project. The picture was commissioned from the artist by New York businessman Charles L. Gould, treasurer of the Ohio & Mississippi Railroad, which explains the presence of a train in the background of the sprawling view

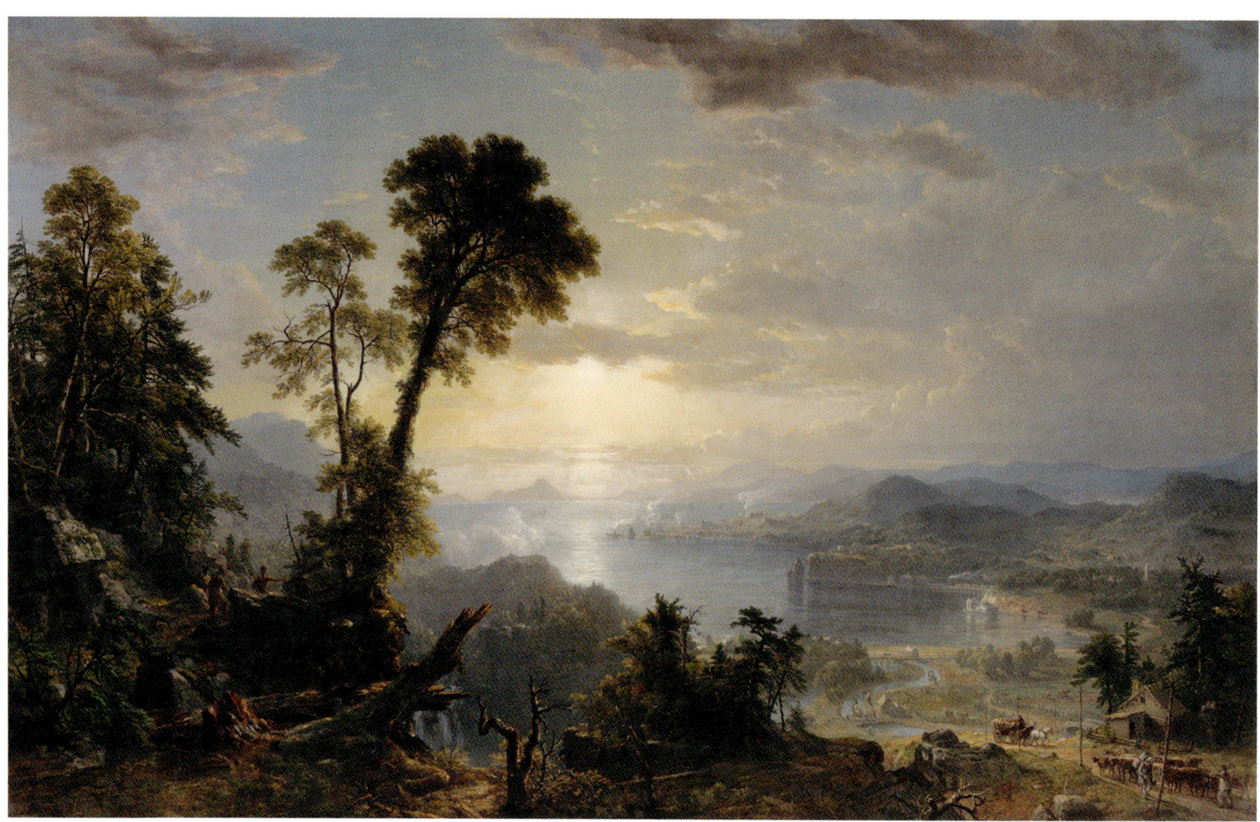

Fig. 7

Asher B. Durand (American, 1796-1886)
Progress (The Advance of Civilization), 1853
oil on canvas
48 × 72 in.
Virginia Museum of Fine Arts, Richmond
Gift of an Anonymous Donor, 2018.547

amidst other signs of Western industrialization, from factories to steamships.[18] In truth, the painting as a whole presents a teleological view of American history: the idea of history as a linear process moving toward a prescribed outcome or final goal. This inevitable end is, avowedly, the settlement of the land by a supposedly rational Euro-American society under the aegis of the US republic. In contrast, a group of passive Indigenous figures depicted in the left foreground occupies a disappearing wild, witnessing history as it unfolds without participating in it. Dwarfed by the bustling colonized landscape,

Fig. 8

Thomas Proudley Otter (American, 1832–1890)
On the Road, 1860

oil on canvas
22⅛ × 45⅝ in.

The Nelson-Atkins Museum of Art,
Kansas City, Missouri

Purchase, William Rockhill Nelson Trust, 50-1

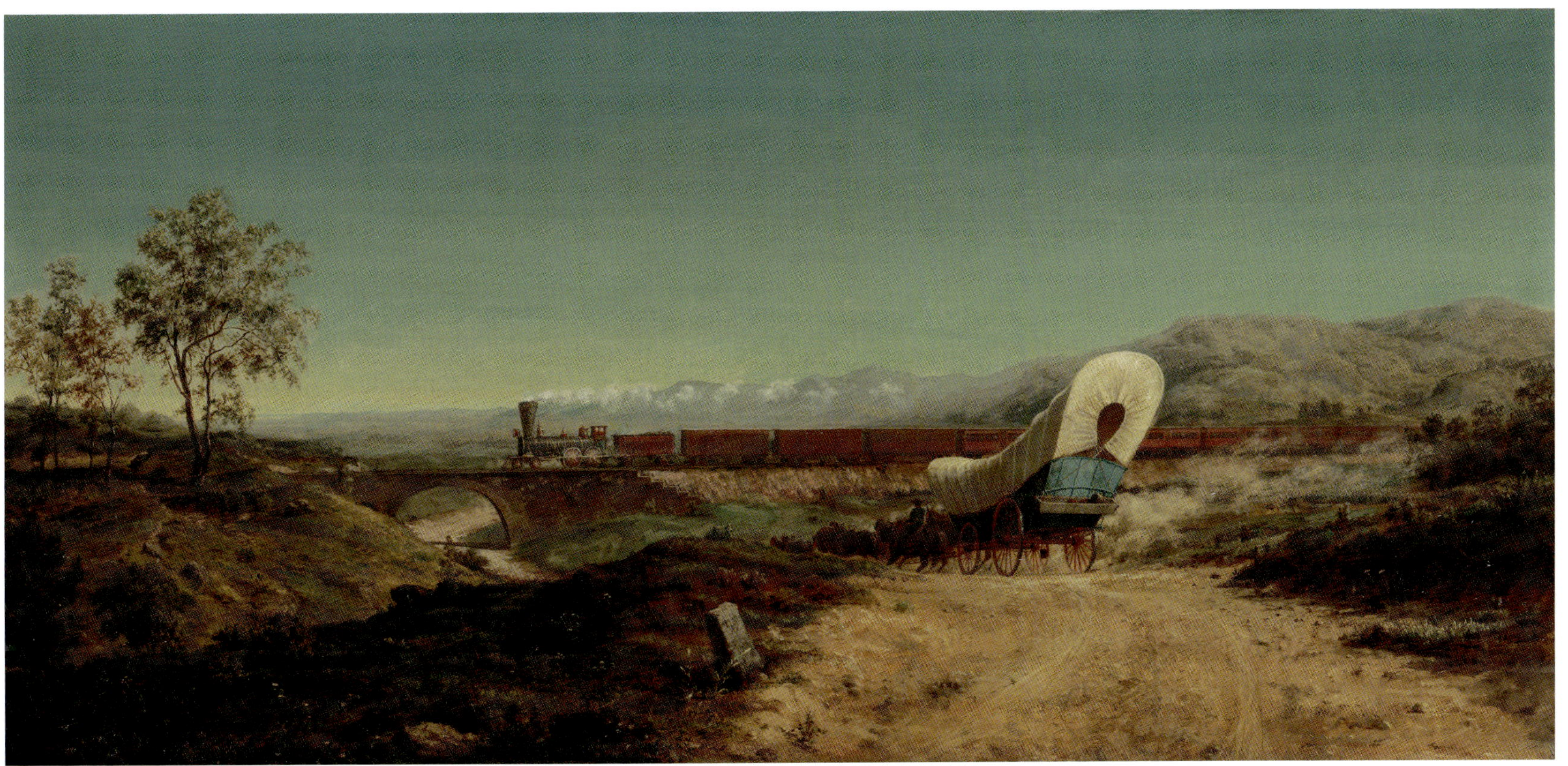

they appear as quasi-mythical beings. As the sun sets on this manufactured world of apparent plenty, Native nations have become mere characters populating the folk tales of a bygone era.

Thomas Proudley Otter's *On the Road* (1860; fig. 8), painted in Pennsylvania, was even more straightforward in presenting the railroad as an instrument of future expansion that would complement and even outdo previous technologies. The painting visually conflates a Conestoga wagon, one of the most enduring symbols of migration to the American interior, and a train crossing a bridge.

Both vehicles are shown heading in the same direction, symbolically the left (westward), thus hinting at their similar function: to assist the US in its continental project of settlement.[19] Railroads, it is implied, have become the new wagons, faster and more dependable.

Council Bluffs, Iowa, chosen as the starting point of a future transcontinental railroad line in the 1860s, would be a case in point of that transition. Celebrating the establishment of the Union Pacific Railroad's new origin station in town, Scottish artist Andrew Melrose's *Westward the Star of Empire Takes*

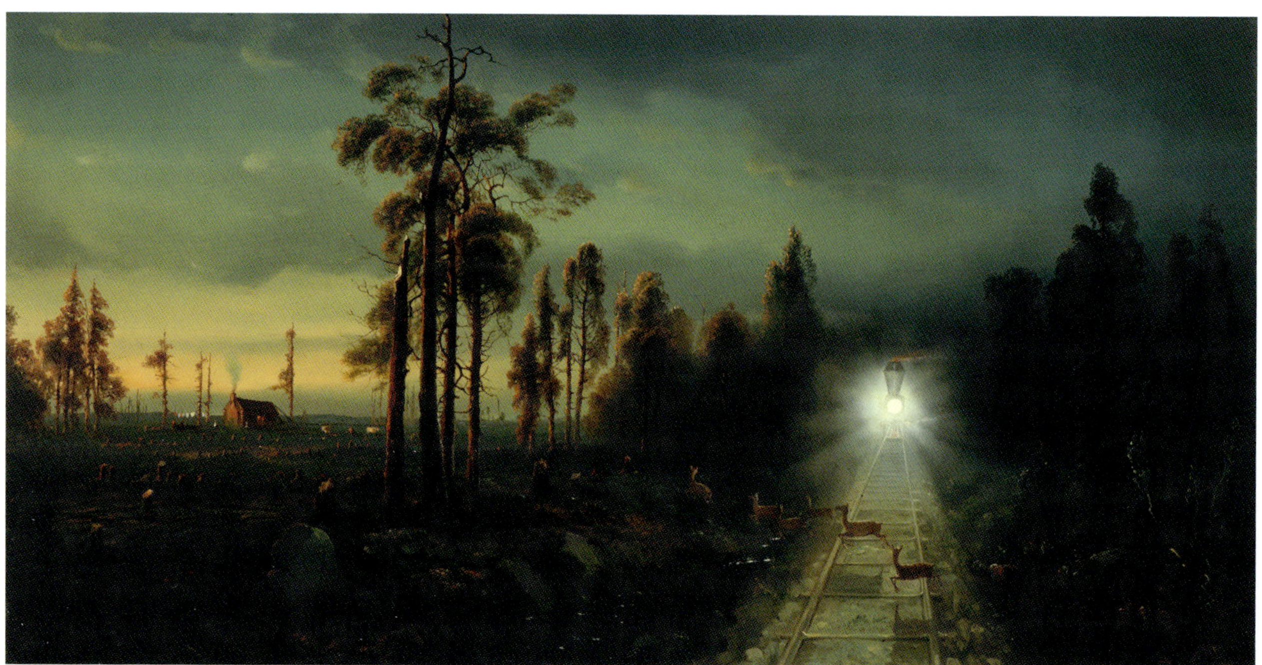

Its Way (1867; fig. 9) confronts its viewers with the blinding light of a rushing locomotive swiftly advancing through cleared woods.[20] Wildlife scatters before the machine, as a homestead of farming settlers stands assertively nearby. All around, trees have been cut down to make way for an agricultural paradise. Yet the days of wagons have gone, as prospective immigrants can now rely on the faster technology of the rail to transport them to the fertile fields of the American West. Founded in the late 1840s as the Mormon settlement of Kanesville, Council Bluffs, which adopted its current name in 1853, was especially attuned to these questions, having served as the departure point of emigration trails to Oregon and California.[21] These trails witnessed an influx of thousands of migrants who gathered on lands appropriated from Umoⁿhoⁿ (Omaha), Očhéthi Šakówiŋ (Dakota), and Báxoje (Ioway) peoples, as well as the forcibly-displaced Bodéwadmi (Potawatomi) of the Great Lakes, who arrived in 1837.[22] The introduction of railroads in the area not

only brought dramatic changes to this existing trail culture, but it accelerated the incorporation of the Missouri River into a US imaginary of white expansion.

The Alsace-born Henry Farny, influenced by both German and French visual art traditions, would have remembered these preoccupations with land, technology, and modernity when confronted with a fast-changing American West at the turn of the twentieth century. In 1907, for instance, the traveling immigrant painter proposed the railroad as an incarnation of the morning of a new day (cat. 3), that of a triumph of the machine over the once-impenetrable landscapes of the Rocky Mountains. Mounted on horses near a ledge, a column of Indigenous figures looks on as a train easily races through a picturesque valley blanketed with snow. The picture, one of Farny's best known, symbolically stages the winter of Native civilizations outpaced by the "iron horse," spectators of their own impending demise.[23] Equally absent from the scene, however, is the manpower necessary to carve the landscape

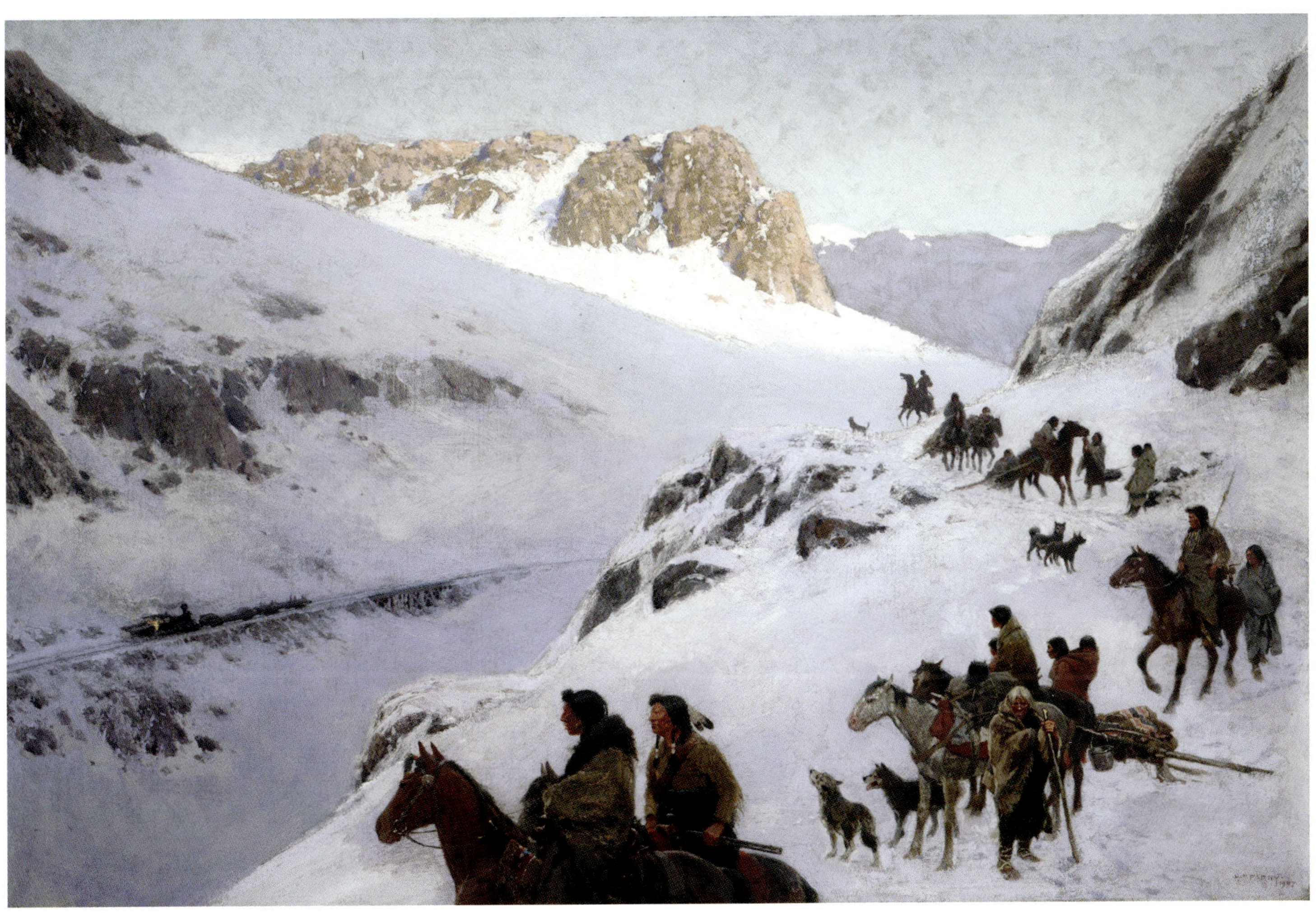

**Henry Farny (American,
born France, 1847–1916)**
Morning of a New Day, 1907

oil on canvas
22 × 32 in.

National Cowboy & Western
Heritage Museum, Oklahoma City

Museum purchase, 1998.72.7

into the shape of a Euro-American settlement. As early as the 1860s, immigrant Chinese laborers, with the addition of a small number of Indigenous and recently emancipated Black workers, toiled away to fulfill the Manifest Destiny promised by the rail. The beauty of the triumphant machine belied a complex reality of labor and resistance.

Derailing Colonialism: Reading Resistance Behind Railroad Views

In February 1869, German readers of the weekly journal *Illustrirte Zeitung* encountered a striking description:

> Through the otherwise so silent, endless expanse of the prairie, the machine carrying civilization yells and groans, and sounds the blow and hammers, and the home world of the "legitimate dwellers" is getting narrower and narrower…. But he still has the weapons of the weak, cunning and deceit, against the overpowering opponent. When the darkness of night lies over the prairie…, the Red Men approach the side of the road, crawling like cats pressed to the ground, so that the stiff, tall grass of the plain hides their creeping bodies.[24]

In florid terms, the article referred to Theodore Kaufmann's painting *Westward the Star of Empire* (1867; cat. 4), a hit on both sides of the Atlantic. Born in Germany but living in the United States since 1851, the artist had worked as an illustrator in New York City before serving as correspondent for the Union Army during the Civil War. It was not as a chronicler or caricaturist, however, that Kaufmann would experience his biggest success. The Reconstruction

Era following the bitter conflict would allow him to leave his mark with a picture presenting a group of Indigenous men involved in an act of sabotage. Emerging from the grass of a prairie under the cover of night, the group has cut and removed two sections of railroad tracks in order to cause an approaching train to derail. As the locomotive's headlight already projects its reddish glow onto the vegetation, one of the figures escapes to the left, leaving behind a stone-head hatchet, or perhaps a tomahawk, that he used to split the metal apart. Kaufmann's Indigenous characters are purposefully not particularized. Their painted faces, their hair adorned with feathers, their attire—all reflect generic accoutrements that most Europeans and Euro-Americans would have associated with Indigenous peoples of the Great Plains. Kaufmann relegated Native Americans to a realm of darkness, crouched down, their heads barely surfacing above untraversable herbage. The depiction implies the futility of this particular act, as American modernity would advance into the vastness of the continent despite attempts to stop it.

Kaufmann's conflictual vision of the railroad captured transatlantic Euro-American fantasies about supposed Indigenous hostility. When his work was displayed in Düsseldorf and Vienna in 1868-69, it elicited visceral responses clearly describing the stakes of introducing railroads in North America as a struggle "for the winning of freedom and the … advancing [of] civilization [against] barbarism."[25] The picture tapped into white anxieties that settler-colonialism may be slowed down by stubborn Indigenous opposition. So successful was this narrative that Kaufmann felt compelled to paint a second version of his scene to be turned into prints.[26] The pair of works was soon renamed

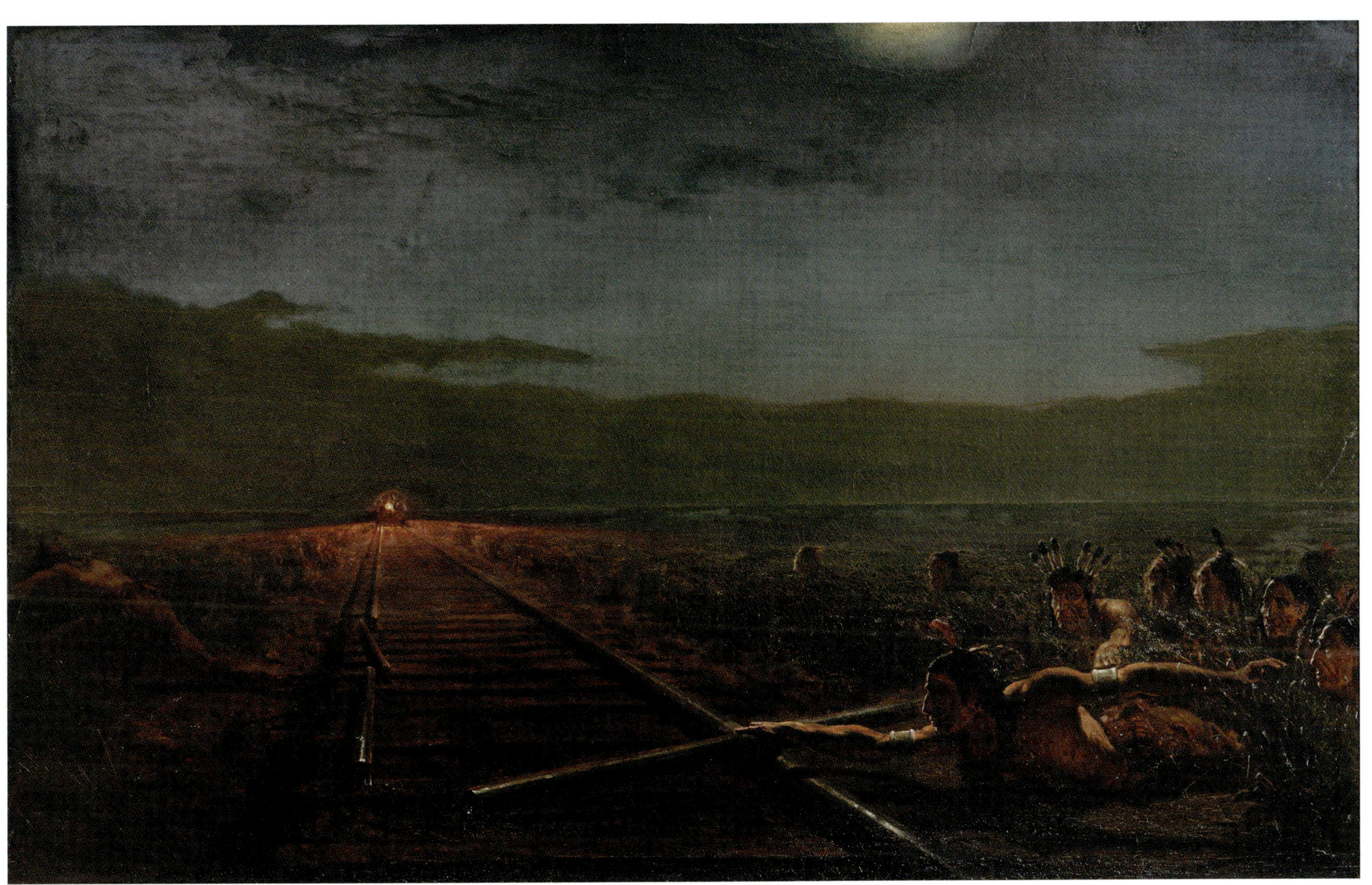

Cat. 4

Theodore Kaufmann (American, 1814-1896)
Westward the Star of Empire, 1867

oil on canvas
35½ × 55½ in.

Collection of the St. Louis Mercantile Library
at the University of Missouri-St. Louis

Gift of James E. Yeatman

Westward the Star of Empire to equate them with Andrew Melrose's contemporary picture. The title under which they were perpetuated reveals the underlying importance of the railroad to the consolidation of the US as an imperial force against competing sovereignties perceived as threatening. In actuality, only two separate actions of resistance by Indigenous people were recorded against the transcontinental railroad: one by a Heévâhetaneo'o (Southern Cheyenne) party in August 1867 and one by Lakȟóta (Lakota) men in September 1868, both of which occurred in Nebraska.[27] Yet sporadic attacks on railroads, especially by Indigenous peoples, had special currency as entertainment, allowing Euro-Americans to regain control of the narrative. Visual dramatization of these incidents served to deprive them of any political relevance—sensationalizing meant disarming.

A similar spirit also underscores Thomas Hill's *The Driving of the Last Spike* (1881; fig. 10), which recreated the meeting of the Union and Central Pacific railroads at Promontory Point, Utah, on May 10, 1869, the official completion of the transcontinental line between Council Bluffs and Sacramento. Surrounding Central Pacific president Leland Stanford, a large crowd of onlookers forms the cast of the scene.[28] The composition emulates European history painting, organized in the manner of a theater stage, with "figures … placed in positions pre-arranged, and not easily varied," as stated in the pamphlet accompanying the work's public presentation in San Francisco in January 1881.[29] Laterally framing Stanford's symbolic hammering of the last spike into the tracks, a US flag and a telegraph pole answer each other, equating the destiny of the country with that of technological development. Noteworthy,

however, is the presence of both Indigenous and Chinese figures. Two of the Asian workers, exoticized by their distinct attire, crouch down near Stanford and seem to look up to him with quasi-reverence. The obvious artificiality of Hill's scene naturalized not only the presence of the railroad in the landscape but also immigrant exploitation by white entrepreneurs, by presenting a false communion around the goal of completing the transcontinental line.[30] As in the case of Indigenous resistance, the backbreaking labor of some 20,000 Chinese railroad employees on the transatlantic lines was neutralized through artistic representations. Both their presence and labor were paradoxically made invisible in plain sight, romanticized in pictures like Hill's.[31] Gone were the days of the Chinese strike that had halted work on the railroad in June 1867, an event that would later justify racial discrimination and management-stirred competition between Asian, free Black, and Indigenous workers.[32]

In this context, the visual arts once again downplayed the discontent of Chinese laborers, by far the largest contingent of the railroad workforce, which effectively diminished the importance of any action they may have taken to improve their condition and the racial discrimination they suffered. Sent out west by *Frank Leslie's Illustrated Newspaper* to portray Asian immigrants in California and the Rockies, painter Joseph Becker, for instance, still applied a measure of the railroad sublime impulse to his subject. A former Civil War correspondent, Becker devoted a series of illustrations to the railroad and its workforce in the years immediately following the conflict.[33] Leaving New York in October 1869 for San Francisco via the newly completed transcontinental rail, Becker started publishing his

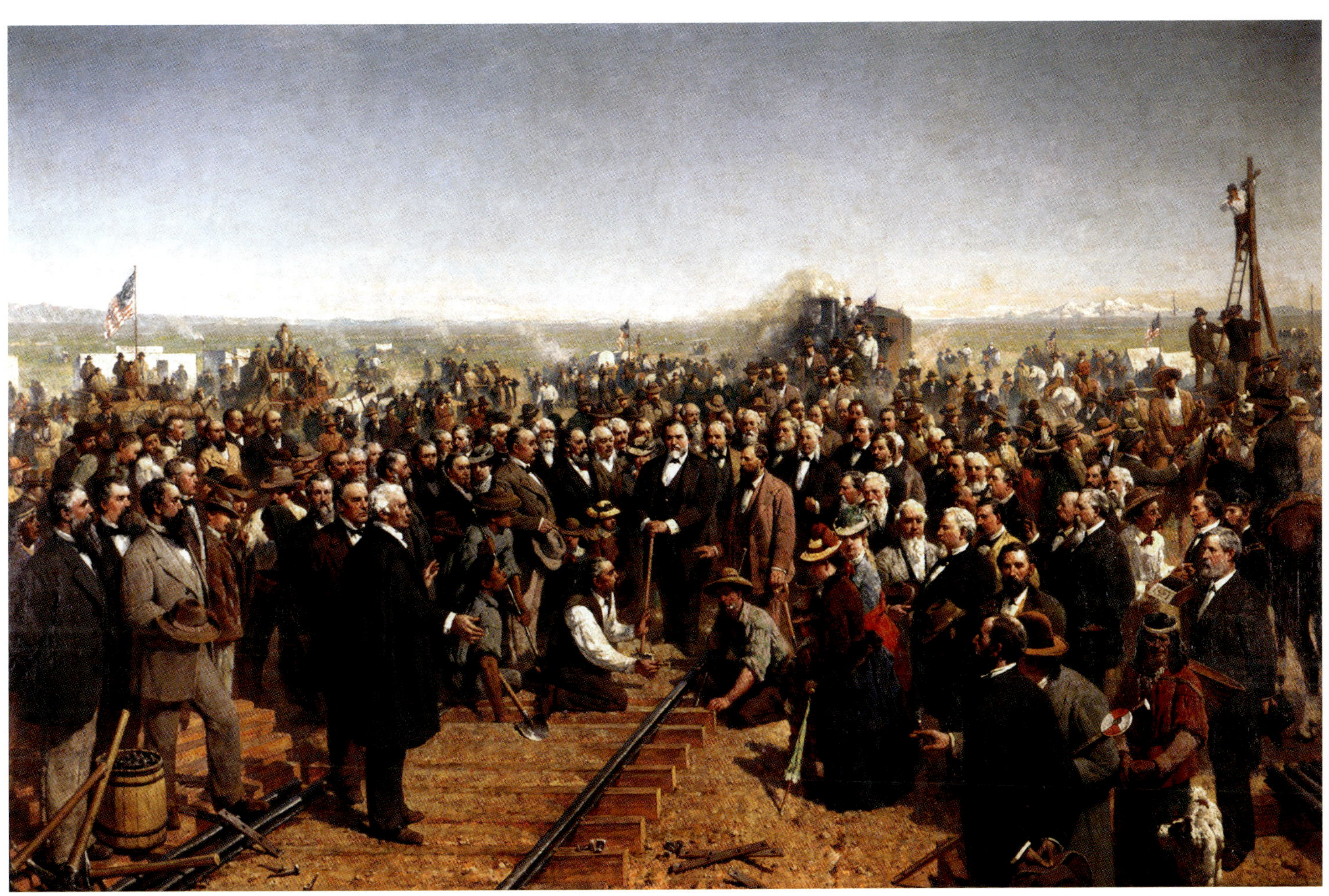

Fig. 10

Thomas Hill (American, born in England, 1829–1908)
The Driving of the Last Spike, 1881

oil on canvas
96 × 144½ in.

California State Railroad
Museum Library & Archives,
Sacramento, California

field sketches in *Frank Leslie's* after the November 13, 1869, issue.[34] Some of these images, like *Chinese Railroad Workers and Landscape* (fig. 11), present a further naturalization of immigrant labor. Here, Becker turned his individual figures into props in a majestic composition that aestheticizes both the surrounding nature and railroad technology of the American West. Set in a picturesque winter landscape, *Snow Sheds on the Central Pacific Railroad in the Sierra Nevada Mountains* (fig. 12), one of the oils that Becker also completed based on his trip, threads the same kind of discourse. A group of workers clearly coded as Chinese, some holding shovels, waves with excitement at the sight of a Central Pacific Railroad train dashing through sheds that they were responsible for building. More than praising of the company's achievements, the painting perpetuates a misleading idea of benevolence towards the laborers, foregrounding the machine as the result of their grateful toil.[35] By the same token, famed landscapist Albert Bierstadt brushed aside the labor required to dig through the towering mountain ranges of California as he completed a painting of Donner Lake commissioned by another railroad magnate, Collis P. Huntington.[36] Once again, both the final canvas and its smaller-scale studies (cat. 5) resorted to a sublime aesthetic of landscape to conceal settler-colonial violence and exploitative commerce behind the sheer awe provoked by a grandiose scene: the illusory symbiosis between raw nature, technique, and human power.

The Burden of the Railroad Sublime

The railroad sublime did not disappear after the American Frontier had been reached, concluding the "first period of American history," to reprise

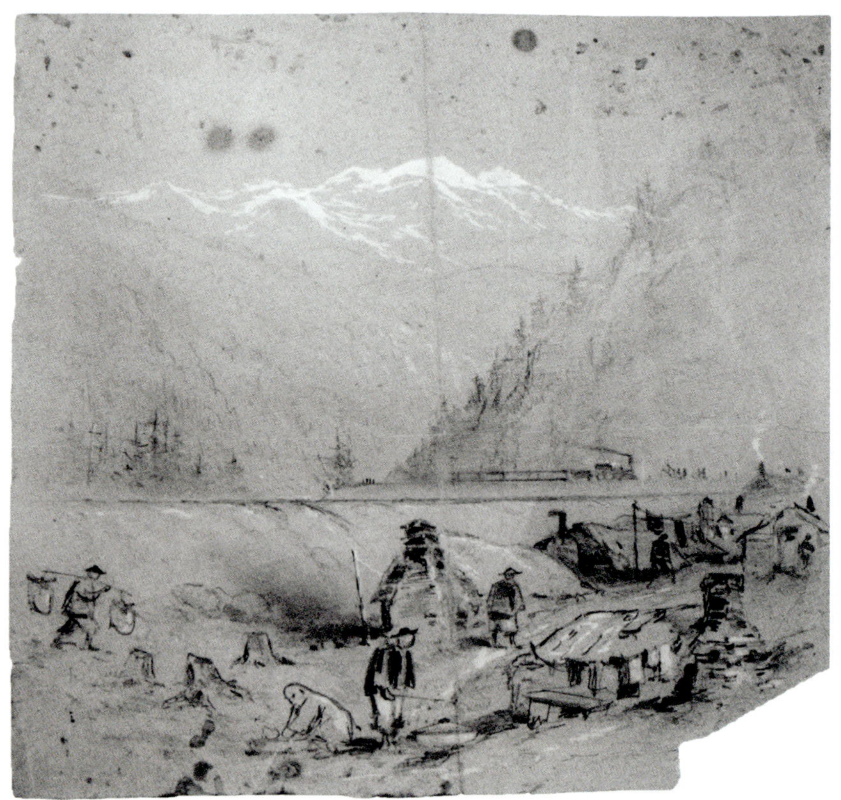

Fig. 11

Joseph Becker (American, 1841-1910)
Chinese Railroad Workers and Landscape, 1869-70

white gouache and graphite on toned paper
9½ × 10 in.

Boston College Libraries

The Becker Collection, 1840-1910.
RR-JB-69-70-10

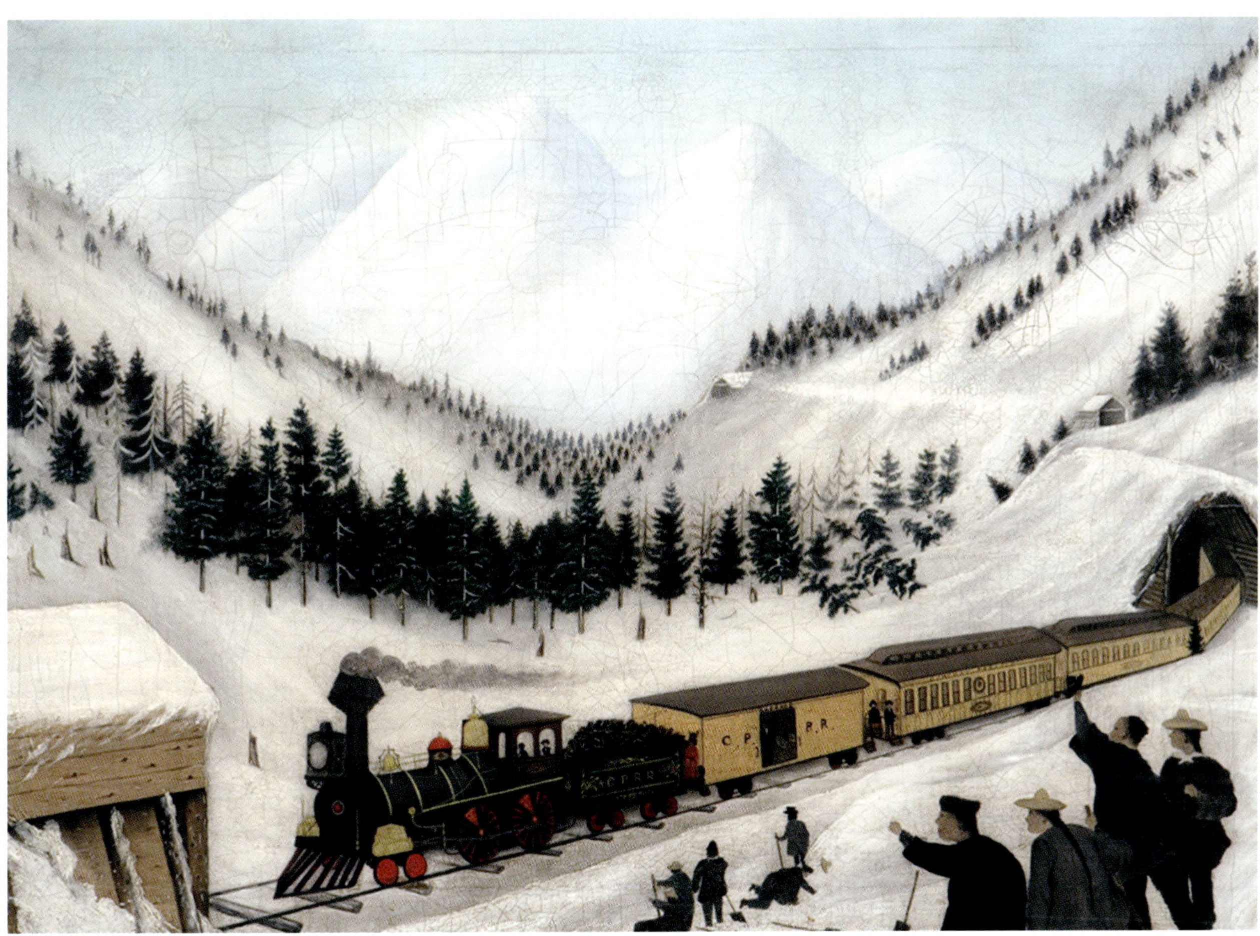

Fig. 12

Joseph Becker (American, 1841–1910)
*Snow Sheds on the Central Pacific
Railroad in the Sierra Nevada
Mountains*, late 19th century

oil on canvas
19 × 26 in.

Gilcrease Museum, Tulsa, Oklahoma

Gift of the Thomas Gilcrease
Foundation, 01.1212

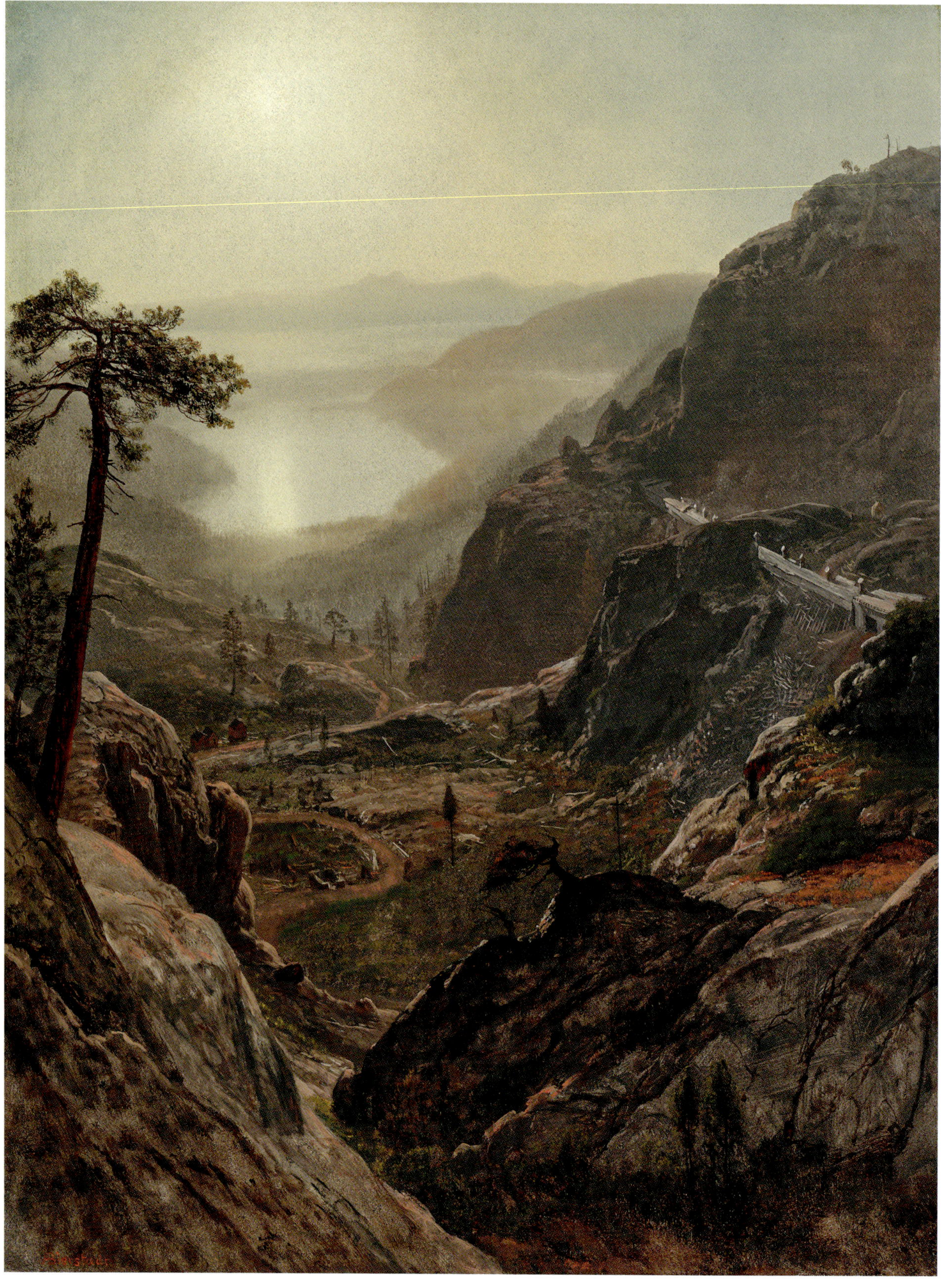

Cat. 5

Albert Bierstadt (American, 1830-1902)
View of Donner Lake, California,
1871-72

oil on paper mounted on canvas
29¼ × 21⅞ in.

Fine Arts Museums of San Francisco

Gift of Anna Bennett and Jessie Jonas in
memory of August F. Jonas Jr., 1984.54

a controversial idea famously developed by historian Frederick Jackson Turner in 1893.[37] By that time, the United States had laid down close to 193,000 miles of tracks, the result of grueling work and an ever-growing encroachment on larger swaths of Native land.[38] Visual artists had often downplayed or sidelined racial and economic injustices, as well as acts of resistance, occurring in response to the infrastructure. Deeply ingrained in US-American identity after decades of representation, trains had become a crucial part of a vast and widespread imagery of American innovation, and nineteenth-century painted views of the technology helped to establish its myths. Sublime railroad imagery would soon be enlisted by American painters to illustrate new imperial and colonial projects, this time outside of the borders of the nation. Large-scale projects involving US intervention abroad allowed for the continued pursuit of Manifest Destiny through technology after the West had already been appropriated.

In the early 1900s, for instance, a wilderness would once again be gutted by American technology to accommodate a large infrastructure, that of the Panama Canal.[39] Here too would railroads enable US commerce to infringe upon seized lands. It was no coincidence that the enterprise should be advocated for by Theodore Roosevelt, the US president perhaps most closely identified with the cultural values of white settlers in the American West, and who had himself tried his luck as a rancher in North Dakota in the mid-1880s.[40] The Panama Canal Zone, administered as an unincorporated territory of the United States between 1903 and 1979, became the theater of renewed Euro-American technological hubris, with railways playing a prominent role. As the United States entered another phase of its history on the world stage, the burden of the railroad sublime continued to impact those excluded from its dominant narratives of plenty and progress, and landscape painters would continue to explore these dynamics.

Endnotes

1   Susan Danly, introduction to *The Railroad in American Art: Representations of Technological Change*, ed. Susan Danly and Leo Marx (Cambridge, MA: MIT Press, 1988), 5-6. See also Kathleen Waters Sander, *John W. Garrett and the Baltimore and Ohio Railroad* (Baltimore: Johns Hopkins University Press, 2017), 63; and Herbert Gottfried, *Erie Railway Tourist, 1854-1886: Transporting Visual Culture* (Bethlehem, PA: Lehigh University Press, 2018), 28-29.

2   David Hunter Strother, "Artists' Excursion Over the Baltimore & Ohio Rail Road," *Harper's New Monthly Magazine* 19, no. 109 (June 1859): 1.

3   On Rossiter's painting, see Susan Danly Walther, *The Railroad in the American Landscape, 1850-1950* (Wellesley, MA: Wellesley College Museum, 1981), 84. See also John R. Stilgoe, *Metropolitan Corridor: Railroads and the American Scene* (New Haven, CT: Yale University Press, 1985), 138-39; John A. Cuthbert, *Early Art and Artists in West Virginia: An Introduction and Biographical Directory* (Morgantown: West Virginia University Press, 2000), 73-74; David E. Nye, *America as Second Creation: Technology and Narratives of New Beginnings* (Cambridge, MA: MIT Press, 2003), 160-62; and Ian Kennedy, "Crossing Continents: America and Beyond," in *The Railway: Art in the Age of Steam*, ed. Ian Kennedy and Julian Treuherz, exh. cat. (New Haven, CT: Yale University Press, 2008), 134.

4   Literature about this painting is abundant, but for a thorough analysis of the work see Ian Carter, *Railways and Culture in Britain: The Epitome of Modernity* (Manchester: Manchester University Press, 2001), 51-70. Carter was inspired by John Gage, *Turner: Rain, Steam and Speed* (London: Allen Lane the Penguin Press, 1972).

5   Among recent volumes and articles dealing with this topic, see Edward M. Spiers, *Engines for Empire: The Victorian Army and Its Use of Railways* (Manchester: Manchester University Press, 2017); Aparajita Mukhopadhyay, *Imperial Technology and "Native" Agency: A Social History of Railways in Colonial India, 1850-1920* (New York: Routledge, 2018); Julio Decker, "Lines in the Sand: Railways and the Archipelago of Colonial Territorialization in German Southwest Africa, 1897-1914," *Journal of Historical Geography* 70 (October 2020): 74-87; and J. P. Daughton, *In the Forest of No Joy: The Congo-Océan Railroad and the Tragedy of French Colonialism* (New York: W. W. Norton & Company, 2021).

6   John R. Stilgoe, "Smiling Scenes," in *Views and Visions: American Landscape before 1830*, ed. Edward J. Nygren with Bruce E. Robertson, exh. cat. (Washington, DC: Corcoran Gallery of Art, 1986), 227. The resorting to a picturesque countryside aesthetic to promote and sell the antebellum American land has also been examined by Ross Barrett, "Bursting the Bubble: John Quidor's Money Diggers and Land Speculation," *American Art* 30, no. 1 (Spring 2016): 35.

7   Leo Marx, *The Machine in the Garden: Technology and the Pastoral Ideal in America* (Oxford: Oxford University Press, 1964), 16.

8   Marx, 35.

9   Alan Wallach, "Thomas Cole's *River in the Catskills* as Antipastoral," *Art Bulletin* 84, no. 2 (2002): 339. See also Kenneth W. Maddox, "Thomas Cole and the Railroad: Gentle Maledictions," *Archives of American Art Journal* 30, no. 1/4 (1990): 147.

10   For a good analysis of the painting, see Andrew Lyndon Knighton, *Idle Threats: Men and the Limits of Productivity in Nineteenth Century America* (New York: New York University Press, 2012), 79-80. On Heade's discourses on rural past, as opposed to technological present, see Sarah Burns, *Pastoral Inventions: Rural Life in Nineteenth-Century American Art and Culture* (Philadelphia: Temple University Press, 1989), 38-39.

11   David E. Nye, *American Technological Sublime* (Cambridge, MA: MIT Press, 1994), 48-50. The concept was originally coined by Marx (*The Machine in the Garden*, 195) and was expanded on by Perry Miller, *The Life of The Mind in America: From the Revolution to the Civil War* (New York: Harcourt, Brace & World, 1965). More recently, Nye completed his 1994 work with a second volume titled *Seven Sublimes* (Cambridge, MA: MIT Press, 2022).

12   Vanessa Meikle Schulman, *Work Sights: The Visual Culture of Industry in Nineteenth-Century America* (Amherst: University of Massachusetts Press, 2015), 27.

13   Barbara Novak, *Nature and Culture: American Landscape and Painting, 1825-1875* (New York: Oxford University Press, 1980), 149.

14   On this painting, see Nancy Price Graff and E. Thomas Pierce, eds., *Charles Louis Heyde, Nineteenth Century Vermont Landscape Painter: With Catalogue Raisonné* (Burlington, VT: Robert Hull Fleming Museum, 2001), 23.

15   Manu Karuka, *Empire's Tracks: Indigenous Nations, Chinese Workers, and the Transcontinental Railroad* (Oakland: University of California Press, 2019), 8.

16   One of the best studies of the rhetoric of the "vanishing Indian" remains Brian W. Dippie, *The Vanishing American: White Attitudes and U.S. Indian Policy* (Middletown, CT: Wesleyan University Press, 1982). Though not focused on the American West, another excellent study is Jean M. O'Brien, *Firsting and Lasting: Writing Indians Out of Existence in New England* (Minneapolis: University of Minnesota Press, 2010). For a perspective centered on the visual arts, see Thomas L. Doughton, "Text, Image and the Discourse of Disappearing Indians in Antebellum American Landscape Painting," *Interfaces* 38 (2017): 195-222, https://doi.org/10.4000/interfaces.323.

17   O'Sullivan was writing in the context of the annexation of the Republic of Texas into the Union: "It is surely to be found … in the manner in which other nations have undertaken to intrude themselves into it …, in a spirit of hostile interference against us, for the avowed object of thwarting our policy and hampering our power, limiting our greatness and checking the fulfillment of our manifest destiny to overspread the continent allotted by Providence for the free development of our yearly multiplying millions." John Louis O'Sullivan, "Annexation," *United States Magazine and Democratic Review* 17, no. 85 (July/August 1845): 5.

18   Rebecca Bedell, "Asher Durand's *Progress* Reconsidered," *Panorama: Journal of the Association of Historians of American Art* 5, no. 1 (Spring 2019), https://doi.org/10.24926/24716839.1688.

19   On Otter's painting, see Kennedy, "Crossing Continents," 126; and Margaret C. Conrads, ed., *The Collections of the Nelson-Atkins Museum of Art: American Paintings to 1945, Volume 2* (Kansas City, MO: Nelson-Atkins Museum of Art, 2007), 181.

20   On Melrose's painting, see William H. Truettner, "Ideology and Image: Justifying Westward Expansion," in *The West as America: Reinterpreting Images of the Frontier, 1820-1920*, ed. William H. Truettner, exh. cat. (Washington, DC: Published for the National Museum of American Art by the Smithsonian Institution Press, 1991), 31-32; William Cronon, "Telling Tales on Canvas: Landscapes of Frontier Change," in *Discovered Lands, Invented Pasts: Transforming Visions of the American West*, ed. Thomas Gilcrease, exh. cat. (New Haven, CT: Yale University Press, 1992), 72-73; and Michael Adas, *Dominance by Design: Technological Imperatives and America's Civilizing Mission* (Cambridge, MA: Belknap Press of Harvard University Press, 2006), 91-92.

21   Lawrence H. Larsen, *Upstream Metropolis: An Urban Biography of Omaha and Council Bluffs* (Lincoln: University of Nebraska Press, 2007), 31-39.

22 Lynn M. Alex, *Iowa's Archaeological Past* (Iowa City: University of Iowa Press, 2000), 223-24. See also John P. Bowes, *Land Too Good for Indians: Northern Indian Removal* (Norman: University of Oklahoma Press, 2016), 161-62.

23 On Farny's painting, see J. Gray Sweeney, "Racism, Nationalism, and Nostalgia," in *Race-ing Art History*, ed. Kymberly N. Pinder (New York: Routledge, 2002), 156-58; Emily B. Neff, *The Modern West: American Landscapes, 1890-1950*, exh. cat. (New Haven, CT: Yale University Press, 2006), 65; and Susan L. Meyn, *Henry Farny Paints the Far West*, exh. cat. (Cincinnati: Cincinnati Art Museum, 2007), 29-30.

24 The original German-language text states: "Durch die sonst so schweigende, endlose Fläche der Prairie gellt und ächzt die culturtragende Maschine und tönt der Schlag und Hämmer, und dem ,Legitimen' wird seine Heimatwelt enger und enger…. Aber die Waffen des Schwachen, die List und Tücke, hat er noch zur gegen den übermächtigen Gegner. Wenn das nächtliche Dunkel über der Prairie lagert …, schleichen katzenartig an den Boden gedrückt, daß das starre, hohe Gras der Fläche ihre hinkriechenden Leiber verbirgt, die rothen Männer heran an die Wegschwellen." [Translation by the author] "Indianer, einen Eisenbahnzug überfallend. Originalgemälde von Theodor Kaufmann," *Illustrirte Zeitung* (Leipzig) 52, no. 1336 (February 6, 1869): 102. This primary source was first quoted in H. Glenn Penny, *Kindred by Choice: Germans and American Indians Since 1800* (Chapel Hill: University of North Carolina Press, 2013), 46-47.

25 "Indianer, einen Eisenbahnzug überfallend," 102. On the exhibition of the painting in Europe, see Alexander Roob, "Thomas Nast and Theodor Kaufmann: Higher Forms of Hieroglyph," Melton Prior Institute, November 10, 2012, https://www.meltonpriorinstitut.org/content/en/thomas-nast-and-theodor-kaufmann-higher-forms-of-hieroglyph-alexander-roob.

26 One version of the scene is in the collection of the St. Louis Mercantile Library at the University of Missouri. The other is in the American Museum of Western Art—The Anschutz Collection, in Denver, Colorado. The latter is reproduced in Joan Carpenter Troccoli, *Painters and the American West: The Anschutz Collection, Volume 1* (Denver: Denver Art Museum, 2000), 75.

27 The first event became known as the Plum Creek Raid and served to build up fears about Indigenous threats to the infrastructure. See Thornton Waite, *Attacking the Union Pacific: The Truth and the Legend behind the 1867 Cheyenne Indian Raid at Plum Creek, Nebraska* (David City, NE: South Platte Press, 2020). Some art historians have suggested that Kaufmann directly referenced that event in his painting. See Julie Schimmel, "Inventing 'the Indian,'" in Truettner, *The West as America*, 167; and Kennedy, "Crossing Continents," 131.

28 A good overview of the history of this painting, its commissioning, and its exhibition is John Ott, *Manufacturing the Modern Patron in Victorian California: Cultural Philanthropy, Industrial Capital, and Social Authority* (Burlington, VT: Ashgate, 2014), 42-45.

29 *"The Last Spike," a Painting by Thomas Hill Illustrating the Last Scene in the Building of the Overland Railroad. With a History of the Enterprise* (San Francisco: Privately printed by the artist, 1881), 33. Hill acknowledged that he had been inspired by European history painters while completing his picture. His brochure names Horace Vernet (1789-1863), Paul Delaroche (1797-1856), Jean-Léon Gérôme (1824-1904), Wilhelm von Kaulbach (1805-1874), and Adolphe Yvon (1817-1893) as models (see p. 38).

30 Schulman, *Work Sights*, 37.

31 On the past invisibility or misconstruing of Chinese labor on the transcontinental railroad, see two recent publications based on reevaluated primary sources: Gordon H. Chang and Shelley Fisher Fishkin, eds., *The Chinese and the Iron Road: Building the Transcontinental Railroad* (Redwood City, CA: Stanford University Press, 2019), and Gordon H. Chang, *Ghosts of Gold Mountain: The Epic Story of the Chinese Who Built the Transcontinental Railroad* (New York: Houghton Mifflin Harcourt, 2019). A theoretical approach to the visual abstraction of Chinese labor for purposes of colonial exploitation in the nineteenth century is Iyko Day, *Alien Capital: Asian Racialization and the Logic of Settler Colonial Capitalism* (Durham, NC: Duke University Press, 2016), 41-72.

32 Karuka, *Empire's Tracks*, 92-93. On the work of emancipated slaves on the transatlantic railroad and their relations with other laborers, see Eric Arnesen, *Brotherhoods of Color: Black Railroad Workers and the Struggle for Equality* (Cambridge, MA: Harvard University Press, 2001), and Theodore Kornweibel, *Railroads in the African American Experience: A Photographic Journey* (Baltimore: Johns Hopkins University Press, 2010).

33 Richard Francaviglia, *Go East, Young Man: Imagining the American West as the Orient* (Logan: Utah State University Press, 2011), 160-61. On Becker's time as war correspondent, see Judith Arlene Bookbinder and Sheila Gallagher, eds., *First Hand: Civil War Era Drawings from the Becker Collection*, exh. cat. (Chestnut Hill, MA: McMullen Museum of Art at Boston College, 2009).

34 Robert Taft, "The Pictorial Record of the Old West: XI. The Leslie Excursions of 1869 and 1877—Joseph Becker, Harry Ogden, and Walter Yeager," *Kansas Historical Quarterly* 18, no. 2 (May 1950), 118-19, https://www.kshs.org/publicat/khq/1950/1950may_taft.pdf.

35 For a more extensive analysis of the painting, and of a corresponding print published in *Frank Leslie's*, see Ryan Dearinger, *The Filth of Progress: Immigrants, Americans, and the Building of Canals and Railroads in the West* (Oakland: University of California Press, 2016), 181-82. Dearinger even compares the figures to a group of "tourists." For further mentions of the painting, see also Nancy K. Anderson, "The Kiss of Enterprise: The Western Landscape as Symbol and Resource," in Truettner, *The West as America*, 260-61; and Cronon, "Telling Tales on Canvas," 75-76.

36 Ott, *Manufacturing the Modern Patron*, 148-49. Bierstadt's painting, titled *Donner Lake from the Summit* (1873), is now in the collection of the New-York Historical Society.

37 Frederick Jackson Turner, "The Significance of the Frontier in American History (1893)," in *The Frontier in American History*, ed. Frederick Jackson Turner (New York: Henry Holt and Company, 1920), 1-38.

38 Kennedy, "Crossing Continents," 119.

39 A recent, though rather laudatory, account of the enterprise is Peter Pyne, *The Panama Railroad* (Bloomington: Indiana University Press, 2021).

40 Roosevelt later published three accounts related to his life in North Dakota between 1884 and 1887. On Roosevelt's relationship to the American West and his embrace of settler-colonial values associated with the region, see Roger L. Di Silvestro, *Theodore Roosevelt in the Badlands: A Young Politician's Quest for Recovery in the American West* (New York: Walker & Company, 2011).

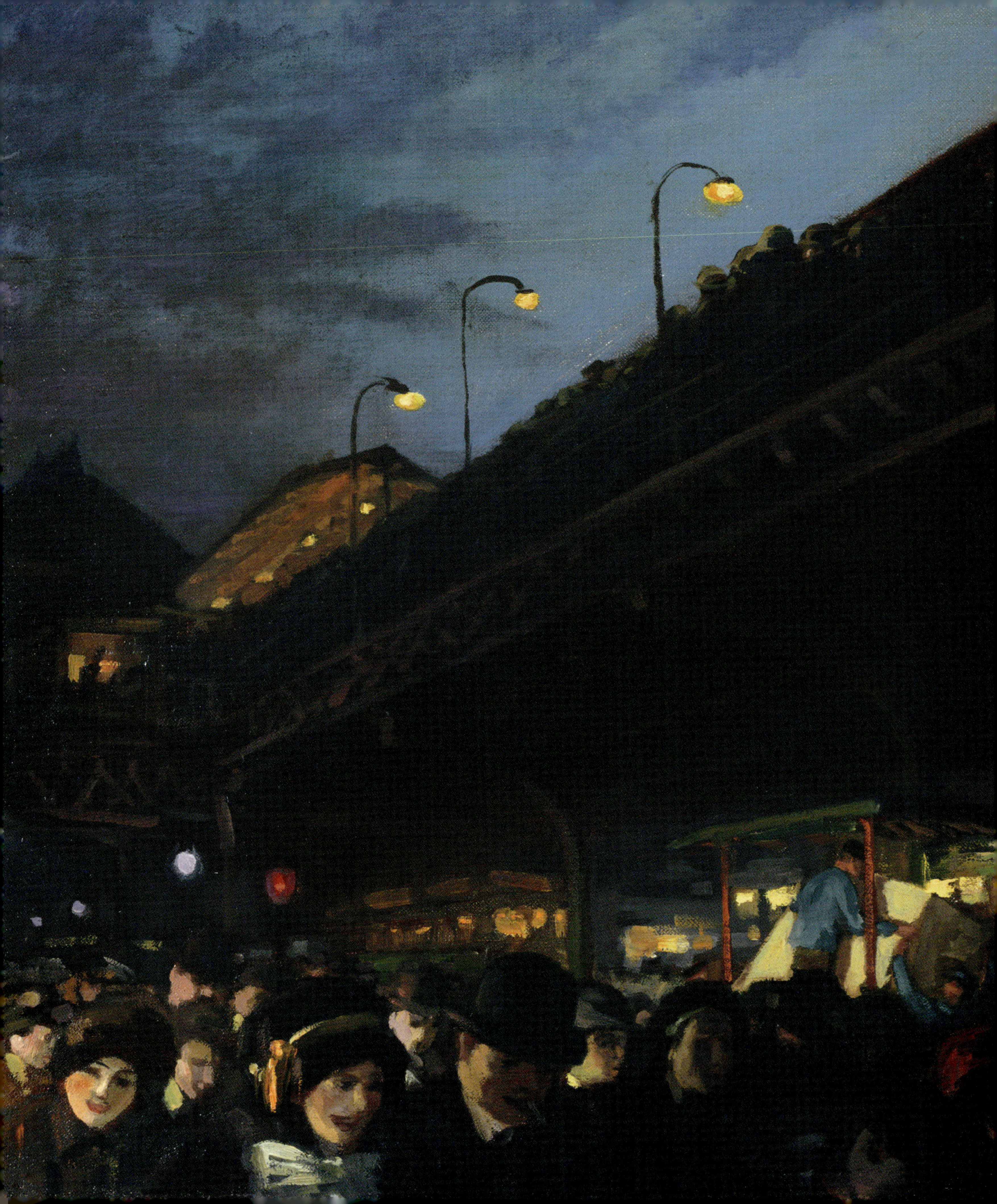

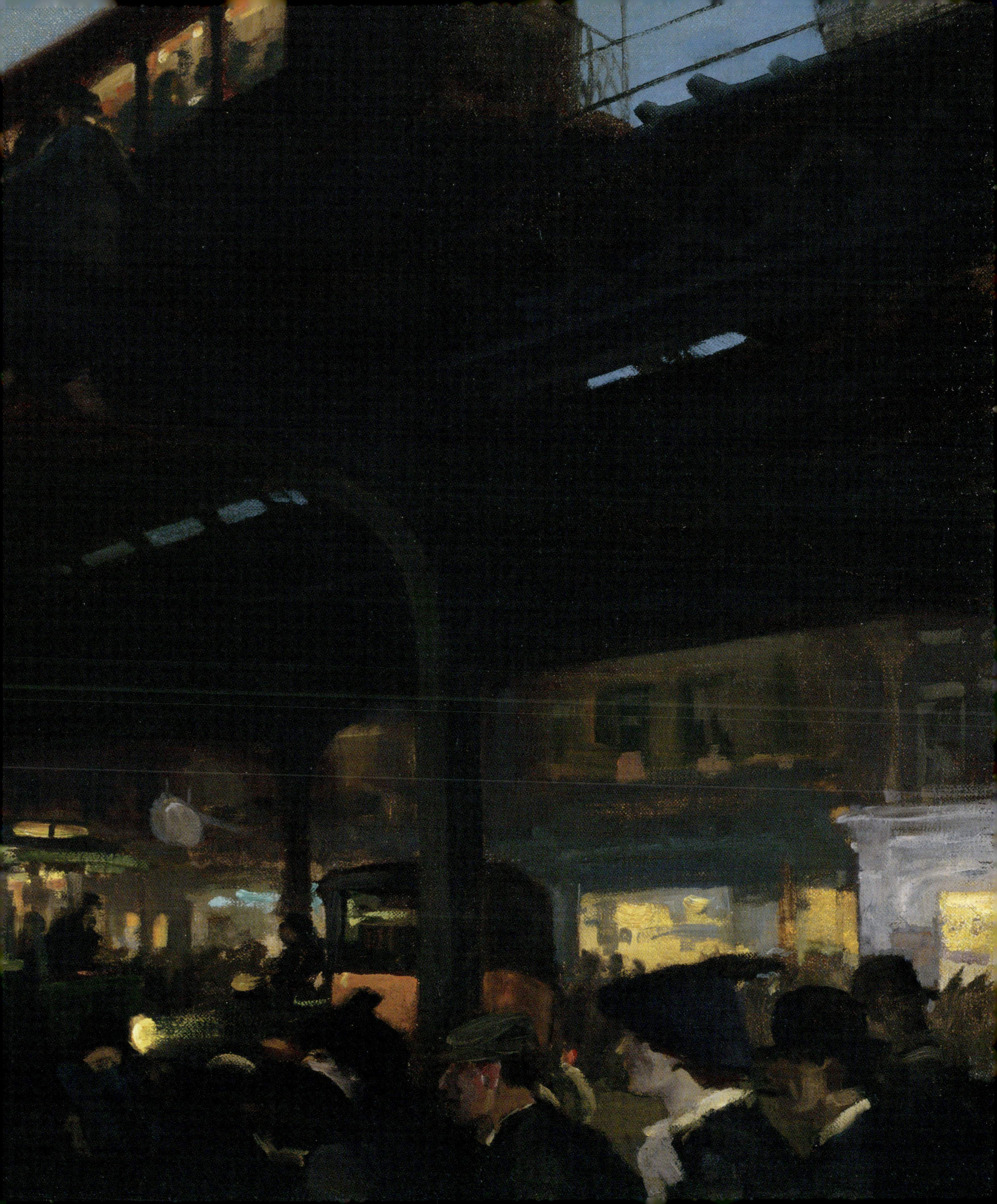

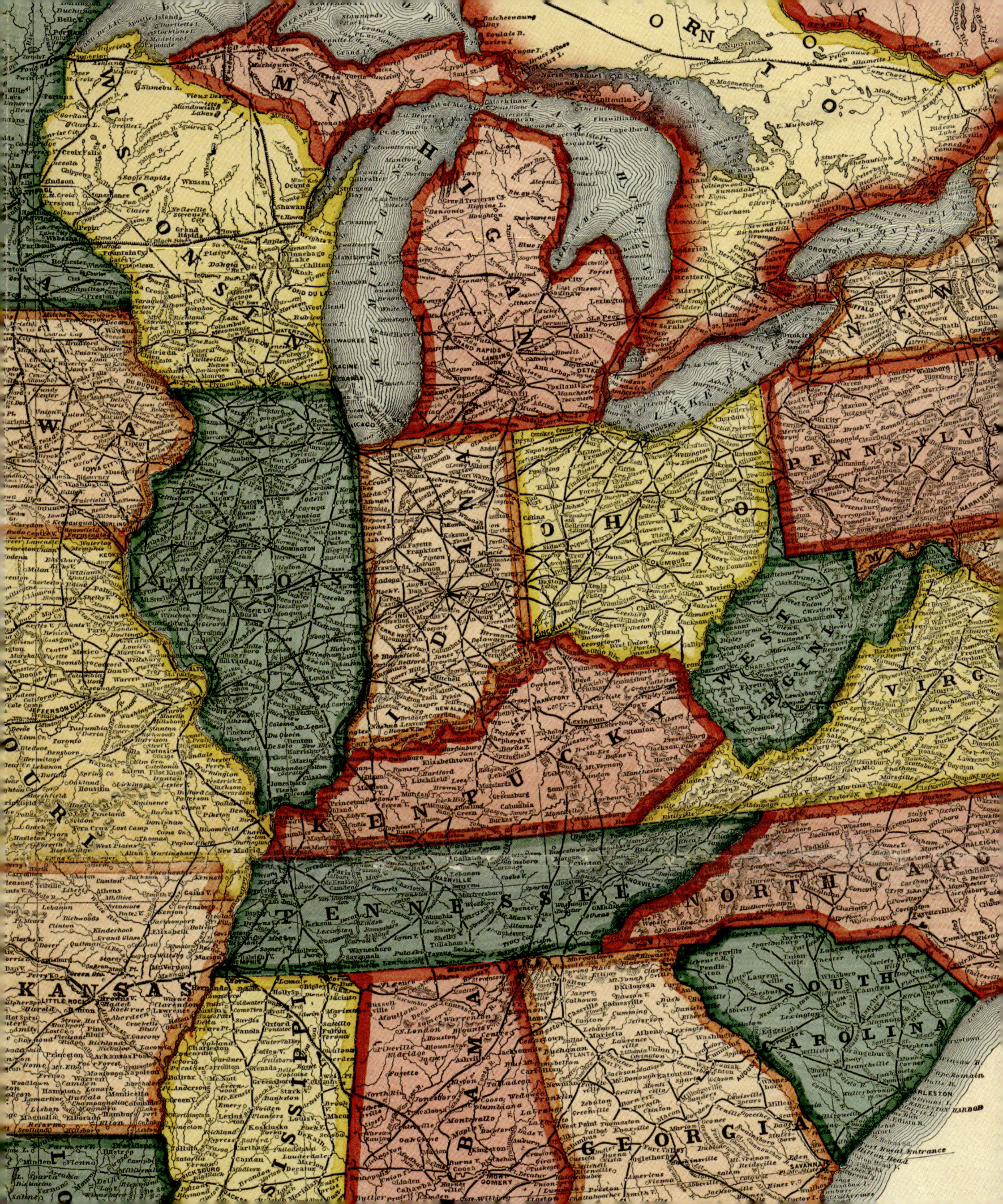

INDUSTRY AND URBANIZATION

The Railroad and American Art in the Progressive Era and Beyond

Julie Pierotti

Men have an indistinct notion that if they keep up this activity of joint stocks and spades long enough all will at length ride somewhere, in next to no time, and for nothing; but though a crowd rushes to the depot and the conductor shouts "All aboard!" when the smoke is blown away and the vapor condensed, it will be perceived that a few are riding, but the rest are run over—and it will be called, and will be, "A melancholy accident."

Henry David Thoreau, *Walden* (1854)[1]

Gaylord Watson (American, 1833-1896), *Centennial American Republic and Railroad Map of the United States and of the Dominion of Canada* (detail), 1875.

Library of Congress Geography and Map Division, Washington, DC

THE DAWN OF THE TWENTIETH CENTURY USHERED IN a new period in American history, focused on advancement in a multitude of ways: social reform, government regulations, and economic expansion. Known as the Progressive Era and generally spanning the mid-1890s into 1917, when the United States entered World War I, this moment witnessed an enormous growth of cities such as New York and Pittsburgh, in terms of their physical sizes, populations, industries, charities, amenities, and amusements. The railroad was central to this growth, providing jobs and the transportation necessary to efficiently move raw materials, goods, and people across the country and among urban areas. By 1902, railroad tracks in the United States measured 200,000 miles, double what they had been just two decades prior, and technology was advancing as well, allowing trains to move more and more passengers and materials ever more quickly toward a growing number of destinations across the country.[2] And while the railroad was crucial to America's rise as a global economic leader, there

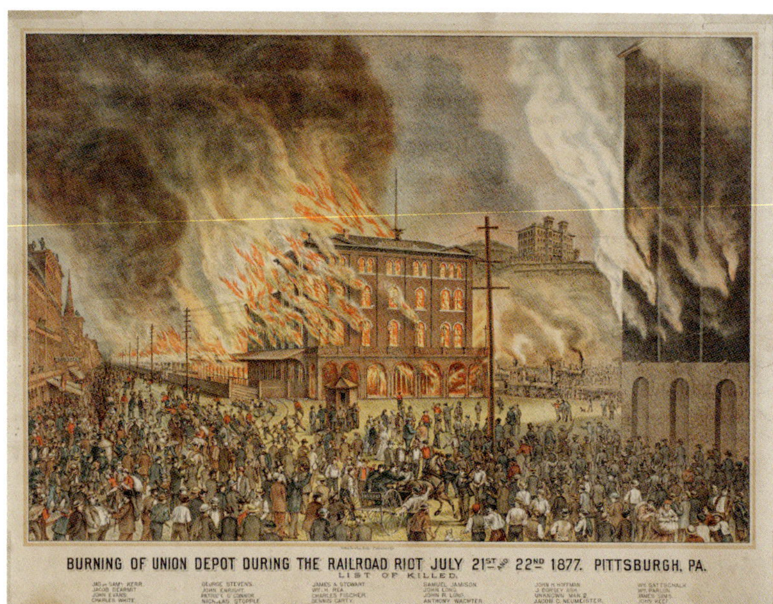

Fig. 13

Otto Krebs (American, 1832-1898)
Burning of Union Depot During the Railroad Riot, July 21st and 22nd, 1877. Pittsburgh, Pennsylvania, ca. 1877

lithograph on paper
22 × 28 in.

Carnegie Museum of Art, Pittsburgh
Bequest of Charles J. Rosenbloom, 74.7.137

Cat. 6

William Robinson Leigh (American, 1866-1955)
The Attempt to Fire the Pennsylvania Railroad Roundhouse in Pittsburgh, at Daybreak on Sunday, July 22, 1877, 1895

oil on canvas on board
28⅜ × 21½ in.

Carnegie Museum of Art, Pittsburgh
Gift of Thomas Mellon Evans, 76.60

were concerns, presciently articulated by Thoreau in the 1850s, over the costs of such progress to the nation's landscape, well-being, and identity.

The rapid expansion of the railroad in the late nineteenth and early twentieth century precipitated unprecedented wealth among rail-line executives such as Alexander Cassatt, Jason "Jay" Gould, Collis Potter Huntington, and Cornelius Vanderbilt, to name only a few. These men exerted enormous influence in their communities and spent lavishly on building extravagant mansions and vast art collections to establish their social position. The term "Gilded Age," drawn from the title of an 1873 novel by Mark Twain and Charles Dudley Warner, has been applied to this era of profligate materialism, brought on by the development of the transportation industry. But this growth did not come without drawbacks, and the United States government responded swiftly with attempts to regulate the industry, which was troubled by monopolies and labor inequities.

Just before the turn of the century, Pennsylvania artist William Robinson Leigh recorded a harrowing and pivotal event from the Great Railroad Strike of 1877 nearly twenty years earlier (cat. 6). The Great Strike, the first major workers' upheaval in American history, had begun in Martinsburg, West Virginia, on July 16, 1877, after a series of job and wage cuts,

but quickly spread throughout the country. Just five days later, on July 21, the protests had spread into Pittsburgh, erupting into an antimonopoly uprising involving more than just railroad workers that the *New York Times* would describe as the "reign of terror in Pittsburgh."[3] When the Pittsburgh police, sympathetic to the workers' grievances, failed to control the crowds, Pennsylvania governor John Hartranft deployed National Guard from Philadelphia to Pittsburgh. Early in the morning of July 22, 1877, the angry mob trapped some of the militia in the Pennsylvania Railroad's roundhouse then set fire to it. The guards managed to escape, shooting their way out, and killing twenty people in the process.[4] William Robinson Leigh, a native of West Virginia, captured the tense moment when flames were blazing around the roundhouse. Though nineteen years had passed, he painted the scene as if he were an eyewitness reporter. The mob of protestors in the foreground are only barely illuminated—the flames pour light onto the National Guard in the background, carrying rifles and ready to fight.

Pittsburgh's July 1877 "reign of terror" had made front-page headlines in newspapers around the country, and its immediate aftermath had been depicted by several illustrators (fig. 13). Why then did Leigh choose to revisit this event nearly two

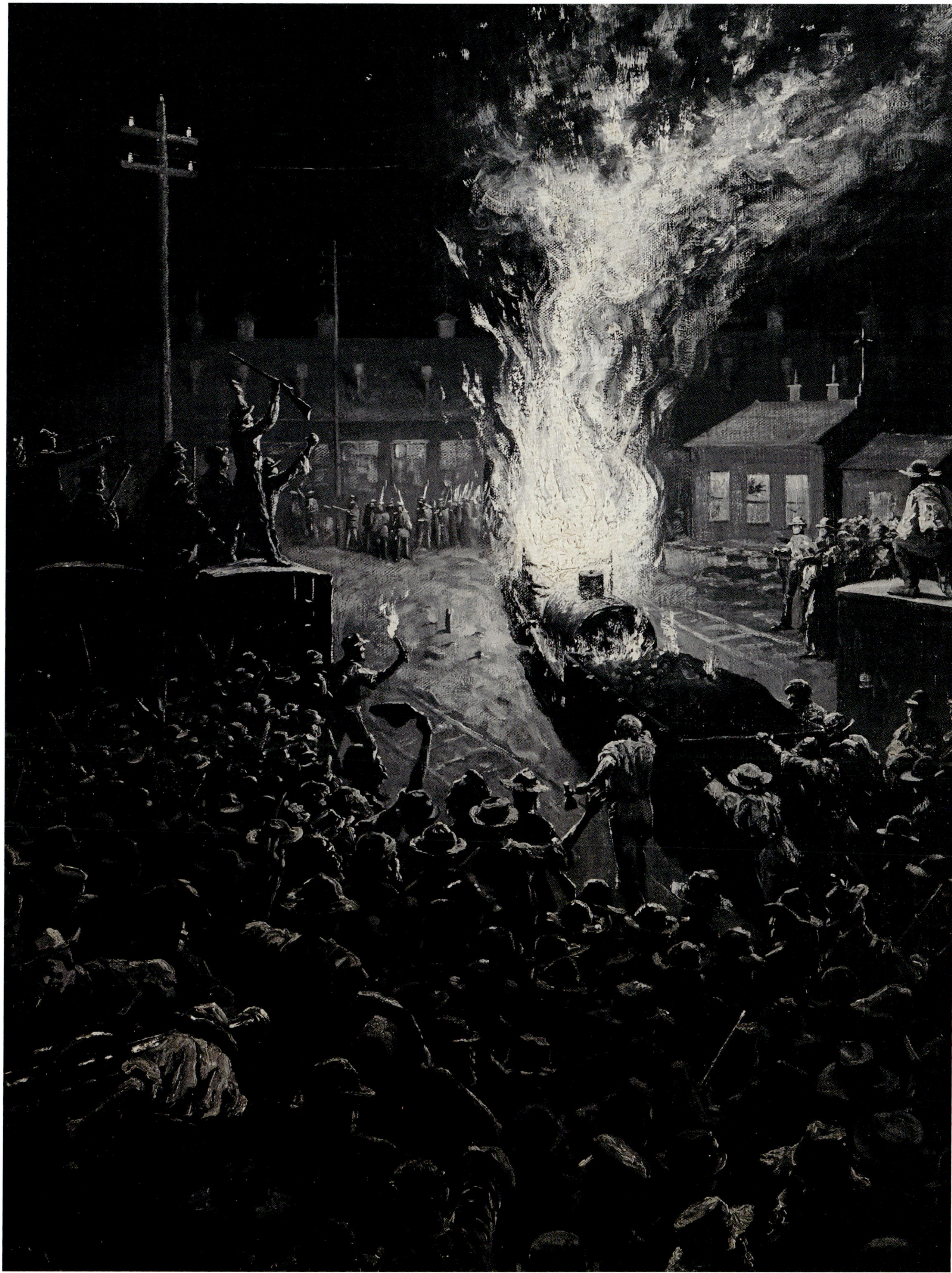

Cat. 7
Colin Campbell Cooper (American, 1856-1937)
Pittsburgh, PA, ca. 1905
oil on canvas
23⅛ × 30¼ in.
The Westmoreland Museum of American Art
Gift in memory of Alex G. McKenna, 1996.19

decades later? He had been a teenaged art student in Baltimore at the time the riots occurred, and spent much of the 1880s and half of the 1890s studying in Europe. When he returned to the United States in the mid-1890s, he found work as an illustrator for *Scribner's* magazine, for which he completed *The Attempt to Fire the Pennsylvania Railroad Roundhouse in Pittsburgh, at Daybreak on Sunday, July 22, 1877*. The painting appeared as an illustration in their July–December 1895 issue in an article entitled "A History of the Last Quarter Century in the United States," by E. Benjamin Andrews, then-president of Brown University, who included in his history a brief discussion of the Pittsburgh rail riots of 1877.[5]

The Great Strike of 1877 was a watershed moment in American labor history and the history of the railroad, but others followed in the late nineteenth century, including the Pullman Strike of May 1894, in which more than 200,000 rail workers protested layoffs and wage cuts. President Theodore Roosevelt signed legislation between 1903 and 1906 that empowered the Interstate Commerce Commission (itself only established in 1887) with a certain amount of control over the private corporations that ran the country's various railroads. For example, the 1903 Elkins Act sought to put an end to the preferential rebates that often were exchanged between railroad companies

and the businesses that shipped large quantities of freight with them. Three years later, Roosevelt supported and signed the Hepburn Act of 1906, which regulated rates for both passengers and shippers using the railroad.

After the violent labor strikes of 1877 were resolved, Pittsburgh remained an important industrial center into the twentieth century, and therefore the railroad was a constant presence. When Colin Campbell Cooper, a Philadelphia native living in New York, returned to his home state to paint Pittsburgh around 1905, the effects of more than one hundred years of factories, foundries, and trains polluting the landscape was evident. *Pittsburgh, PA* (cat. 7) is characterized by grime: on a dreary winter day, clouds of black and white smoke puff out of trains crossing the murky waters of the Allegheny and Monongahela Rivers only to dissipate into equally dark clouds in the sky. Another train chugs toward the viewer in the foreground, carrying just a few coal cars behind it, surrounded by the muck that has accumulated along the riverbanks.

Cooper's view of Pittsburgh is honest and bleak, but not without its moments of beauty. By 1905, he had become one of the leading American artists embracing Impressionism, particularly known for his ability to render modern architecture with a soft sensitivity. *Pittsburgh, PA* draws upon industrial

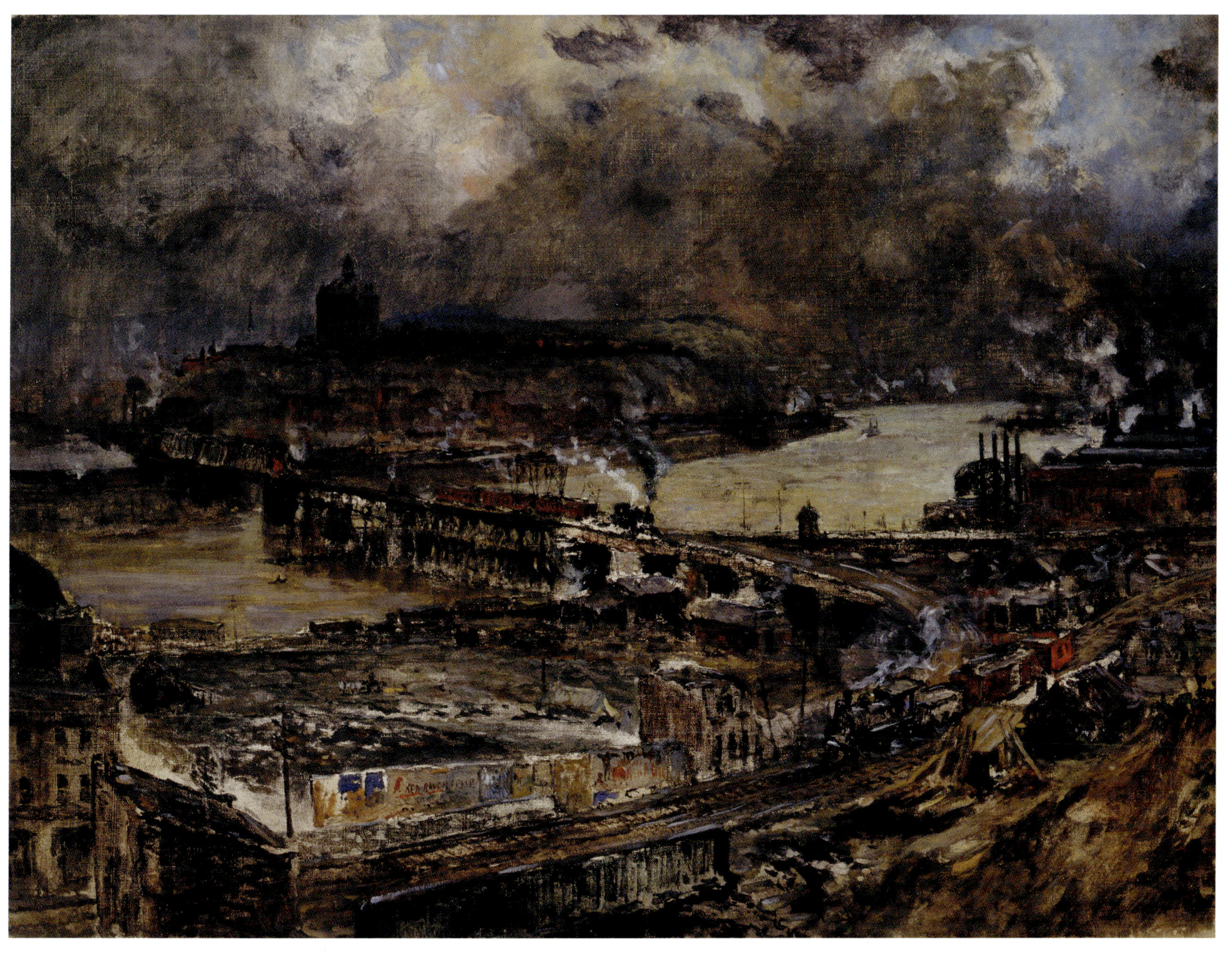

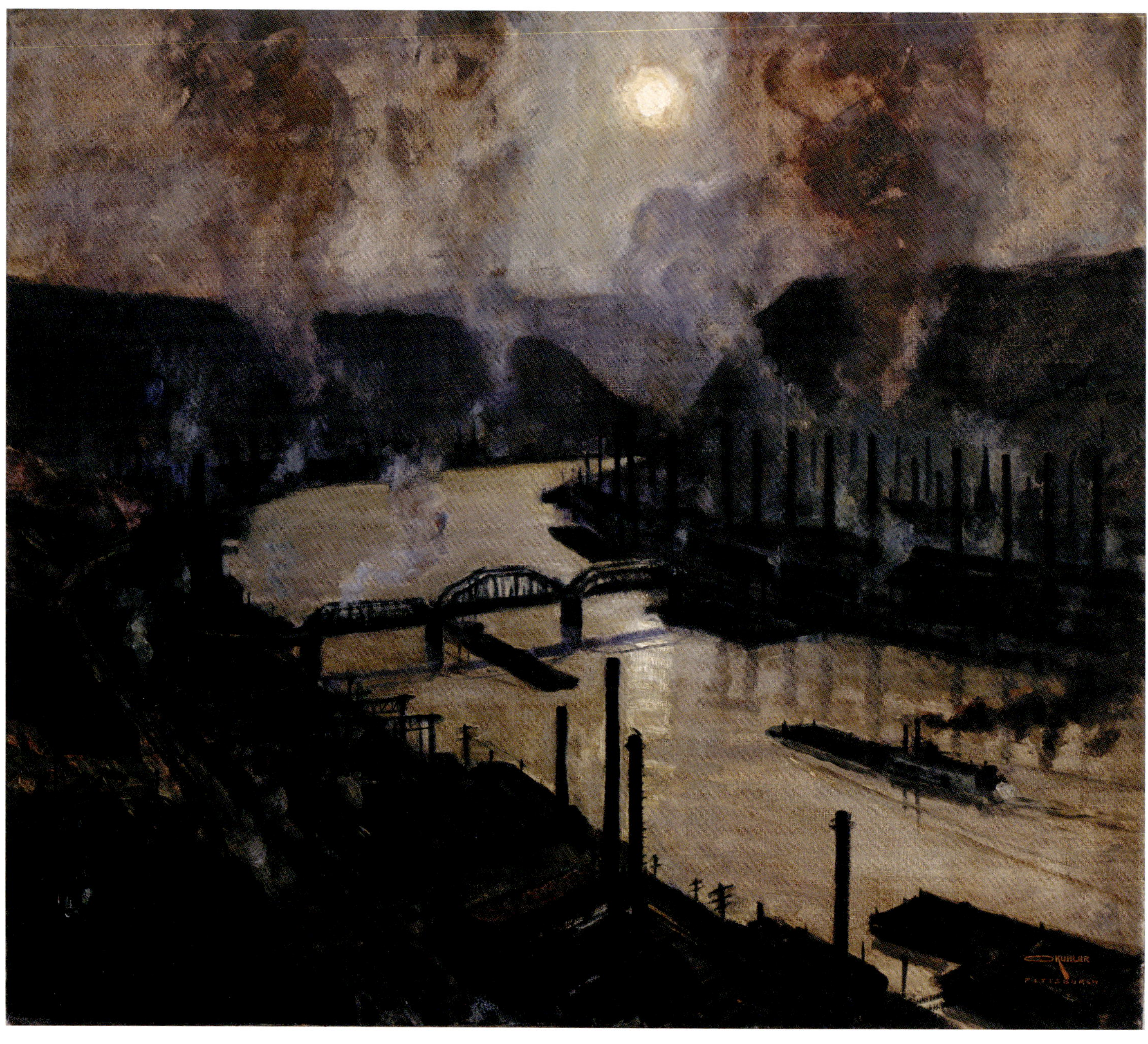

landscapes painted by French Impressionists such as Claude Monet and Alfred Sisley; the heavy, polluted clouds break way in some areas for clear light, and the waters of the river offer a sense of visual tranquility in an otherwise humming scene. As the main source of that active energy, the trains running through *Pittsburgh, PA* are a critical element in the painting—not just as a visual focal point, but also as a source for the dirt, smoke, and ash that pervade the scene.

As if he were in the position of the viewer of Cooper's painting, twentieth-century writer R. L. Duffus described Pittsburgh thus:

From whatever direction one approaches the once-lovely conjunction of the Allegheny and the Monongahela, the devastation of progress is apparent. Quiet valleys have been inundated with slag, defaced with refuse, marred by hideous buildings. Streams have been polluted with sewage and waste from the mills. Life for the majority of the population has been rendered unspeakably pinched and dingy. This is what might be called the technological blight of heavy industry.[6]

Cooper painted a larger and more detailed version of *Pittsburgh, PA* around the same time in 1906. Seven years later, after the artist became a full academician at the National Academy of Design in 1912, he presented the larger version, now titled *Pittsburgh, Pennsylvania*, to the National Academy's collection as his diploma submission.[7]

German-born designer and painter Otto Kuhler painted a view of Pittsburgh (cat. 8) that consciously expands upon Cooper's efforts to find beauty amid the consequences of industrialization. Kuhler immigrated to the United States in 1923, and found work in Pittsburgh as a commercial artist focusing on industrial landscapes such as *Steel Valley, Pittsburgh*. The railroad was a constant presence in Kuhler's art from his earliest years in Germany, and therefore his view of Pittsburgh was more optimistic—or at least less apocalyptic—than Cooper's. In this large but somehow still quiet painting, a train makes its way over the Monongahela River, framed on either side by the smokestacks of factories billowing clouds of brown and gray smoke into the air. The rising sun illuminates the landscape and gives the mirror a glassy surface that borders on the beautiful. Kuhler eventually would be hired by the American Locomotive Company, first in their advertising department and eventually as a designer of passenger trains, but his knowledge and respect for trains and their role in American industry was already apparent. Kuhler eventually moved to the American West, where he continued

Fig. 14
Mary Cassatt (American, 1844–1926)
Alexander J. Cassatt, ca. 1880
oil on canvas
25¾ × 36⅜ in.
Detroit Institute of Arts
Founders Society Purchase,
Robert H. Tannahill Foundation Fund,
1986.60

making paintings exploring the railroad and its encroachment into such unique and majestic landscapes as New Mexico's Wagon Mound butte (cat. 9).

Pittsburgh may have drawn the most commentary on the effects of its industrialization on the landscape, but it certainly was not the only city to experience such a shift. The kind of industrial growth illustrated in Cooper's paintings of Pittsburgh precipitated the growth of urban centers as a whole. To accommodate the laborers needing transport to factories, often located outside of residential boroughs, metropolitan-area rail systems were also expanding, most notably in New York City. The city's role as the most important commercial city in the country and its growing number of commuters led Pennsylvania Railroad CEO Alexander Cassatt (fig. 14) to initiate the building of a large, centralized station that would allow his trains to access Manhattan (previously it was only by ferry from Jersey City, New Jersey, that Pennsylvania Railroad passengers could get to the city) by a series of tunnels running under the Hudson and East Rivers. Construction began in 1904 on what would ultimately be named Pennsylvania Station, designed by the eminent architectural firm McKim, Mead & White, who proclaimed that their plans "would provide the most perfect and much the largest railroad passenger station in the world."[8]

The construction of Pennsylvania Station and its tunnels was a long and complicated process that was chronicled for millions of readers in the press, drawing comparisons to a still more massive contemporary project: the Panama Canal.[9] The building process became such a ubiquitous presence in New York that artists attuned to modern urban life could not ignore it and sought to immortalize it on canvas. The railroad had certainly had an impact on American society and its art in the nineteenth century, but in the Progressive Era, artists engaged with the railroad in a different way. As the Hudson River

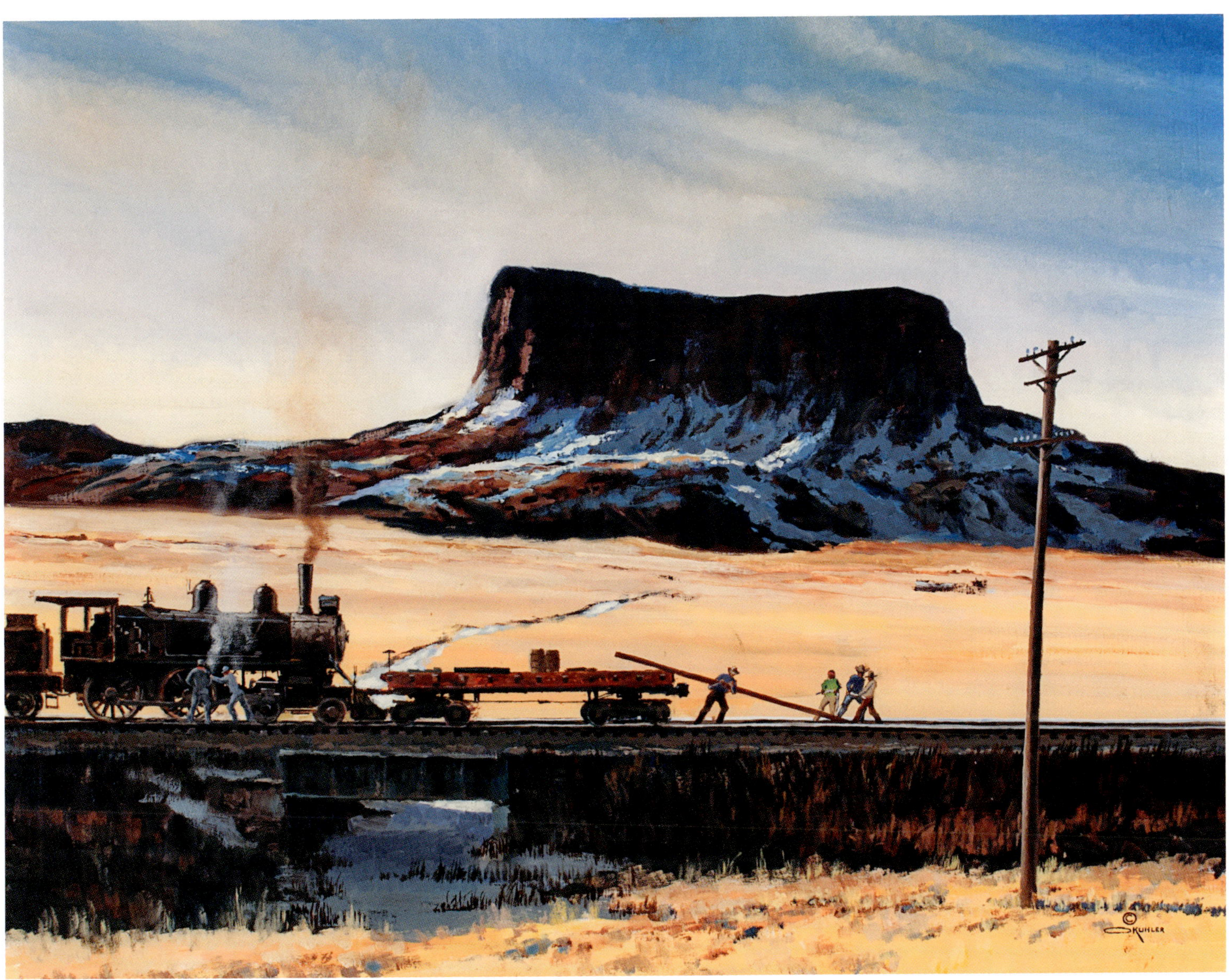

Cat. 9

**Otto Kuhler (American,
born Germany, 1894-1977)**
Work Train at Wagonmound, n.d.

oil on canvas
23⅝ × 29⅝ in.

Collection of the New Mexico Museum of Art

Gift of Otto August Kuhler, 1976, 3648.23P

school gave way to Impressionism and realism as the dominant aesthetics in American art, the way in which the railroad was portrayed shifted as well. Instead of wide, sweeping views of a majestic American landscape, painters cropped their compositions much more closely, focusing on the intensity of the sounds, vibrations, environmental impact, politics, and even some of the danger surrounding the railroad.

Merging the observational realism of his Ashcan contemporaries with his own preference for the Impressionist approach to landscape painting, Ernest Lawson captured some of the construction of Pennsylvania Station around 1906 (cat. 10). Amid the snow of winter, man and machine labor over one of the many excavation sites required for the tunnels that would service the station. A small engine chugs across the foreground, aiding in the excavation and also serving as a visual reminder of the reason for the labor. Lawson's point of view in *Excavation—Penn Station* is drawn back, with the workers seen at such a distance that they lose their individual characteristics and take on an ant-like collective energy, and the enormity of the project is somewhat diminished. Lawson's light palette and heavy impasto—the influence of Impressionists such as Alfred Sisley—render the scene almost abstract (or at least illegible in areas) and counterbalance the painting's gritty realism.

Lawson's image of the construction of Pennsylvania Station was praised by critics for its uniquely American honesty. Bayard Boyesen, writing for *Putnam's* in 1908, extolled Lawson as fully embracing the American realists' "frank and enthusiastic acceptance of the conditions of life, and a subsequent realization that beauty lives most vigorously in those manifestations of human energy which are stripped of the accident of the picturesque."[10] Writing about the laborers in *Excavation—Penn Station*, Boyesen went on:

How different are those workmen from the sentimentalized figures of a Millet or a Meunier, as they droop with the Weariness of stupidity and resignation, or sit in dull, animal sorrow, broken with toil! And how perfectly is their movement (they are mere dots, a brushstroke here and there) subordinated to the service of the poetic idea. Here is the romance of nature and man in their eternal conflict expressed with the rugged joy of one who realizes the exigencies and hardships of life only as a challenge to his understanding and his greatness.[11]

Lawson was by no means the only American artist to immortalize the construction of Pennsylvania Station, yet he was one of the few artists to

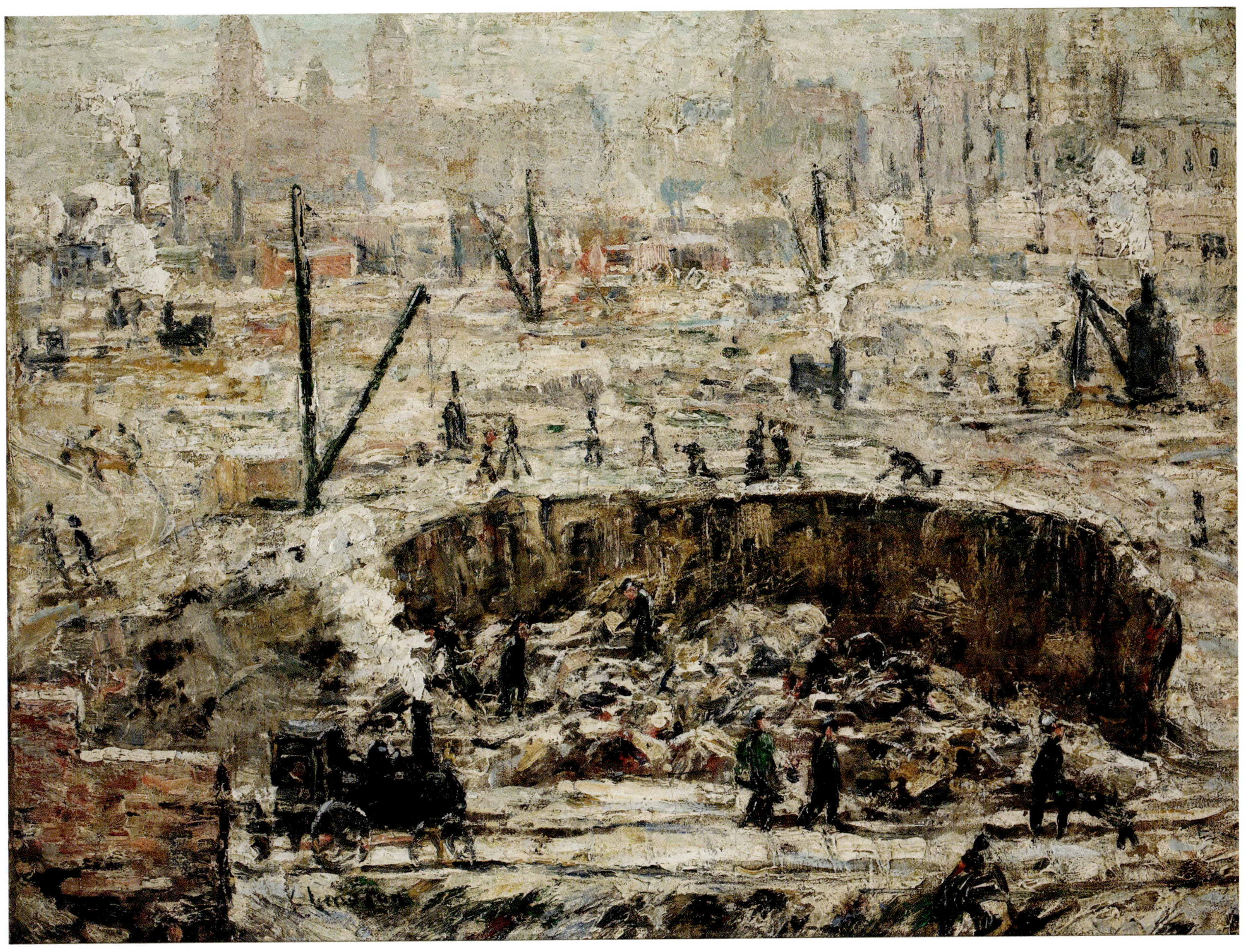

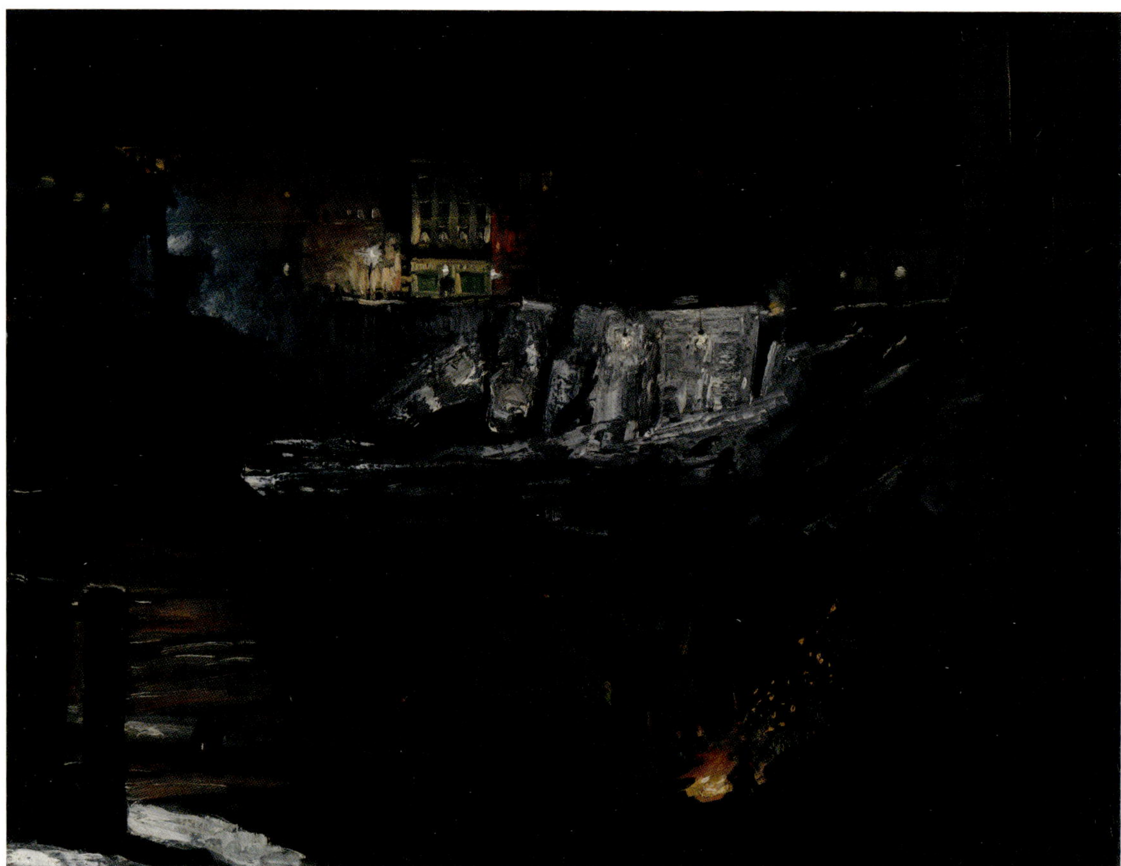

Fig. 15

**George Bellows
(American, 1882-1925)**
Excavation at Night, 1908

oil on canvas
34 × 44 in.

Crystal Bridges Museum of
American Art, Bentonville,
Arkansas

2010.77

interpret it through a more traditional Impressionist aesthetic. By contrast, George Bellows's views of the excavations for the station's tunnels are dark (whether or not they were set at night), bleak, and raw, with no attempts to aestheticize or glamorize either the harsh conditions faced by those involved in its construction or the undeniable effects this massive project had on New York's landscape (fig. 15). In examining the effects of the railroad on New York life, Bellows alternated between close-up, eyewitness-style views and more sweeping landscape surveys. *Rain on the River* (fig. 16) is part of a series of paintings Bellows completed in 1908 examining the working aspects of the Hudson River, but instead of the river dominating the scene, it recedes into an expanse of gray.[12] White smoke streams from a train that cuts diagonally through the canvas, commanding the viewer's attention. The train serves as the border between the gritty working-class nature of the Hudson and the idyllic

(if saturated) greenspace of Riverside Park, which itself had been converted from the Hudson River Railroad railyards beginning in the 1870s by landscape architect Frederick Law Olmsted.[13]

Rain on the River with its near bird's-eye view, displays not the scars on the environment caused by the railroad seen in Bellows's Pennsylvania Station paintings, but a more well-rounded visual perspective of the effects of industry and urbanization on the landscape. Though the railyards had once consumed the land along the Hudson River, through the intervention of forward-thinking citizens in the mid-nineteenth century it had been transformed into a public space for leisure, and a cause for civic pride.[14] The train running alongside the river is neither a menace nor a marvel, but its presence cannot be denied.

Alexander Cassatt died in December 1906 before he could see his vision realized when Pennsylvania Station officially opened to riders on September 8,

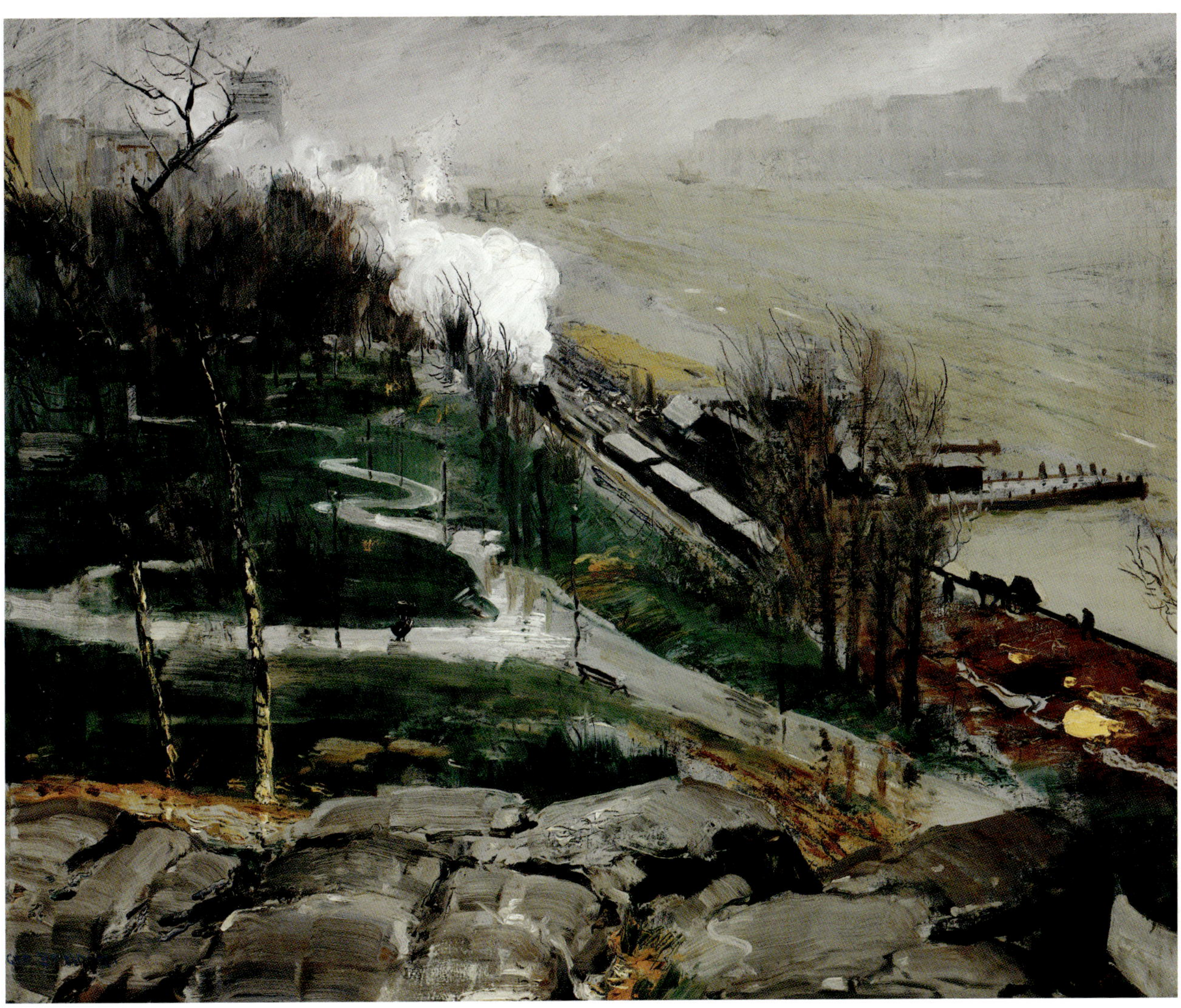

Fig. 16

George Bellows (American, 1882–1925)
Rain on the River, 1908

oil on canvas
32⅜ × 38¼ in.
RISD Museum, Providence, Rhode Island
Jesse Metcalf Fund, 15.063

1910. The Beaux-Arts behemoth was heralded as "the largest building in the world ever built at one time" and a "monumental gateway and entrance to a great metropolis."[15] With the station's completion, New York's hive-like network of locomotive activity reached new heights—on its first day of service, some 35,000 passengers traveled on 196 separate trains, with the *New York Times* reporting that many of those riding the trains that day were doing so "for the novelty of the ride."[16]

Artists sensitive to the subtle and not-so-subtle shifts in urban living recognized the potential in painting the effects the expanded rail system had on New York life. Elevated trains had provided a backdrop for some of John Sloan's quintessential

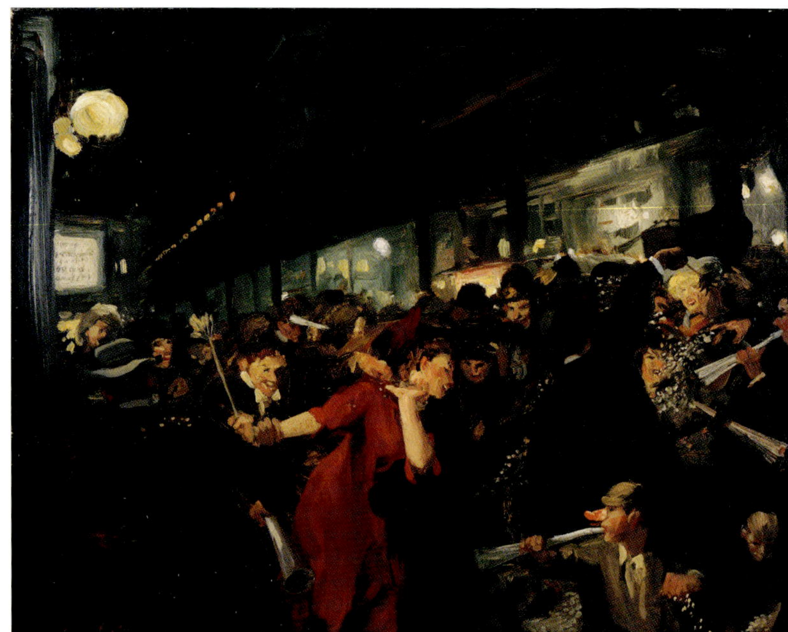

Fig. 17

John Sloan (American, 1871–1951)
Election Night, 1907

oil on canvas
26⅜ × 32¼ in.

Memorial Art Gallery of the
University of Rochester

Marion Stratton Gould Fund,
1941.33

Ashcan paintings of the 1900s, including *Election Night* (fig. 17), in which he joined a crowd of revelers in Herald Square in November 1907. By 1912, when the artist completed *Six O'Clock, Winter* (cat. 11), he was still standing among the masses of New Yorkers, but he had shifted his focus upward to the Third Avenue elevated train, or "el." Sloan structured his composition into three horizontal bands or zones: the fading blue winter sky, the massive el and its track, and the workaday people and storefronts of the ground level. Though stopped and shrouded in darkness, the el is the powerful force and focal point of the painting. It is also somewhat of a threatening presence, looming over the heads of oblivious or at least distracted men and women. Elevated trains had been in common operation in New York since the 1870s, providing relief from the traffic that plagued the city's streets.[17] Even with the opening of subterranean rail lines in 1904, elevated trains remained an important artery for intercity transport. The el in *Six O'Clock, Winter* is a powerful beast of a machine, swelling with faceless commuters waiting to ride home at the end of a cold workday.

As time went on, elevated trains became less of a curiosity to Sloan and more of a ubiquitous presence in his New York. By 1922, when he completed *The City from Greenwich Village* (cat. 12), his work had evolved from the more narrative paintings of the 1900s and 1910s, but he still retained an observational perspective, looking out at Greenwich Village from the roof of his studio—a common vantage point. Sloan had, just a few years prior, moved his studio from the Varitype Building that appears at the right of the composition to another studio close by, and he contrasted the still relatively quaint charm of Greenwich Village with upper Manhattan's cluster of skyscrapers in the distance.[18] But he also captured some of the magic of a city still humming with life and (artificial) light as evening settles in, with the elevated train serving as a noisy conduit clanging through it all.

New York City's vast train network spread into surrounding regions such as Weehawken, New Jersey, which Leon Kroll depicts in his 1912–13 canvas *Terminal Yards* (cat. 13). By that time, Kroll had studied at the Art Students League with John Henry Twachtman, followed by two years in Paris, and had exhibited in New York with artists including William Glackens, Robert Henri, Edward Hopper, and George Luks—he was on his way to becoming one of the most successful artists in the country.

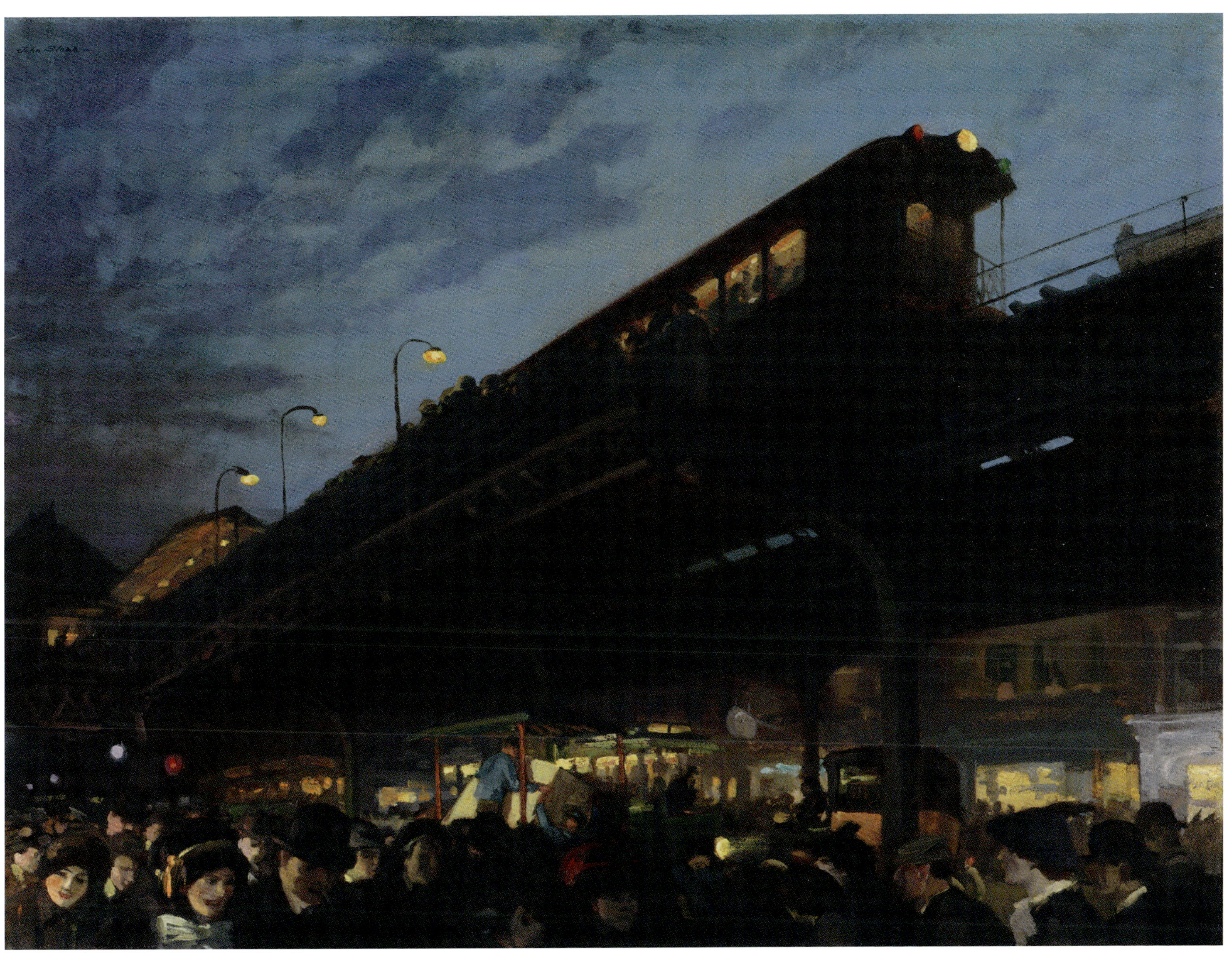

Cat. 11

John Sloan (American, 1871–1951)
Six O'Clock, Winter, 1912
oil on canvas
26⅛ × 32 in.
The Phillips Collection, Washington, DC
Acquired 1922

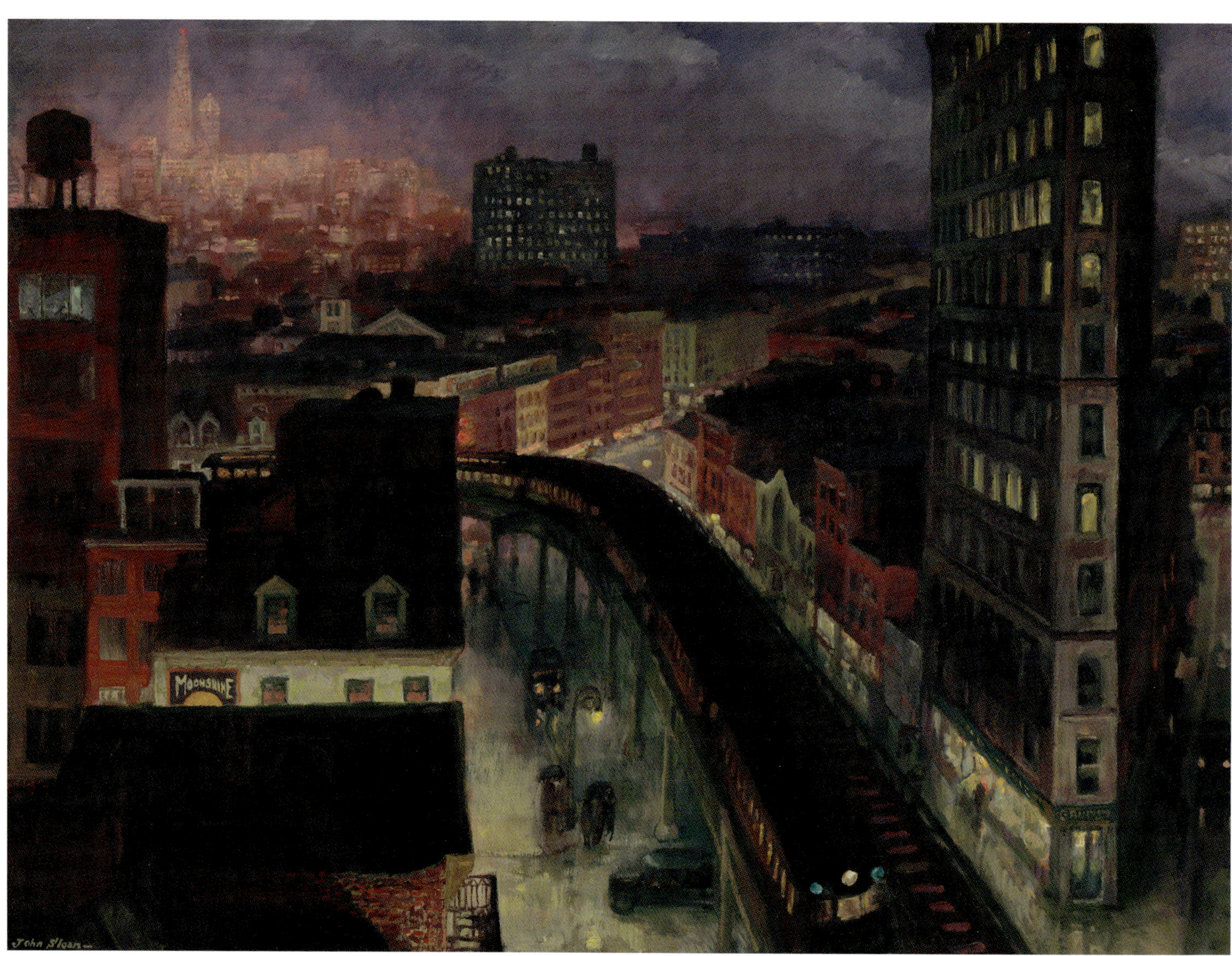

Cat. 12

John Sloan (American, 1871–1951)
The City from Greenwich Village, 1922
oil on canvas
26 × 33¾ in.
National Gallery of Art, Washington, DC
Gift of Helen Farr Sloan, 1970.1.1

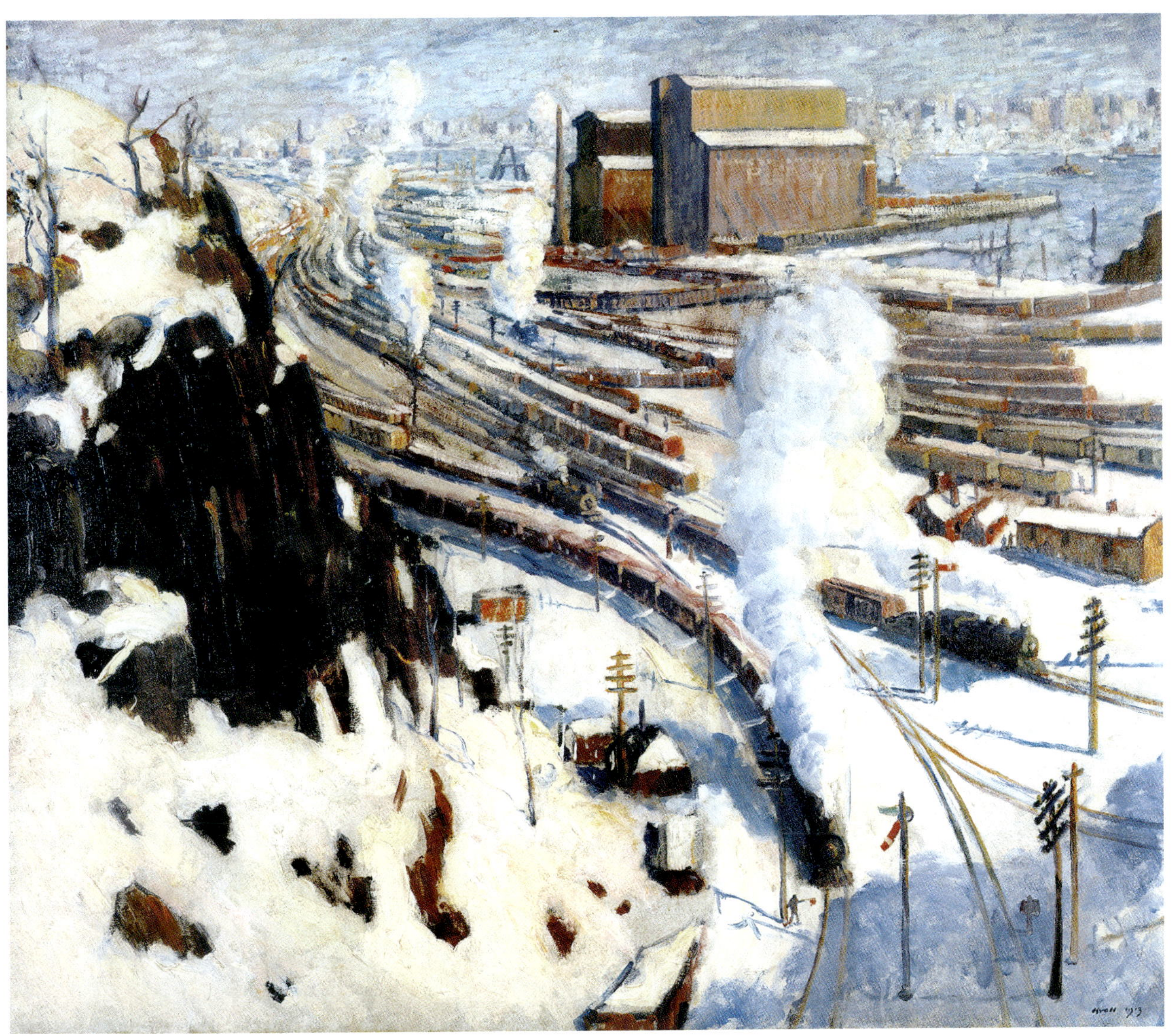

Cat. 13

Leon Kroll (American, 1884–1974)
Terminal Yards, 1912–13

oil on canvas
46 × 52⅛ in.

Flint Institute of Arts, Flint, Michigan

Gift of Mrs. Arthur Jerome Eddy, 1931.4

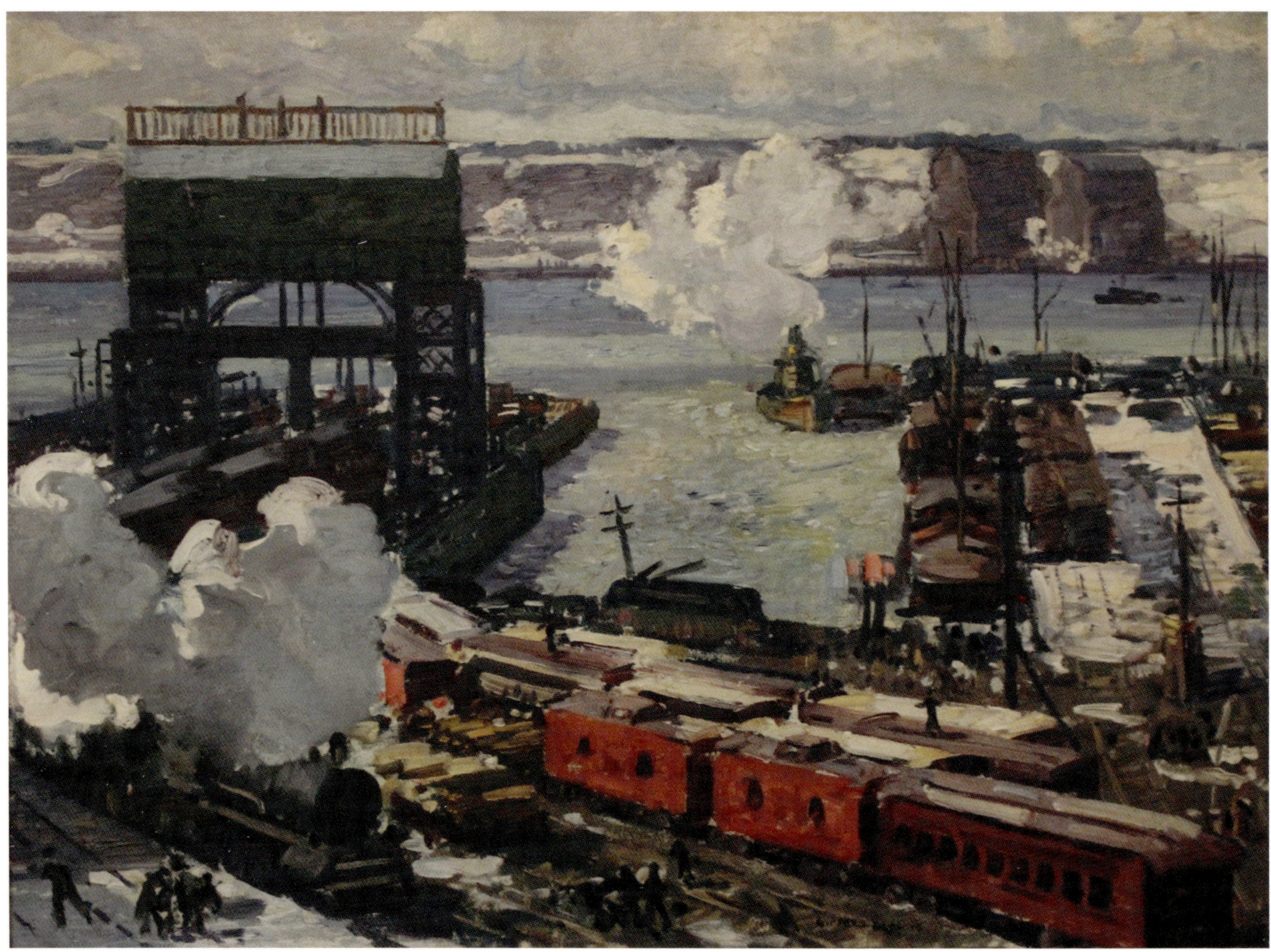

Cat. 14

Gifford Beal (American, 1879–1956)
Freight Yards, 1915

oil on canvas
45 × 57 in.

Collection of the Everson Museum of Art

Museum purchase by the Friends of
American Art Fund, PC 15.80

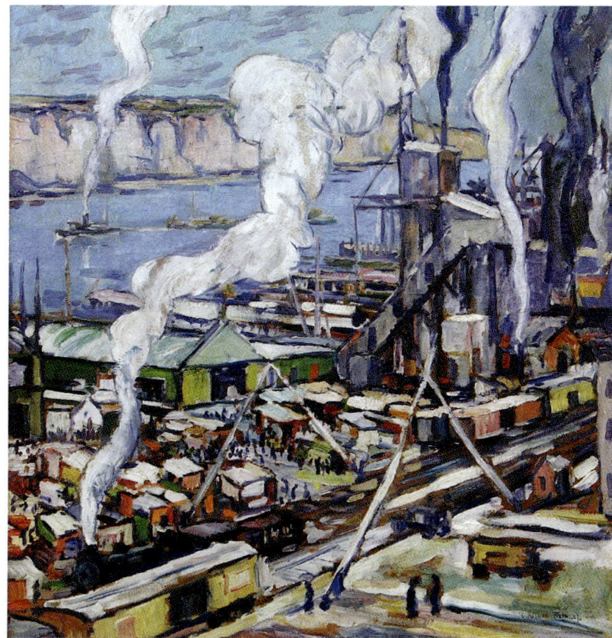

Fig. 18

Daniel Putnam Brinley (American, 1879–1963)
Hudson River View (Sugar Factory at Yonkers), ca. 1915

oil on canvas
30⅛ × 31⅞ in.

Collection of the Hudson River Museum
Museum Purchase, 1995, 95.3.1

His paintings from the early 1910s, combining a sharp eye and great technical skill with a keen sensitivity, often involve urban themes, a product of his own association with the Ashcan artists. *Terminal Yards* depicts a bright and busy winter day at the Weehawken Terminal, the vast transportation hub across the Hudson River from Manhattan, which included an extensive network of both train and ferry connections.

Kroll's view of Weehawken is true, marked by puffs of smoke, crisscrossing lines, station buildings, and the perpendicular forms of electric poles all sandwiched between the Hudson and the rocky bluff. But it bears little of the grittiness and grime that defined Lawson's and Bellows's explorations of the railroad in the urban landscape. Rather, *Terminal Yards* is in many ways a gleaming celebration of American industry. Kroll's view is taken from the top of Weehawken's palisade, overlooking the rail lines, and along the horizon the viewer can recognize the expansive Manhattan skyline, itself a sign of American ingenuity and prowess.

Terminal Yards is one of three canvases of the Weehawken Terminal that Kroll completed in 1913, along with *West Shore Terminal* (Orlando Museum of Art) and *View of Manhattan from the Terminal*

Yards, Weehawken, New Jersey (Montgomery Museum of Fine Arts). They reveal a particular interest in this new form of landscape, and, in a way, like Lawson, seek to present an American interpretation of the Impressionist paintings of trains he saw while studying in Paris at the turn of the century. For French painters such as Gustave Caillebotte, Édouard Manet, Claude Monet, and Camille Pissarro, the train was an emblem of modern urban life.[19] Likewise, Kroll recognized the railroad's ubiquity and focused on capturing it, not only as a sign of progress but also as an ever-present factor in the landscape.

Kroll completed and signed *Terminal Yards* in 1913 and immediately sent it to the New York's *International Exhibition of Modern Art* (known as the Armory Show), his only work to be included in that landmark exhibition. In a show that shocked American audiences with its daring European modernity, Kroll's *Terminal Yards* struck a balance between contemporary subject matter and representational style. And it proved effective— the painting received praise as "one of the most striking" works in the show by former president Theodore Roosevelt, who noted that Kroll's "seeing eye was there, and the cunning hand."[20] *Terminal Yards* was purchased from the Armory Show by Arthur Jerome Eddy, a prominent Chicago lawyer and prescient collector of modern art.[21]

Similarly, other artists found inspiration in the new American landscape of the railyards. Gifford Beal's *Freight Yards* (cat. 14) and Daniel Putnam Brinley's *Hudson River View (Sugar Factory at Yonkers)* (fig. 18) were both completed around 1915 and feature the railroad as an omnipresent element of urban life. Beal's *Freight Yards* results from his *plein air* training under William Merritt Chase, but as Kroll had done a few years prior, he chose for his subject not the bucolic American countryside but a bustling port along the Hudson River, serviced by both trains and ferries. Snow visible in the background indicates winter, as does the bluish-gray smoke from the engines hitting the clear, cold air. Beal's energetic brushwork and deft application of impasto aligns with the activity of the painting—trains move across the foreground as miniscule rail workers scurry about their business, some even riding on top of the trains.

Likewise, the painter and muralist Daniel Putnam Brinley depicted an active industrial landscape in *Hudson River View (Sugar Factory at Yonkers)*. The trains that deliver raw materials and laborers to the sugar factory cut a diagonal across the foreground, with one engine puffing an impossibly long cloud of smoke into the air. As early as the 1860s, in many ways thanks to the rail system, Yonkers had been the site of various sugar refineries, and production had expanded at the turn of the century. Brinley had a sharp eye for color and interpreted the New York town's industrial riverfront with vibrant colors and loose geometric forms—a shift in his style visible after the Armory Show that particularly suited this modern view of Yonkers.[22]

The railroad made the growth of industrial towns such as Yonkers possible, and the presence of the many trains that traveled across the country was constantly felt, even when they were not actively passing through. Ernest Lawson would continue to incorporate the railroad, or at least implicate its presence, in his Impressionistic canvases for years. In the mid-1910s, he completed a series of paintings of New York's Washington Bridge (cat. 15) that reveal the influence of French Impressionists such as Camille Pissarro and Alfred Sisley, who commonly painted rail bridges. By that point, Lawson was at the height of his career and the railroad was perhaps at the pinnacle of its importance to American life. *Washington Bridge, Harlem River* incorporates the marvel of engineering into his landscape, yet it avoids becoming an "industrial landscape." The railcars and automobiles that would normally move across the scene are either absent or have been abstracted; the workers that would normally bustle about the riverbanks are not present; and even the small structures along the water appear quaint.

Lawson successfully integrated the industrial into his landscapes while maintaining a sense of romance. The works of Beal, Brinley, Kroll, and Lawson, all painted within a few years of each other, follow an artistic notion described in the 1960s by historian Leo Marx as the "technological sublime."[23] Building on their predecessors in the Hudson River school, which sought to capture the awe-inspiring

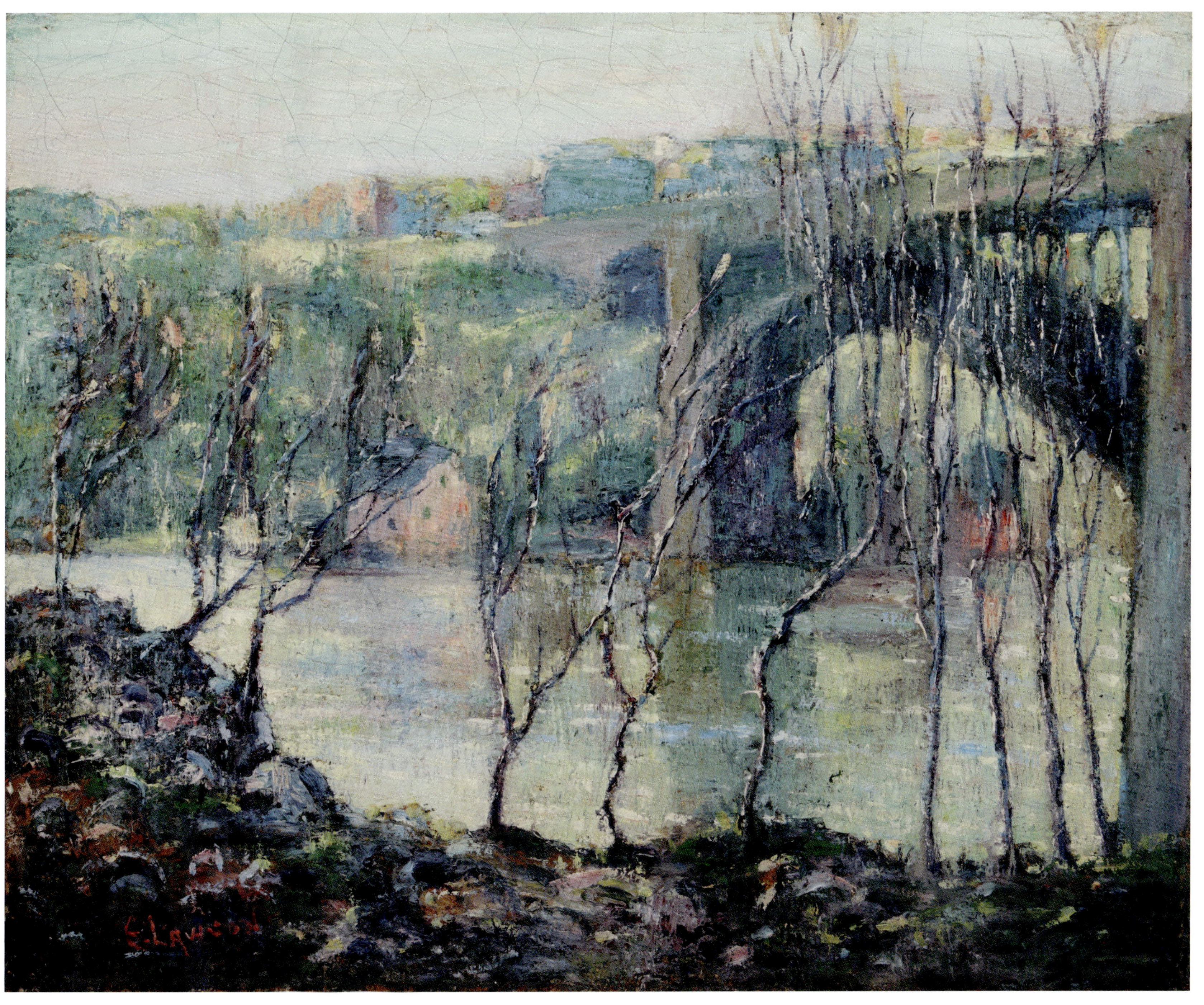

beauty of a virginal American wilderness, artists in the early twentieth century recognized something equally breathtaking (for better or for worse) in the same landscape (often the Hudson River) completely transformed by machine. The skyscrapers, factories, ferries, and railroads that now defined and often blocked access to the river's once-quiet banks called for a new way of seeing, inspired by J. M. W. Turner's singular, emotional interpretations of the landscape and humankind's new impositions on it. Progressive Era American artists were in cautious awe of the scale of industrial-age machinery, the uniformity of its mechanisms, the deafening noise it produced, and its overwhelming power.

The workers who operated the trains, ferries, and factories that dominate American technological or industrial sublime canvases are often miniscule, and in truth, labor conditions on railroads were anything but sublime. After decades of fiery protests and costly labor strikes, in 1916 the Adamson Act was passed, limiting rail workers to an eight-hour workday and mandating overtime pay. There was fierce opposition to the bill, but fears over strikes halting production of war materials pressed President Woodrow Wilson into signing it into law on September 3, 1916, incidentally while seated in his private rail car, the Federal, at New York's Union Station.[24]

Less than one year later, the United States declared war on Germany, and the railroad's far-reaching logistical capacity became even more crucial to the war effort. In December 1917, President Wilson placed the railroads under US government control for the duration of the war, forming the United States Railroad Administration through the Federal Possession and Control Act to ensure uninterrupted operations.[25] Industrial use of the country's various railroads escalated during this time. The end of the Great War and the dawn of the 1920s brought a renewed energy into the nation's urban centers. Though the continued rise of the automobile was signaling the end of the railroad's dominance as the primary means of transportation, trains were still a completely common factor in everyday urban life. In March 1920, the Esch-Cummins Act returned control of the railroads to private corporations, and it mandated the arbitration of railroad labor disputes, which contemporary writers acknowledged was "always charged with political dynamite," to avoid interruptions in service, though it stopped short of making strikes unlawful.[26]

Throughout the 1920s, the railroad remained central to American life, though access to railcars was not equally shared. Throughout the South, Jim Crow laws, initially upheld by the 1877 Supreme Court *Hall v. DeCuir* ruling but expanded upon in the early twentieth century, relegated Black Americans to separate cars that nearly always lacked the basic amenities enjoyed by white travelers. And in many towns throughout the country, railroad tracks served as "iron borders" between Black and white communities.[27] These demarcations emerged in the late nineteenth century during Reconstruction, but the practice continued in the years after World War I and its effects remain visible in cities today.

The international fascination with machine-age modernity escalated in the 1920s, and it was during that time that the American illustrator and painter Reginald Marsh began exploring locomotives as an independent subject of his work. While some

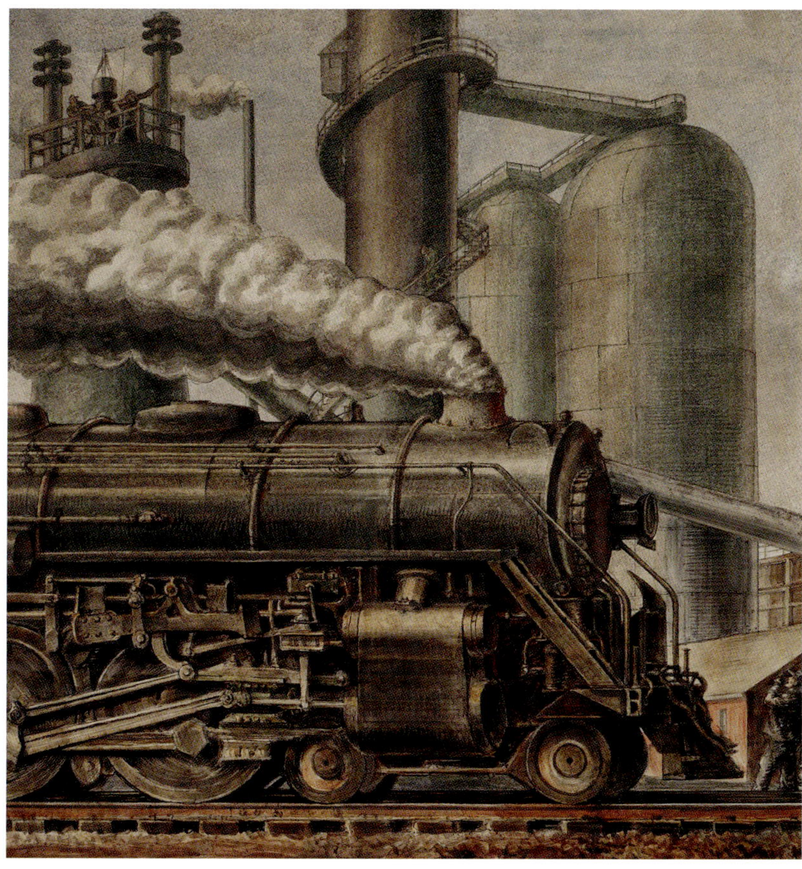

Fig. 19

Reginald Marsh (American, 1898–1954)
The Locomotive, 1935

tempera fresco or tempera on concrete plaster
58 × 53½ in.

The Huntington Library, Art Museum,
and Botanical Gardens

Purchased with funds from the Art Collectors'
Council, the Virginia Steele Scott Foundation
Acquisition Fund for American Art, and The
Trustees of Associated Foundations. Gift of
Mr. Theodore C. Coleman, Estate of James C.
McCormick III, in memory of James Campbell
McCormick, Jr. and Bessie Specht McCormick,
and Doris and Mike Simon, by exchange, 2013.4

of his fascination with trains can be traced to his time studying with Ashcan artists John Sloan and George Luks, it was clearly piqued in the early 1920s by seeing illustrations of trains in publications such as *The Dial* by contemporaries including poet e. e. cummings and watercolorist Charles Burchfield.[28] From that point forward, he mined various aspects of the railroad industry for subjects in a variety of media.[29] Much like his work as an illustrator, some of Marsh's train images depict busty women loitering in rail stations or offer theatrical, frieze-like views of various riders on a subway. But his images focused on the trains themselves (often steam trains), including and perhaps especially *The Locomotive* (fig. 19) from 1935, offer a mechanical counterpart to these works: just as realistic but also exhibiting a kind of polish and beauty that borders on the sublime. *The Locomotive*, both its subject and the work itself, is large and powerful—it was a study for a mural commissioned by the Treasury Relief Art Project for the main rotunda of the Alexander Hamilton U.S. Custom House in New York.[30] The engine is gleaming, almost pristine, as it departs from an industrial station, releasing steam so thick it appears cotton-like. The image is mostly devoid of human presence, save for one diminutive worker along the track and a few more who observe the action from a higher perspective.

Marsh often visited Jersey City's railyards to observe and sketch steam trains, but rarely did he incorporate the Precisionist influence as much as in *The Locomotive*. In the 1920s, a new aesthetic had emerged in American painting that looked to the machine as the embodiment of a new modernity. These canvases, by artists including Charles Goeller (see cat. 25) and Charles Sheeler (see fig. 23), walk a line between enamored attraction to complex machinery and anxiety over its effects, but their pristine and gleaming surfaces betray none of the muck and grime that had defined industrial landscapes earlier in the century. Much like Marsh himself, *The Locomotive* is somewhat hard to classify—it reveals the artist's idiosyncratic draftsmanship, but also eschews his trademark bawdiness in favor of a more streamlined, gleaming industrialism in which the powerful train dwarfs the presence of a few small human figures.

The notion of powerlessness in the modern landscape (which is explored more fully in Kevin Sharp's essay in this volume) offered a striking counterpoint to the bustling industrial landscapes of the early twentieth century. Harry Leith-Ross, a British citizen born on the island of Mauritius, served in the United States Infantry during World War I, and after being discharged spent the remainder of the war years teaching in Woodstock, New York, before ultimately settling in New Hope, Bucks County, Pennsylvania, in 1935. There, around the late 1930s, he produced *Tenant's House and Tracks* (cat. 16), a much more personal and lonely view of life along the railroads than the industrial sublime or Precisionist images of just a few years prior. In the midst of the Great Depression, Leith-Ross found something poignant in a solitary worker going about his daily routine, walking along railroad tracks on a bright winter day. Though likely painted around New Hope, *Tenant's House and Tracks* displays a certain universality—this scene could have been played out in any number of American towns—that made his work so popular with collectors and respected by colleagues and critics.

Aaron Bohrod's 1938 *Slag Heaps* (cat. 17) presents a lone miner, slightly hunched over as he trudges along quiet rail tracks to work. Rather than Leith-Ross's quaint Pennsylvania setting, Bohrod fashioned a bleak and apocalyptic landscape. Behind the worker are the titular "slag heaps," a slang term for the mounds of rocks and refuse that surround a depleted mine. Bohrod's desolate landscape mirrors the desperate situation in which many Americans found themselves during the recession of 1937 and 1938, when unemployment climbed to nearly 20 percent and industrial production fell sharply.[31] The painting was a commission from the Works Progress Administration's Federal Art Project, which provided artists such as Bohrod with employment during the Depression by commissioning works of art that both celebrated and scrutinized American labor. The quiet railroad, lonely worker, and lifeless mounds present this section of middle America as a surreal wasteland depleted by exploitation, betraying the ominous national climate and the "lost promise" of the golden age of railroads.

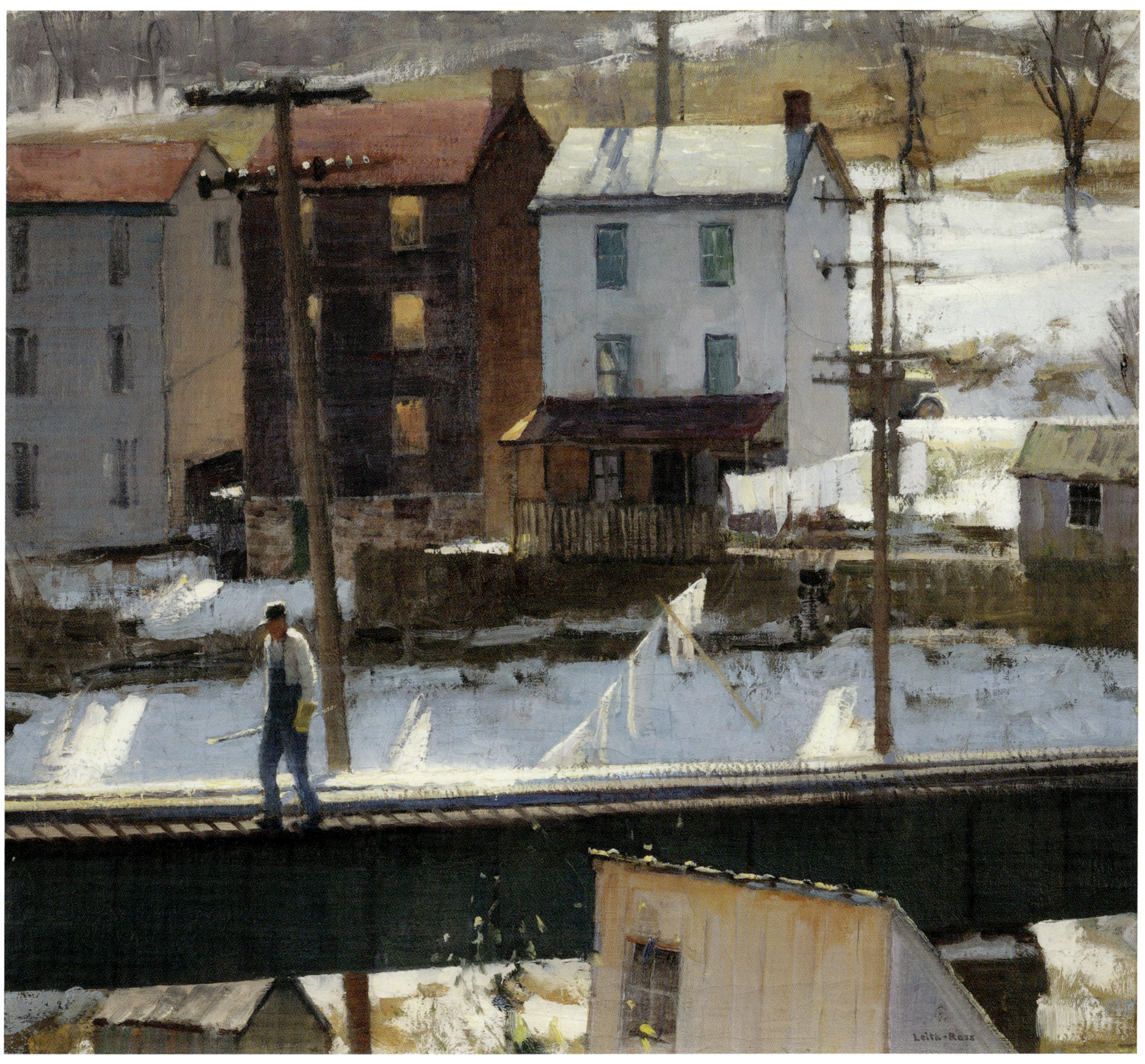

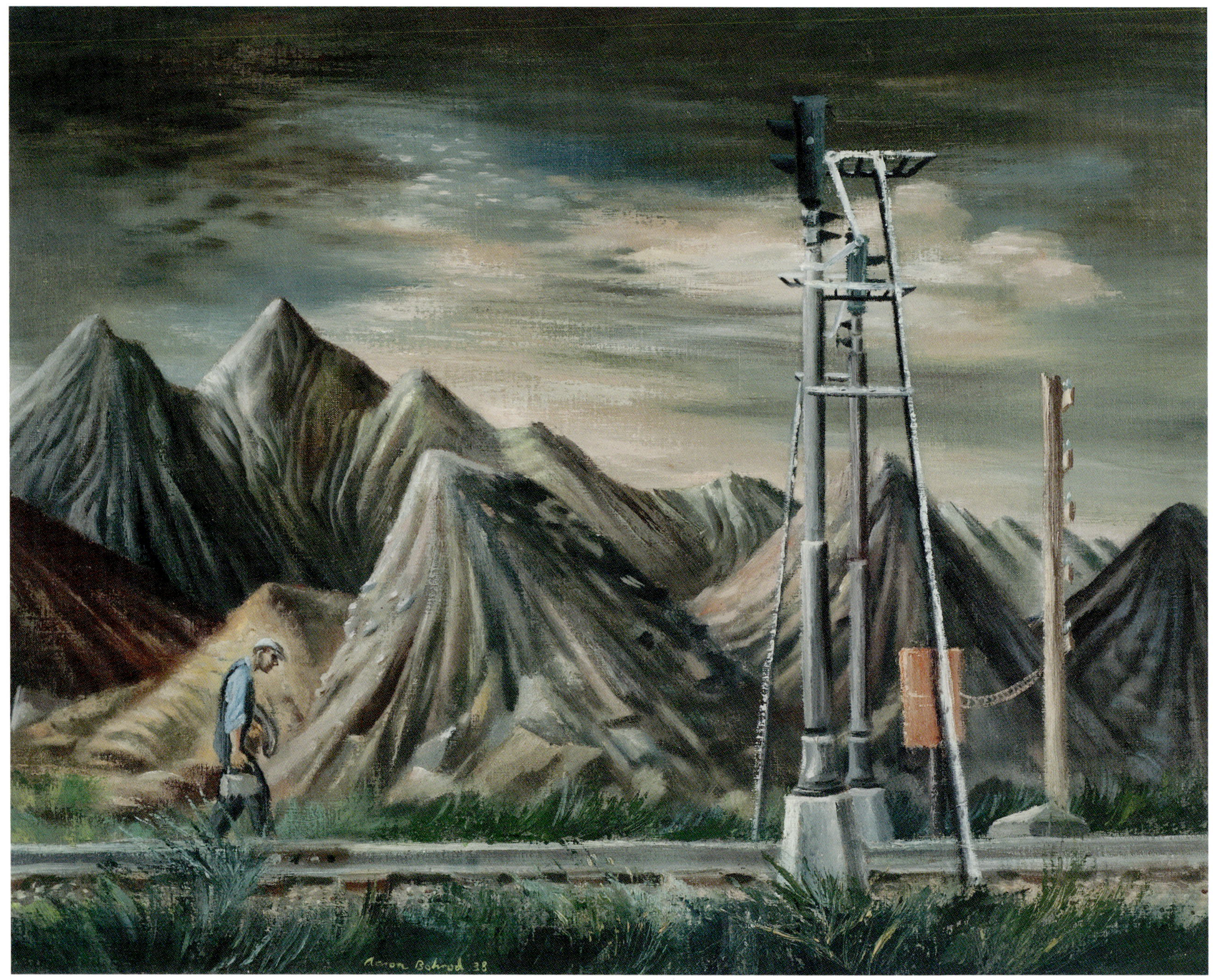

Cat. 17

Aaron Bohrod (American, 1907-1992)
Slag Heaps, 1938
oil on canvas
24 × 30 in.
Sheldon Museum of Art,
University of Nebraska-Lincoln
Allocation of the U.S. Government,
Federal Art Project of the Works Progress
Administration, WPA-106.1943

Railroads were, by the late 1930s, still important in daily life, but the industry was declining. A good many of the country's smaller rail lines failed in the Great Depression, facing competition from automobiles, trucks, and airplanes. The United States' involvement in World War II brought the railroad back into service of the war effort, transporting military personnel and freight at twice the rate that it had during World War I.[32] Cleveland painter Carl Gaertner's 1944 *Swamp Spur* (cat. 18), like Bohrod's *Slag Heaps*, is a damp winter landscape so cold and desolate that it borders on the surreal. But the small train cutting through the center of the composition, bookended by a red caboose with one passenger, sets the otherwise still scene into motion. The "spur" in Gaertner's title is a secondary train line providing access to industrial areas, in this painting the cluster of buildings and smokestacks visible along the painting's horizon. So in spite of its bleak, marshy setting (likely what is now Cuyahoga Valley National Park), *Swamp Spur* walks a poetic line between nostalgia for the past, anxiety about the present, and hope for—or at least movement toward—a better future.

In the postwar years, investment in diesel engines for freight signaled a new era for the American railroad, but by mid-century it was more a symbol of a fading past than the industry that had fueled American growth in the Gilded Age or the gleaming engine of modernity it had been just two decades earlier. Yet in less than a century, the railroad had transformed American life, the American landscape, and therefore American art. Artists' attitudes toward trains shifted and evolved just as the nation's policies and dependencies did, but ultimately it served as the embodiment of progress, the disruptor of traditional notions of time and space, and the symbol of a new Industrial Age from which the nation, its people, its landscape, and its art could never return.

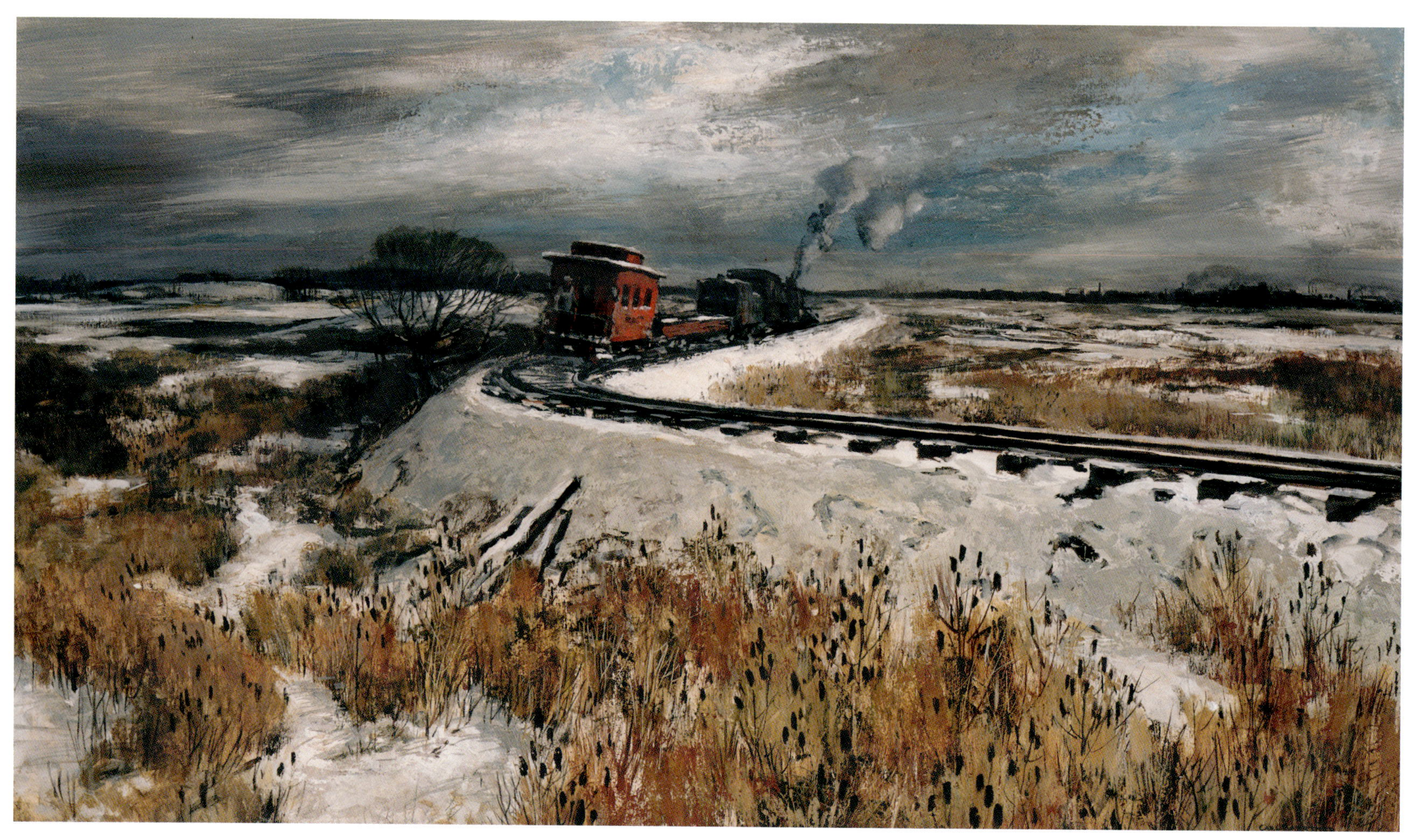

Cat. 18

**Carl Frederick Gaertner
(American, 1898–1952)**
Swamp Spur, 1944

oil on canvas
24 × 40 in.

The John and Susan Horseman
Collection, Courtesy of the
Horseman Foundation

Endnotes

1   Henry David Thoreau, *Walden; or, Life in the Woods* (Boston: Ticknor & Fields, 1854), 58-59, https://archive.org/details/waldenorlifeinwo1854thor.

2   By 1902, American railroads were transporting more than 607 million passengers annually. The US Bureau of the Census report Historical Statistics of the United States, Colonial Times to 1957, chapter Q, "Transportation" (Washington, DC: Government Printing Office, 1960), https://www2.census.gov/library/publications/1960/compendia/hist_stats_colonial-1957/hist_stats_colonial-1957-chQ.pdf, provides a wealth of statistics on the railroad, including mileage, number of rail cars in operation, passenger statistics, and revenue. In 1893, an all-time land speed record of 112.5 miles per hour was set by a train in Genesee County, New York.

3   David O. Stowell, *Streets, Railroads, and the Great Strike of 1877* (Chicago: University of Chicago Press, 1999), 117; "The Great Railroad Riots," *New York Times*, July 23, 1877, 1.

4   "The Great Railroad Riots."

5   E. Benjamin Andrews, "A History of the Last Quarter Century in the United States," *Scribner's Magazine* 18 (July–December 1895). Leigh's painting is printed on p. 83.

6   R. L. Duffus, "Is Pittsburgh Civilized?" *Harper's Monthly* 161 (October 1930): 537.

7   Colin Campbell Cooper, *Pittsburgh, Pennsylvania*, 1906, oil on canvas, 33 × 45 in., National Academy of Design, New York, 270-P.

8   "Tunnel Station of Pennsylvania Railroad," *New York Times*, March 27, 1903, 16.

9   Marianne Doezema, *George Bellows and Urban America* (New Haven, CT: Yale University Press, 1992), 20-21.

10   Bayard Boyesen, "The National Note in American Art," *Putnam's Monthly* 4, no. 2 (1908): 133.

11   Boyesen, 134. Boyesen is referencing the French Barbizon school painter Jean-François Millet (1814-1875) and the Belgian social realist painter and sculptor Constantin Meunier (1831-1905).

12   See also George Bellows, *North River*, 1908, oil on canvas, 32⅞ × 43 in., Pennsylvania Academy of the Fine Arts, 1909.2; and George Bellows, *Up the Hudson*, 1908, oil on canvas, 35⅞ × 48⅛ in., Metropolitan Museum of Art, New York, 11.17.

13   For a complete history of the park, see "Riverside Park History," Riverside Park Conservancy, accessed September 8, 2023, https://riversideparknyc.org/riverside-park-history/.

14   Marianne Doezema, "The Excavation," in Doezema, *George Bellows and Urban America*, 9-66.

15   "New Pennsylvania Station Is Opened," *New York Times*, August 29, 1910, 4.

16   "Day Long Throng Inspects New Tube," *New York Times*, September 9, 1910, 5.

17   Elevated trains debuted in New York in July 1868 but were not reliable or expanded upon until as late as 1878. See "The Elevated Railway," *New York Times*, July 4, 1868, 2; and Sonia Kahn, "What Goes Up Must Come Down: A Brief History of New York City's Elevated Rail and Subway Lines," *Worlds Revealed: Geography and Maps at the Library of Congress* (blog), Library of Congress, May 19, 2022, https://blogs.loc.gov/maps/2022/05/what-goes-up-must-come-down-a-brief-history-of-new-york-citys-elevated-rail-and-subway-lines/.

18   Susan Danly Walther, *The Railroad in the American Landscape: 1850-1950*, exh. cat. (Wellesley, MA: Wellesley Museum, 1981), 120.

19   Auguste Renoir recounted to his son his memory of Monet's inspiration to paint Paris's Gare Saint-Lazare: "I'll show it just as the trains are starting, with smoke from the engines so thick you can hardly see a thing. It's a fascinating sight, a regular dream world." Jean Renoir, *Renoir, My Father*, trans. Randolph and Dorothy Weaver (1958; New York: New York Review of Books, 2001), 163.

20   Theodore Roosevelt, "A Layman's Views of an Art Exhibition," *Outlook* 103 (March 29, 1913): 718-20.

21   "Armory Show 1913 Complete List," New-York Historical Society, 2012, https://armory.nyhistory.org/armory-show-1913-complete-list/. Eddy was a native of Flint, Michigan; his widow left the painting to the Flint Institute of Arts in 1931.

22   Brinley served on the Domestic Committee, the Publicity Committee, and the Reception Committee for the Armory Show, and he exhibited there.

23   See Leo Marx, *The Machine in the Garden: Technology and the Pastoral Ideal in America* (Oxford: Oxford University Press, 1964). See also Kiersten M. Jensen, *Industrial Sublime: Modernism and the Transformation of New York's Rivers, 1900-1940* (New York: Fordham University Press, 2013).

24   "Wilson, at Station, Signs Bill That Averted Strike," *Washington Times*, September 3, 1916, 1.

25   See "Records of the United States Railroad Administration (USRA)," in *Guide to Federal Records in the National Archives of the United States* (Washington, DC: National Archives and Records Administration, 1995), https://www.archives.gov/research/guide-fed-records/groups/014.html.

26   Edgar J. Rich, "The Transportation Act of 1920," *American Economic Review* 10, no. 3 (September 1920): 510.

27   Emily Badger and Darla Cameron, "How Railroads, Highways and Other Man-Made Lines Racially Divide America's Cities," *Washington Post*, July 16, 2015, https://www.washingtonpost.com/news/wonk/wp/2015/07/16/how-railroads-highways-and-other-man-made-lines-racially-divide-americas-cities/.

28   Deedee Wigmore, *Reginald Marsh (1898-1954): Urban Realist, Master of Many Media* (New York: D. Wigmore Fine Art, 2008).

29   Wigmore.

30   Marsh's *The Locomotive* as a mural study was painted with tempera onto the wall of his mentor Olle Nordmark's studio in New Jersey. See Harriet Irgang, "Considering Artist's Intent in the Public Arena," *1994 AIC Paintings Specialty Group Post-Prints* (Washington, DC: Paintings Specialty Group of the American Institute for Conservation of Historic and Artistic Works, 1994), 42-49, https://www.culturalheritage.org/publications/books-periodicals/library/specialty-group-publications/paintings-specialty-group-postprints/docs/default-source/publications-periodicals/painting-specialty-group/paintings-specialty-group-postprints-vol-7-1994. It does not appear that *The Locomotive* was ever translated into a mural for the Custom House frescoes. The Alexander Hamilton U.S. Custom House now houses the Smithsonian Institution's National Museum of the American Indian. See Reginald Marsh papers, 1897-1955, box 7, folder 15: Volume 3 (Custom House and Post Office Murals), circa 1935-1937, Archives of American Art, Smithsonian Institution, https://www.aaa.si.edu/collections/reginald-marsh-papers-9072/subseries-8-3-1/box-7-folder-15.

31   Michael D. Bordo and Joseph G. Haubrich, "Deep Recessions, Fast Recoveries, and Financial Crises: Evidence from the American Record" (working paper 18194, National Bureau of Economic Research, Cambridge, MA, June 2012), https://www.nber.org/papers/w18194.

32   See Association of American Railroads, "Chronology of America's Freight Railroads," accessed September 6, 2023, https://www.aar.org/chronology-of-americas-freight-railroads/.

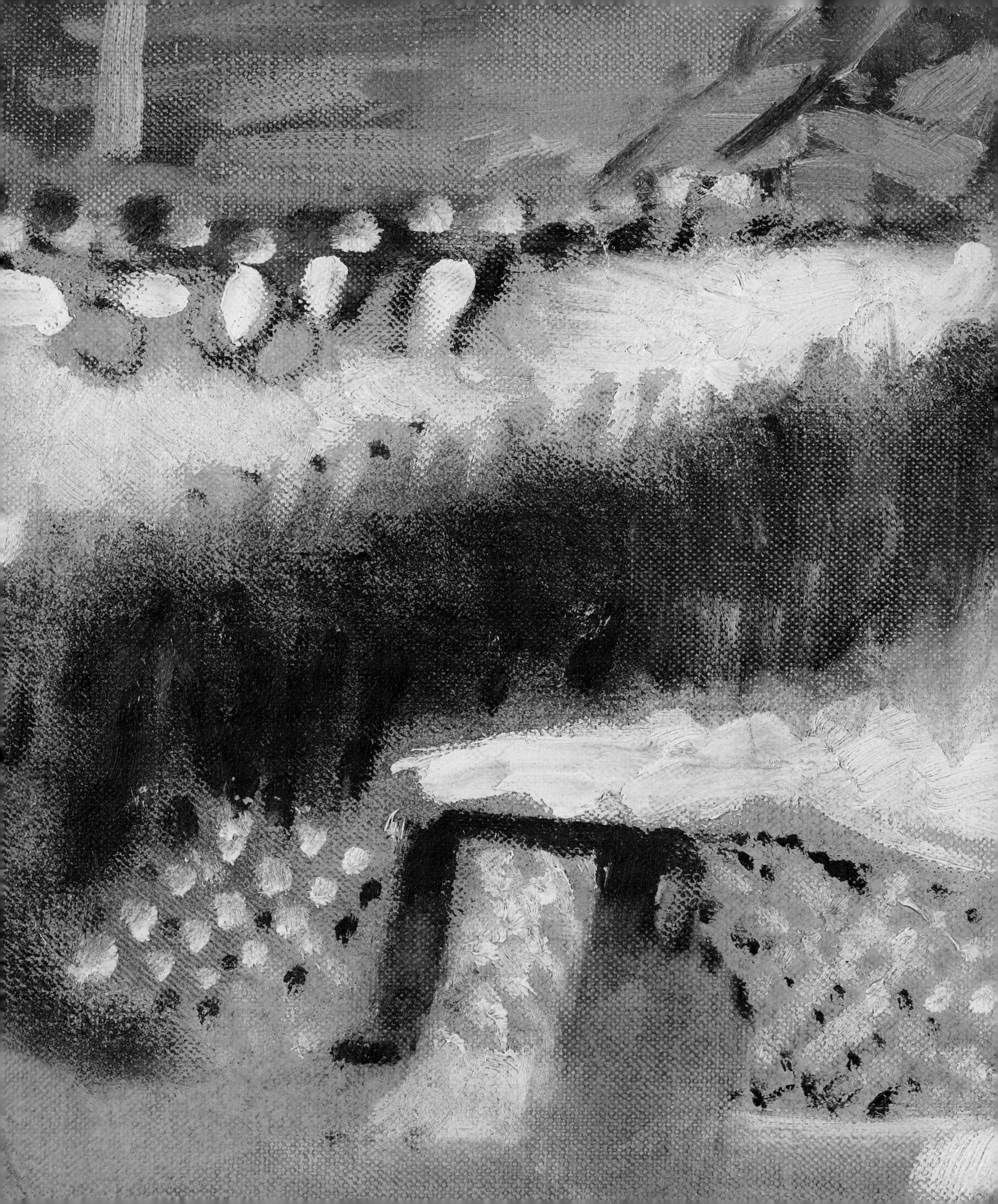

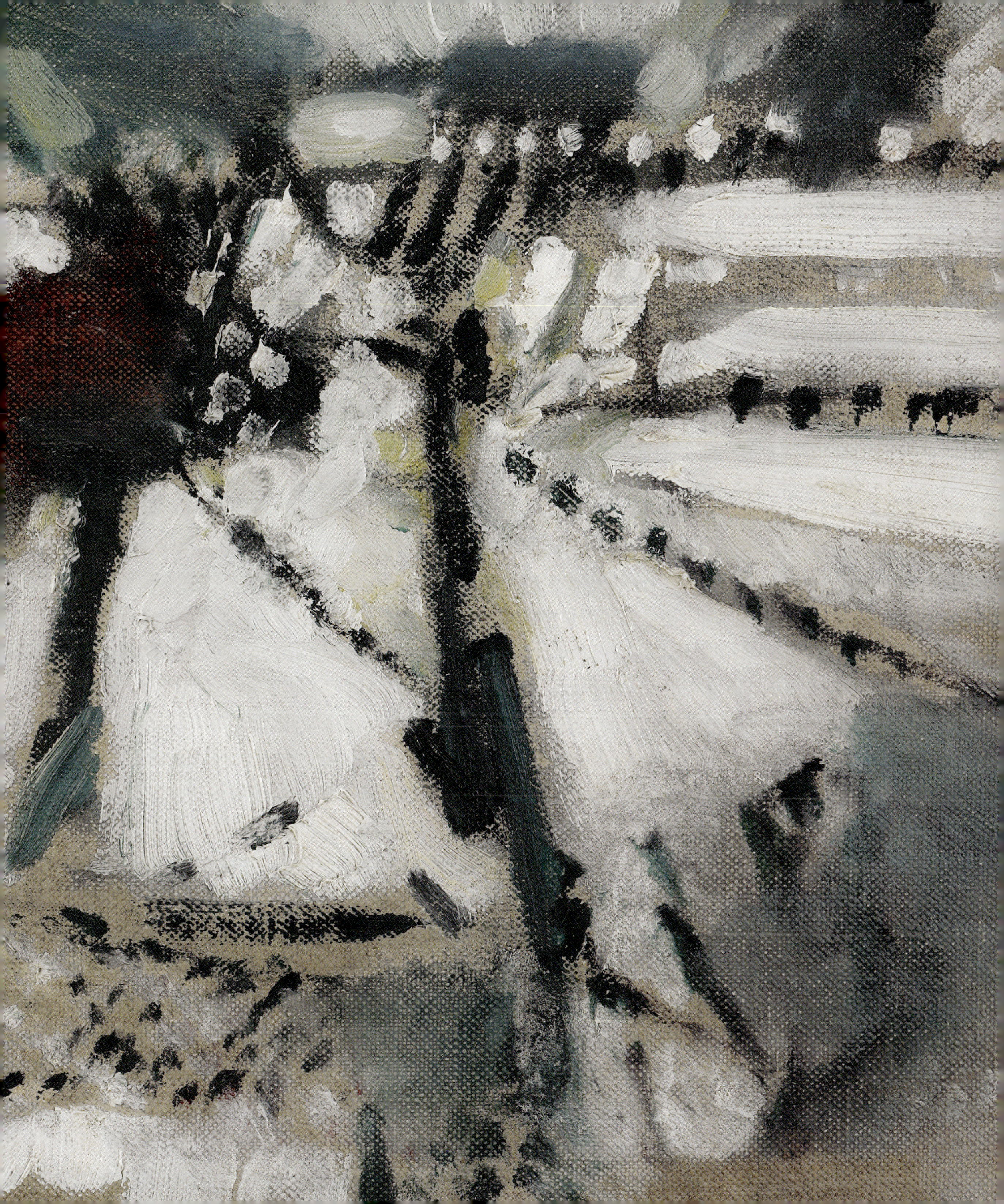

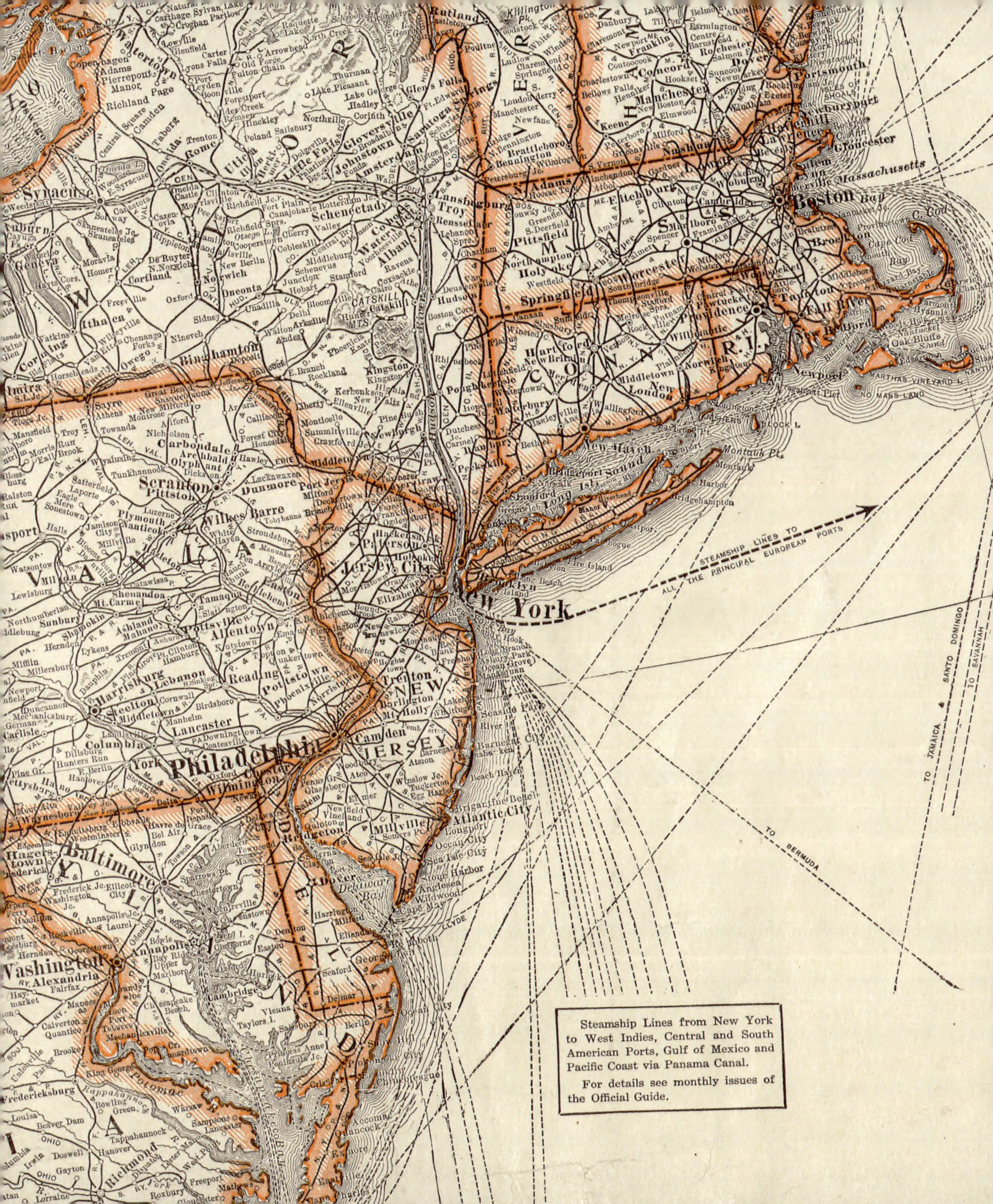

Steamship Lines from New York
to West Indies, Central and South
American Ports, Gulf of Mexico and
Pacific Coast via Panama Canal.
For details see monthly issues of
the Official Guide.
STEAMSHIP LINES TO
ALL THE PRINCIPAL EUROPEAN PORTS
TO BERMUDA
TO JAMAICA
SANTO DOMINGO
TO SAVANNAH
New York
Boston
Philadelphia
Baltimore
Washington
Jersey City
Trenton
Scranton
Wilkes Barre
Harrisburg
Reading
Allentown
Lancaster
Atlantic City
Albany
Troy
Schenectady
Syracuse
Binghamton
Hartford
New Haven
Providence
Worcester
Springfield
Bridgeport Sound
Long Isl'd Sound
Long Isl.
Montauk Pt.
Block I.
Newport
MARTHAS VINEYARD I.
NO MANS LAND
Massachusetts Bay
Cape Cod
Buzzards Bay
Fall River
Taunton
Brockton
Newburyport
Gloucester
Portsmouth
Manchester
Concord
Rochester
Dover
VERMONT
N. H.
MASS.
CONN.
R. I.
NEW YORK
PENNSYLVANIA
NEW JERSEY
MARYLAND
DELAWARE
VIRGINIA
Richmond
Fredericksburg
Alexandria
Annapolis
Cambridge
Baltimore
Hagerstown
Frederick
Carlisle
Gettysburg
York
Columbia
Wilmington
Camden
Vineland
Millville
Camden
Chesapeake Bay
Delaware Bay
Potomac
Rappahannock
OHIO
CATSKILL MTS.
Kingston
Poughkeepsie
Newburgh
Middletown
Port Jervis
Paterson
Elizabeth
Ithaca
Elmira
Corning
Cortland
Auburn
Geneva
Oneonta
Utica
Rome
Amsterdam
Saratoga Springs
Glens Falls
Rutland
Keene
Brattleboro
Bennington
Pittsfield
Northampton
Holyoke
New London
Norwich
Middletown
New Britain
Stamford
Hudson
Catskill
Kingston
Hook
Sandy Hook
Fire Island
Barnegat
Absecon
Cape May
Cape Charles
Wildwood
Ocean City
Sayre
Towanda
Carbondale
Pittston
Dunmore
Easton
Bethlehem
Pottsville
Pottstown
Norristown
Burlington
Mt. Holly
Seaside Park

3

THE LONELY RAIL

Kevin Sharp

National Railway Publication Company, *General Railway Map Engraved Expressly for the Official Guide of the Railways and Steam Navigation Lines of the United States, Porto Rico, Canada, Mexico and Cuba* (detail), 1918.

Library of Congress Geography and Map Division, Washington, DC

AFTER DECADES OF INDUSTRIAL INNOVATION, phenomenal expansions of track miles, almost complete corporate domination, spectacular wealth creation, and, in the minds of many reformers, delirious corruption, by the dawn of the twentieth century, America's railways were facing their most serious existential challenges. With the creation of the Interstate Commerce Commission in 1887 and the more vigorous enforcement of the 1890 Sherman Antitrust Act by the justice departments of Presidents Theodore Roosevelt, William Howard Taft, and Woodrow Wilson that started in 1901 and did not relent until the United States' entry into the Great War in 1917, American railways saw rates regulation, consumer protections, and their ability to strangle competition stymied for the first time. Fifteen years of federal trustbusting, as it was called, was followed by the even more stunning nationalization of the American railway system in 1917—the Wilson administration's effort to hurry and bolster the nation's readiness to enter the war in Europe. Even after the armistice in November 1918 and the eventual return of American railways to corporate management and control in March 1920, the great age of railroad hegemony was clearly a thing of the past.[1]

For most Americans coming of age in the early 1920s, the railroad had always been a substantial presence in the cities, towns, and farms from which they hailed. The tracks and trains they knew were as much a part of their everyday existence as shops, roads, churches, and schools. Just thirty years earlier, however, American railways would have appeared to the parents of the flapper generation to be a still-developing, visibly maturing, and powerful industry. At the end of the Civil War in 1865, there were roughly 35,000 miles of functioning track in the United States. By 1900, there were more than 200,000 miles. As late as the 1890s—even with an economic depression in 1893 and a strengthening labor movement—railway lines were yet under construction and others were still being planned, mostly in the West. These two perceptions of America's railways, separated by a single generation, could scarcely have been more

"

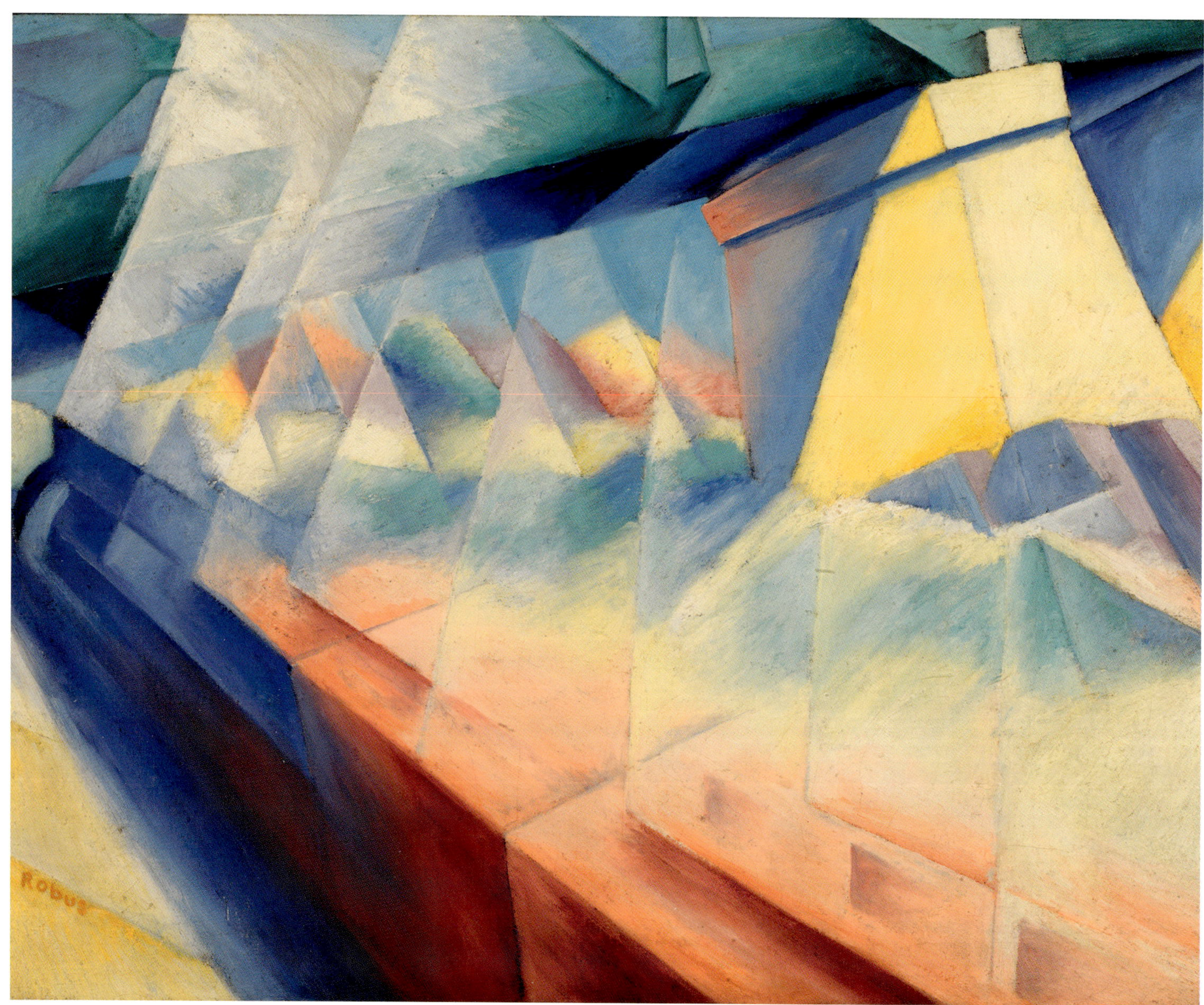

Cat. 19

Hugo Robus (American, 1885-1964)
Train in Motion, ca. 1920

oil on canvas mounted on fiberglass
26¼ × 32⅛ in.

Smithsonian American Art Museum

Gift of Mr. and Mrs. Hugo Robus, Jr., 1978.153.2

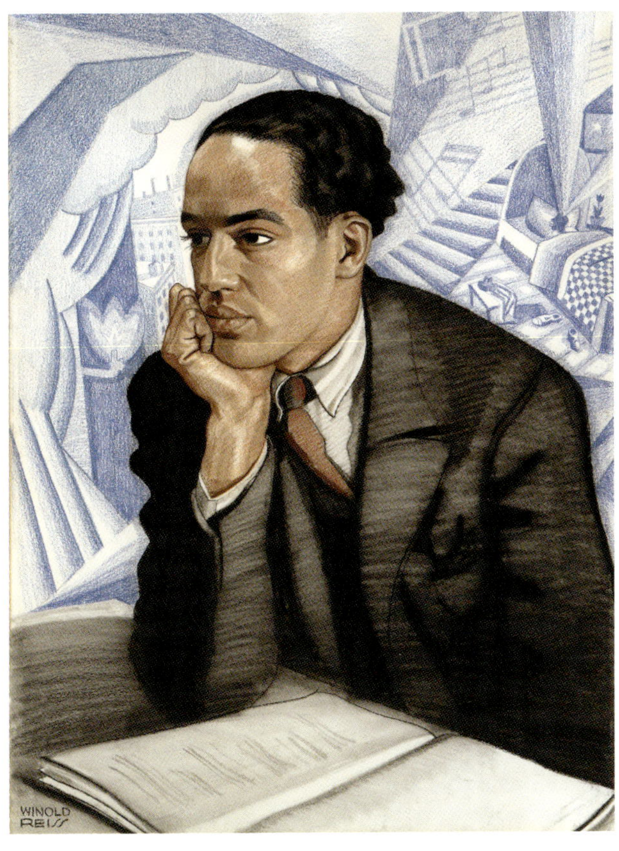

Fig. 20

Winold Reiss (American, born in Germany, 1886-1953)
Langston Hughes, ca. 1925

pastel on illustration board
sheet: 30⅛ × 21⅝ in.

National Portrait Gallery, Smithsonian Institution

Gift of W. Tjark Reiss, in memory of his father, Winold Reiss

different. One generation saw explosive growth and corporate might, while the next witnessed an industry that was in a form of stasis, under siege, and seemingly in decline.

The American railway system in 1920 was as large as it would ever be, covering more than a quarter of a million miles of track in the United States alone, employing a million and a half people, and reaching virtually every corner of the country with service of some kind. But that mammoth scale was mostly residue of an earlier and more productive era, and the system would grow no larger. Increasingly, in the 1920s, ordinary Americans began to identify with the freight and passenger trains that rattled through town, their sights and sounds frequent, abundantly familiar, and suddenly, it seemed, steeped more in nostalgia than in an expansive future.[2] That familiarity helped establish associations, feelings, and memories in ways the transportation juggernaut could never have expected to occur at the height of its land-

grabbing, union-busting, and politician-bribing power in the late nineteenth century.[3] Moreover, by mid-decade people were leaving rural lives in the South in massive numbers for the hope of greater opportunity and less discrimination in the industrial North. Many of those travelers arrived in northern cities by train, as the *Chicago Defender* noted in its national edition in May 1925: "The great migration is on. Every train pulling into stations of northern cities unloads migrants fresh from the cotton fields, foundries, and lumber camps of the South."[4]

Even as American railways could feel themselves contracting, any given train roaring by could still seem formidable to a bystander. Hugo Robus's brilliant abstract painting *Train in Motion* (cat. 19) of about 1920 captured the railroad as the industry may have wanted to see itself—a still-vital form and the very symbol of speed and efficiency. Robus placed a string of rolling boxcars diagonally across the lower register of the composition, the closer cars in red and those further away in shadowy blue. Abstracted bridges and trestles and trusses fill the upper reaches of the painting while shafts of light pour through the architecture and cast broad shadows upon it. In its complete absence of a human presence, the painting speaks to the loneliness Americans would eventually come to associate with the railroads, even if only obliquely. But Robus's emphasis on muscle and locomotion, and his embrace of Cubist abstraction in *Train in Motion*, largely ignores the nostalgia for the railways that many if not most were coming to feel.[5]

It may have been the poet Langston Hughes (fig. 20) who was the first to grasp and capitalize artistically on the shifting American perception of the railroads. He first gained notice for a poem he called "The Negro Speaks of Rivers," written in 1918 when he was only seventeen years old. The poem was inspired by Hughes's travel aboard a passenger train from New York to Mexico (to see his father) as it was crossing the Mississippi River.[6] The short verse was initially published in *The Crisis* in 1921 but later appeared in Hughes's first volume of poetry, *The Weary Blues*, in 1926.[7] That volume became one of the literary touchstones of the Harlem Renaissance. Hughes followed that success with a second book that controversially made ample use of Black vernacular language and included the poems "Homesick Blues" and "Railroad Avenue," both of which assigned expressive meaning to some element of the railway. In "Homesick Blues," a railroad bridge and the sound of a passing train conjure a desire to be "somewhere," seemingly anywhere.

> De railroad bridge's
> A sad song in de air.
> De railroad bridge's
> A sad song in de air.
> Ever time de trains pass
> I wants to go somewhere.[8]

Born in Joplin, Missouri, and raised in Lawrence, Kansas, the child of separated parents frequently on the move in search of work, Langston Hughes understood that Americans saw the railroad differently than they once had—or at least he saw it differently. It had become recognizable to his readers as a perfectly adaptable agent for metaphoric meaning beyond power and speed. It was now capable of establishing a sense of longing in his verse, as a growing segment of his readership was living somewhere other than the place where they had been born. Hughes effectively embroidered upon this shifting vision of the railway as a catalyst for separation, loss, and loneliness, as many other poets, writers, musicians, and visual artists eventually would as well. They increasingly saw the rails as a viable thematic symbol as many Americans adjusted to an accelerating age of mobility and migration.

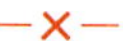

The painter, watercolorist, and printmaker John Marin had reached maturity long before the 1920s. Born in 1870, he had worked as an architect of sorts, designing houses in Union Hill, New Jersey, and studying art sporadically in Philadelphia and New York. In 1905, he traveled to Europe, where he would remain for the next five years, mostly based in Paris, where his art training continued. But Paris was also where Marin, past age thirty-five, finally launched his career as a visual artist. By 1907 and 1908, Marin was experiencing some success, showing his watercolors at the Salon d'Automne and seeing one of his etchings reproduced in the *Gazette des Beaux-Arts*. Marin went back and forth between Paris and New York in 1909 and 1910 before returning to the United States permanently in the fall of 1910 as a fairly well-established artist with strong prospects.[9]

New York was very different in 1910 than the city Marin had left five years earlier. In his usual colorful terms, he described the changes he was now discovering anew:

> The Woolworth Building was under construction; two new bridges had been swung across the East River; horse and cable cars were now almost entirely replaced by electric ones; there was an elevated railway rattling overhead and subway growling underfoot.[10]

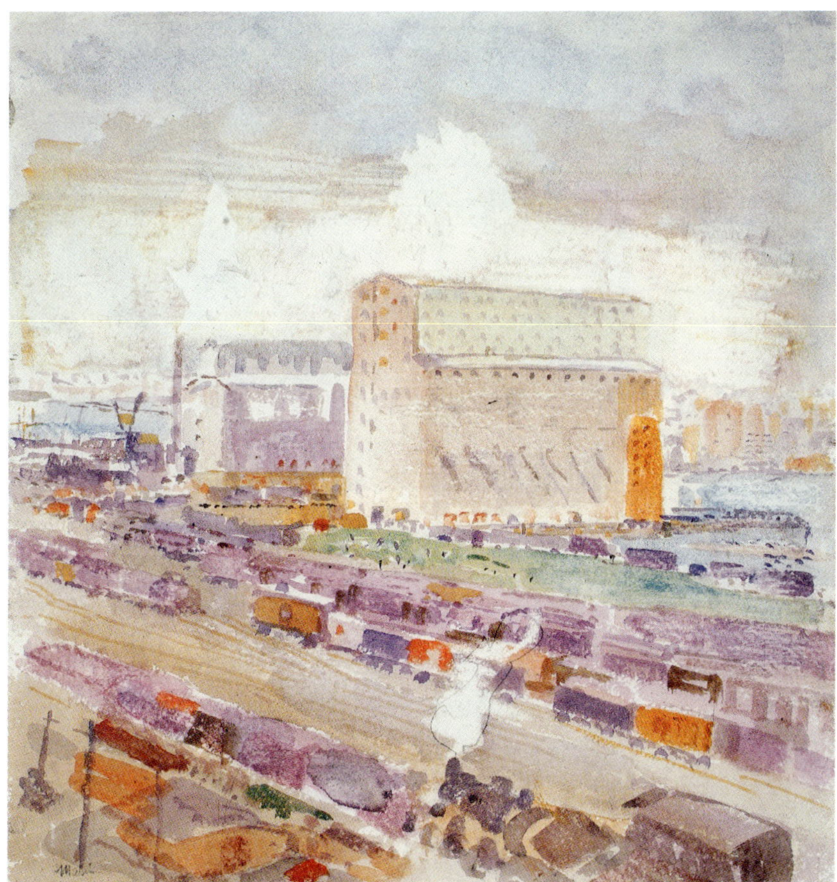

Fig. 21

John Marin (American, 1870–1953)
Weehawken Railroad Yards and Grain Elevator, 1910
watercolor and graphite on paper
14⅞ × 13¾ in.
Private collection

Marin was a sensitive and attuned observer of rhythm and pattern, whether natural or manufactured, and he eloquently translated those forms into increasingly abstracted works of art. Not long after returning to the United States, he established the first of a series of studios in New Jersey and made frequent painting excursions to the Palisades, high bluffs above the Hudson River on the Jersey side that he had known since childhood. Before the end of 1910, Marin painted an impressive watercolor of Weehawken, looking down on the busy section yard, railroad sidings filled with boxcars and a locomotive puffing steam, and the vast West Shore Elevator on Pier 7 looming over the Hudson River (fig. 21). The great grain elevator would have been among the structures new to Marin in 1910. Its construction had been announced in the *New York Times* on September 11, 1901, and it was trumpeted as the largest such facility in the country.[11] The elevator would have been completed at the time Marin first left for Europe.

In his later oil painting *Grain Elevator*, from his *Weehawken Sequence* (cat. 20), Marin may have come off the Palisades and worked from the section yard. He captured the great storage facility in streaks of red paint, pushed into the upper left of the composition, and surrounded by a shrouded hush of winter snow. The dozen or more sets of siding tracks running alongside the West Shore Elevator were more or less abstracted by Marin into networks of dots and dashed lines. The boxcars that populated his 1910 watercolor were nowhere to be found.

The dating of the works in Marin's *Weehawken Sequence*, a group of perhaps one hundred paintings and many more watercolors, has been the subject of much discussion over the ensuing century. *Grain Elevator* is usually dated between

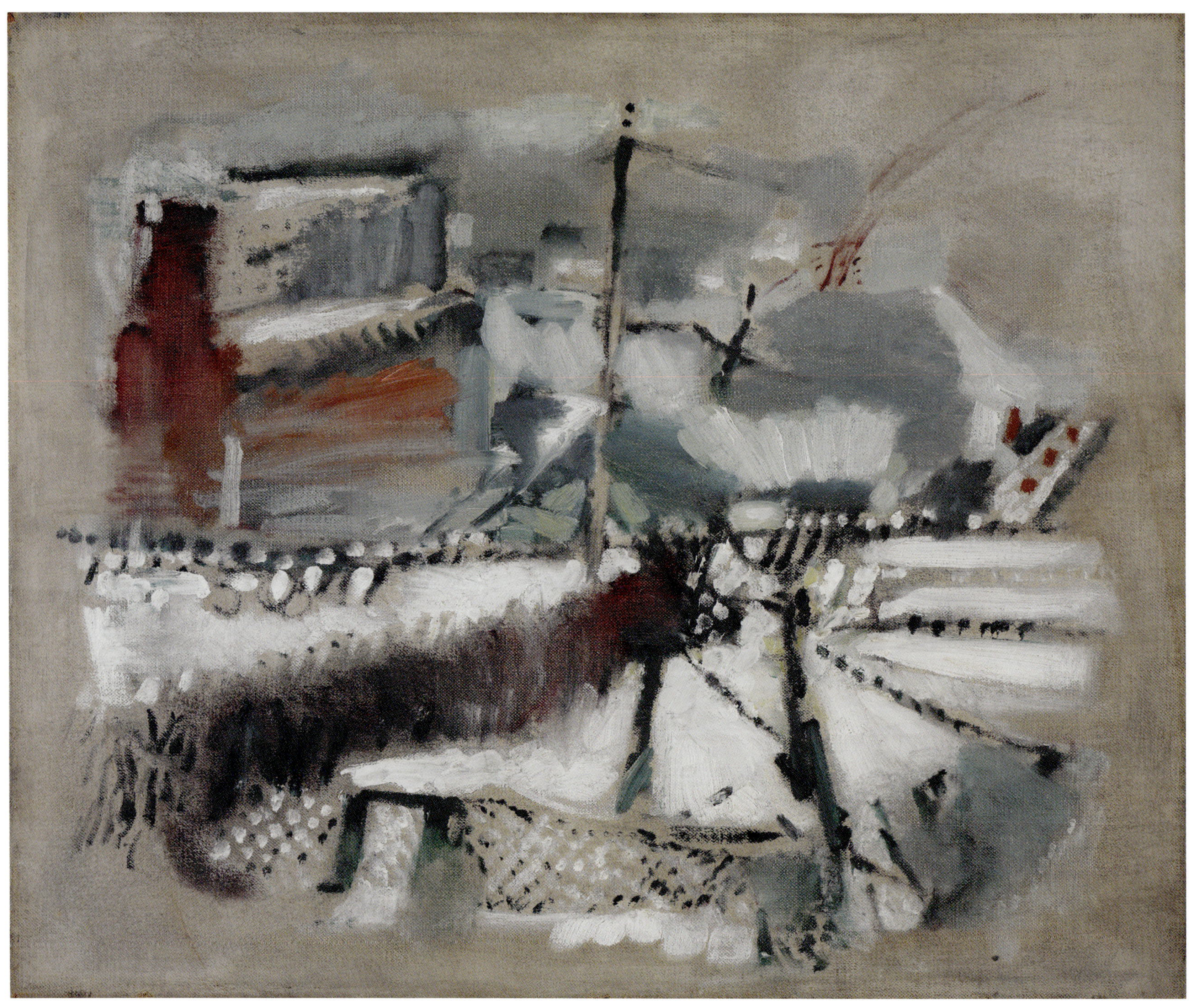

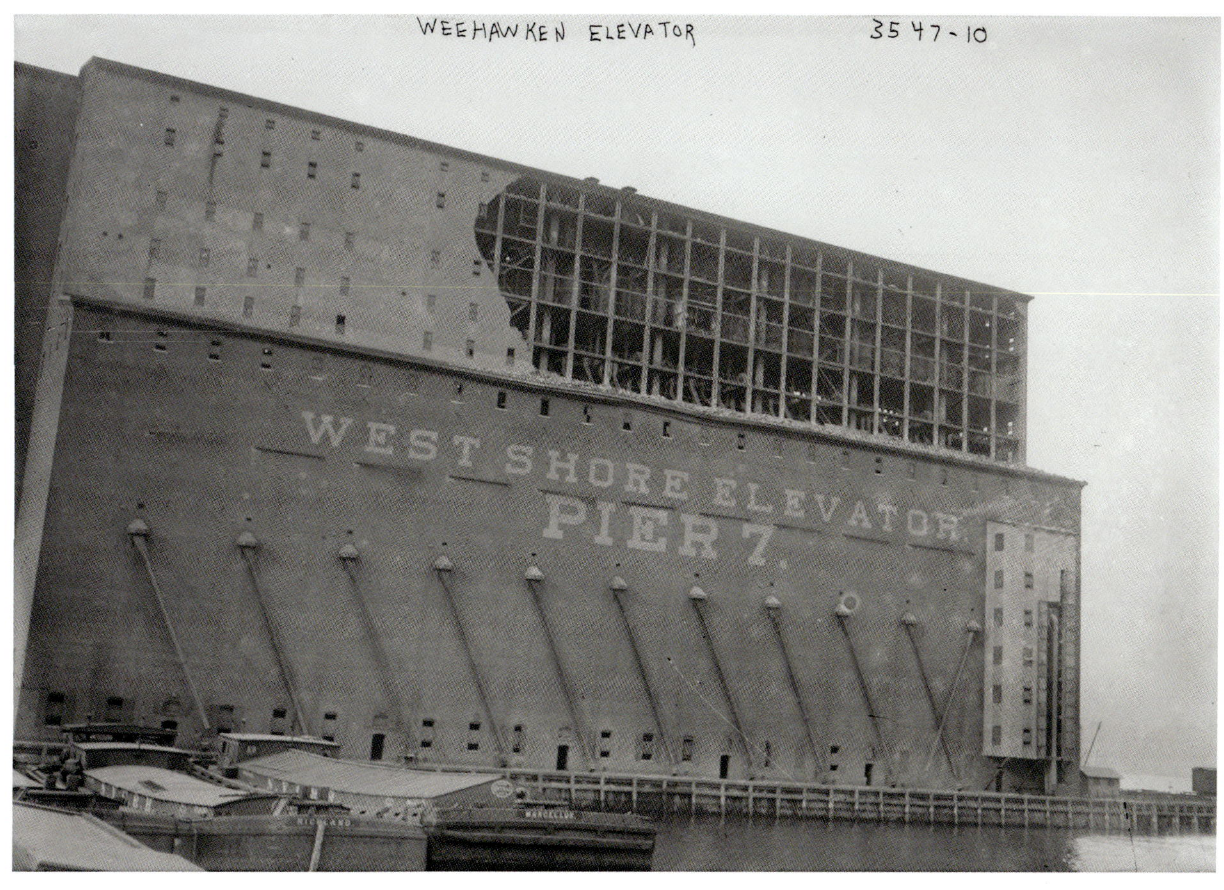

Fig. 22

Bain News Service, publisher

Weehawken Elevator, July 15, 1915

glass negative

Library of Congress Prints and
Photographs Division, Washington, DC

Cat. 20

John Marin (American, 1870-1953)

Grain Elevator, ca. 1910-15

oil on canvas
16⅜ × 19⅜ in.

Promised Gift to Crystal Bridges Museum
of American Art, Bentonville, Arkansas

1910 and 1915, but it was almost certainly produced in the latter year or possibly even in early 1916. On July 15, 1915, a massive explosion at the West Shore Elevator echoed up and down the Hudson, rocking anchored boats along both sides of the river, and the damage to the storage facility itself was severe enough that engineers feared collapse. Much of the cladding and many of the windows on the upper five-story cupola were blown into the air and onto neighboring boats and buildings. The explosion was initially thought to have been a bomb set off by German saboteurs (a frequent subject in the press at the time) trying to limit grain supplies to Allied forces in Europe; the blast was later found to have been caused by grain dust and an electrical spark.[12] A photograph taken of the Weehawken Elevator just after the explosion reveals the extent of the damage (fig. 22), and in Marin's *Grain Elevator*, the building is still missing its cladding and windows.

Cat. 21

Georgia O'Keeffe (American, 1887-1986)
Train Coming in—Canyon, Texas, 1916
watercolor on paper
9¾ × 8¼ in.

Collection of the Amarillo Museum of Art

Purchased with funds from the National
Endowment for the Arts, Amarillo
Area Foundation, Amarillo Art Alliance,
Fannie Weymouth, Santa Fe Industries
Foundation and Mary Fain, AM.1982.1.4

Marin tended to see the spirit in all things, including inanimate objects and architecture, but in *Grain Elevator*, he nonetheless lent the scene a sense of snowy quiet. That feeling may have related less to the changing perception of the railroad than to the wintery time of year, the recent explosion and transfer of grain to other facilities, or any number of other possibilities. Given how impressed he was by the vitality of New York, he may not have seen anything in the railroad at that point to suggest the isolation and loneliness that others heard and saw in it.

Painted at almost the same time as the works in Marin's *Weehawken Sequence*, Georgia O'Keeffe's extraordinary watercolor *Train Coming In—Canyon, Texas* (cat. 21) is an essay in simplicity. The railroad tracks are merely three arcing lines that move quickly out of the composition while a locomotive, little more than a circle, releases massive swirls of colorful smoke into the Texas sky. The work speaks both to O'Keeffe's powerful affinity for the Southwest and the sense of isolation it could offer. She wrote to Alfred Stieglitz, eventually her husband, not long after arriving in Canyon, Texas: "The Plains—the wonderful great big sky—makes me want to breathe so deep that I'll break—There is so much of it…" A week later, she wrote to her friend Anita Pollitzer: "Tonight I walked into the sunset—to mail some letters—the whole sky—and there is so much

of it out here—was just blazing … Well I just sat there and had a great time all by myself."[13]

O'Keeffe's correspondence from this period describes her vacillation between feeling the creative value of separateness and independence but still needing the stimulation of the New York artistic milieu to which Stieglitz had introduced her. She struggled to locate her equilibrium and often found herself on trains between Texas and New York and back before finally settling in Manhattan in 1918 with Stieglitz at her side. They married in 1924.

—✕—

The curious nostalgia for the railroad's bygone days continued in the United States throughout the 1920s. Railroad men of every stripe set down memoirs of their days driving engines, laying track, designing trestles and bridges, hunting buffalo to feed rail workers, and leading whole companies.[14] The first railroad hobbyists emerged in the 1920s, collecting histories and books, but also timetables, postcards, and other bits of ephemera to expand their knowledge and feed their hunger to understand the heyday of the rails. Toy electric trains were available by the turn of the century, but they became increasingly popular in 1920s as more homes had the electricity necessary to drive them. In that newest of cultural forms in the 1920s, the movies, some of the more ambitious

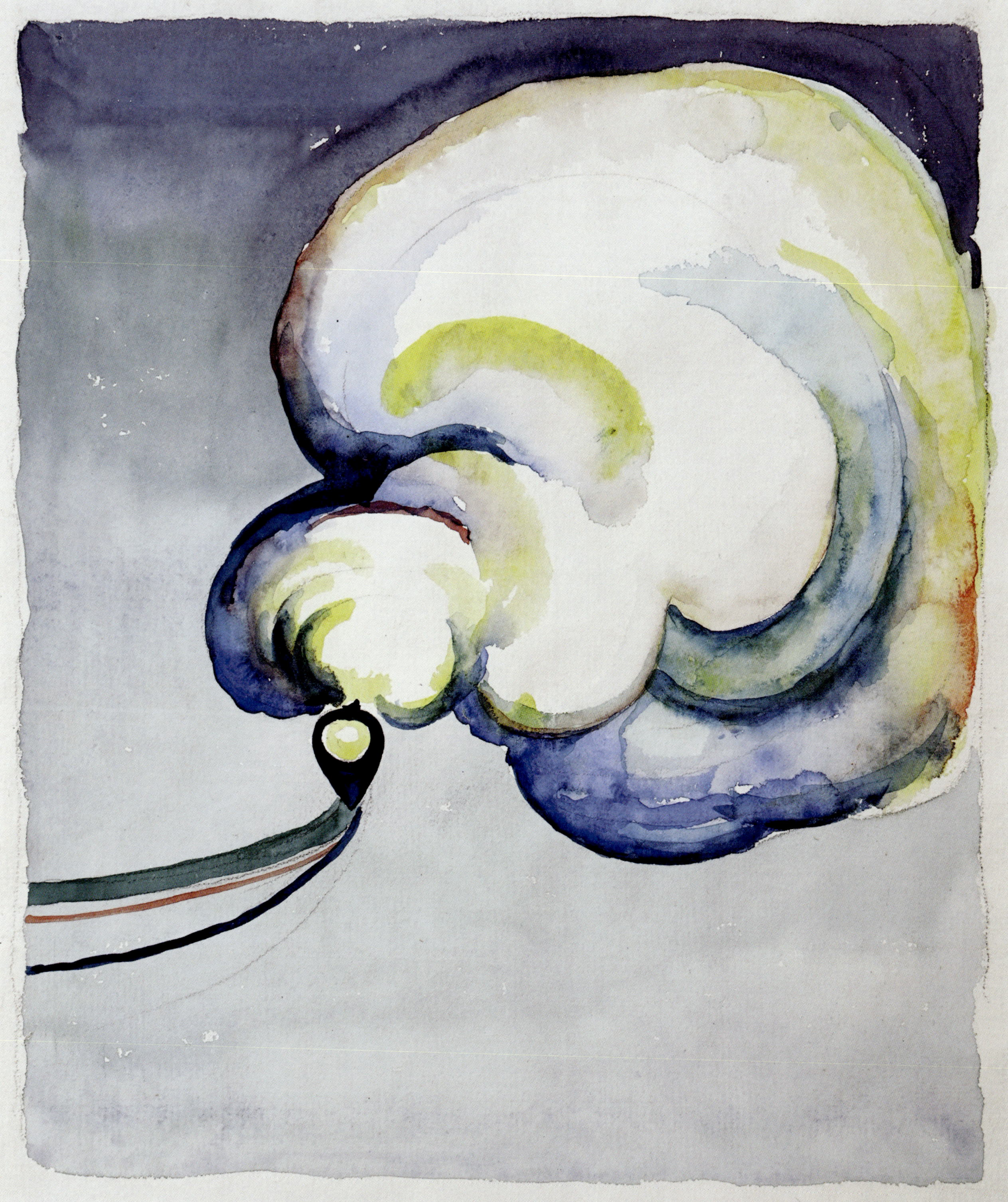

silent films of the era focused on the history of the American railroad, including John Ford's *The Iron Horse* (1924), which fictionalized the construction of the transcontinental railroad in 1869, and Buster Keaton's *The General* (1926), a comedic reenactment of an important Civil War action. And in 1925, Slason Thompson published his taut *A Short History of American Railways: Covering Ten Decades*, which he dedicated to "The Two Million and More Railway Employe[e]s" who may also have been his principal audience.[15]

American painters were as prone to nostalgia as Hollywood producers and directors, but that quality is sometimes overlooked in their competing interest in giving expression to modernist sensibilities. Thomas Hart Benton was born in the small town of Neosho, Missouri, a county seat on the western edge of the Ozarks that traced its origins to the late 1820s. By the time Benton was a child growing up there in the 1890s, Neosho had become a busy railroad hub where the San Francisco and St. Louis line crossed the Kansas City Southern. Listening to trains rumbling through town would have been common fixtures of Benton's early life. Moreover, the future artist's father, Maecenas Eason (M. E.) Benton, was a United States congressman from Missouri's fifteenth district, and from 1896 until 1904, young Tom Benton often found himself on passenger trains in one direction or another between Neosho and Washington, DC.[16] His experience of the rails and what they meant to him early on would eventually be transformed into images that expressed something fundamental about rural life in middle America.

For Benton, the artist, the railroad was a place of adventure, excitement, stories, and songs. Speeding locomotives, railroad workers, train robbers, and legendary engineers featured frequently in his paintings, prints, and murals across the long expanse of his career.[17] But in what may have been among the first of Benton's railroad subjects as a fully mature artist, *New Mexico (Landscape)* of 1926 (cat. 22), a lonely locomotive in a remote landscape pulls five cars and a caboose and coughs black smoke into a hazy western sky. Passing through largely empty terrain, the short train is witnessed only by a single skinny cow standing among soaptree yuccas and sagebrush.

The desolate character of *New Mexico (Landscape)* was almost certainly informed by the circumstances of Benton's life in the mid-1920s. His formidable father had died in 1924, well before the artist had achieved the national recognition that would justify his dubious (to M. E. anyway) choice of careers.[18] Benton had returned to Missouri from New York during his father's final illness and rediscovered in the rusticity of the Ozarks subjects that allowed him to again showcase the wit, spontaneity, and directness he had sacrificed to formalism and technique during his education and early career.

In the spring of 1926, Benton left his wife Rita behind on Martha's Vineyard, where they had summered for the previous five years, and went on a long one-person ramble through Louisiana, Arkansas, Missouri, Texas, and presumably New Mexico. He was seeking inspiration and subject matter that were both authentic to the character of the country and true to himself. He took every kind of conveyance during the five months he was away, including trains, but most often Benton walked, sometimes as much as twenty miles per day. He stayed in rustic mountain hotels or with agreeable

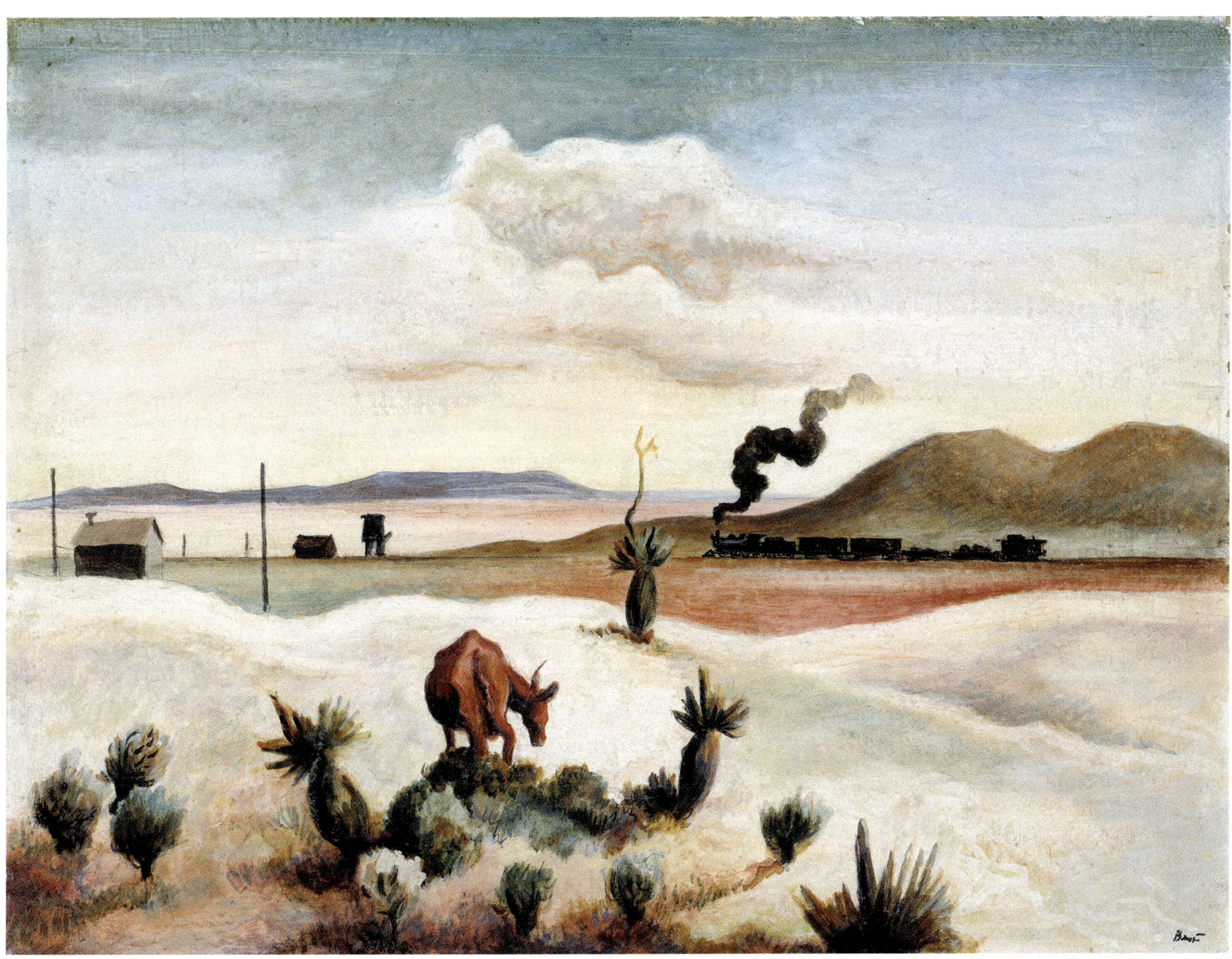

Cat. 22

Thomas Hart Benton (American, 1889-1975)
New Mexico (Landscape), 1926
oil and tempera on panel
20 × 26 in.
Denver Art Museum
Funds from Hellen Dill bequest, 1937.2

farmers, later commenting, "The plain people of the hills, like all plain people in lonely places, are hospitable and friendly."[19] Benton was alive to the changes gripping the country in 1926, fully aware of its restlessness as well as his own, and in *New Mexico (Landscape)*, he expressed it through the vehicle of a lonely rail.

The painters associated with the Precisionist movement were particularly drawn to themes of transportation, and the railroad featured in some of their most impressive works. George Ault's *From Brooklyn Heights* (cat. 23) of 1925 captures the New York waterfront and the view across the East River to Manhattan in all of its grit and loneliness. Train tracks curve around isolated buildings in the foreground, a single boxcar sits idle and disconnected, and a tugboat is moored at a storage building on a pier. As a black and white steam ship belches dark smoke into the air, Manhattan is shrouded in low-hanging clouds and early morning steam vented from anonymous gray buildings. Ault himself described New York as "the inferno without the fire," and that is very much what he presents in *From Brooklyn Heights*.[20]

Ault enjoyed a measure of success during his lifetime, but he also struggled with depression, especially after a series of deaths of close family members. His younger brother, Harold, committed suicide in 1915 and his mother died in a mental hospital in 1920. Ault's tendency to be despondent to the point of melancholy, and drunken and difficult at times, left him alienated from much of the New York art world. Despite his erratic behavior, he was represented by Edith Halpert and her Downtown Gallery, at least until he broke ties with her in 1934.[21] A critic for the *New York Times*, reviewing Ault's November 1928 exhibition at Halpert's space, noted his distinct preference for the artist's watercolors, where "he injects more warmth and energy," over his paintings, which "are for the most part done in sombre, uninviting harmonies."[22] But Ault's talent was unmistakable and *From Brooklyn Heights* was acquired by the Newark Museum of Art that same year, quite possibly from the Downtown Gallery show, despite the dark and brooding nature of its subject and of the artist who produced it.

Charles Sheeler's brand of Precisionism, while sunnier in palette and mood than Ault's, was as equally austere. In *Classic Landscape* (fig. 23), a brilliant work from 1931, Sheeler captured a fairly nondescript section of the Ford Motor Company's River Rouge plant in Dearborn, Michigan, just west of Detroit. Sheeler, who was also a talented photographer, had been commissioned by Ford in 1927 to produce a series of photographs of the then-new facility, which employed more than 75,000 workers, and built Model A Fords, the popular successor to the Model T. The vast River

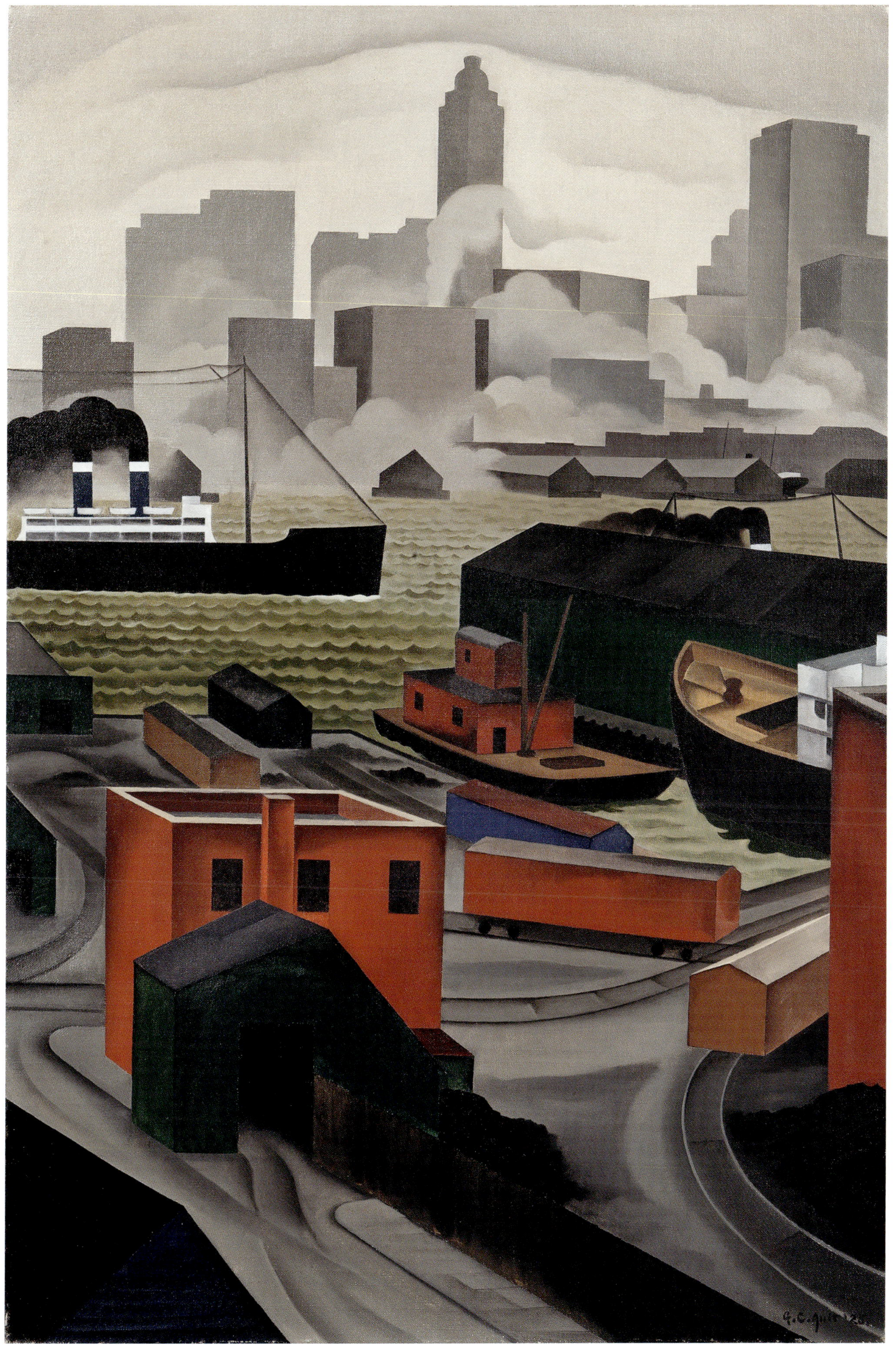

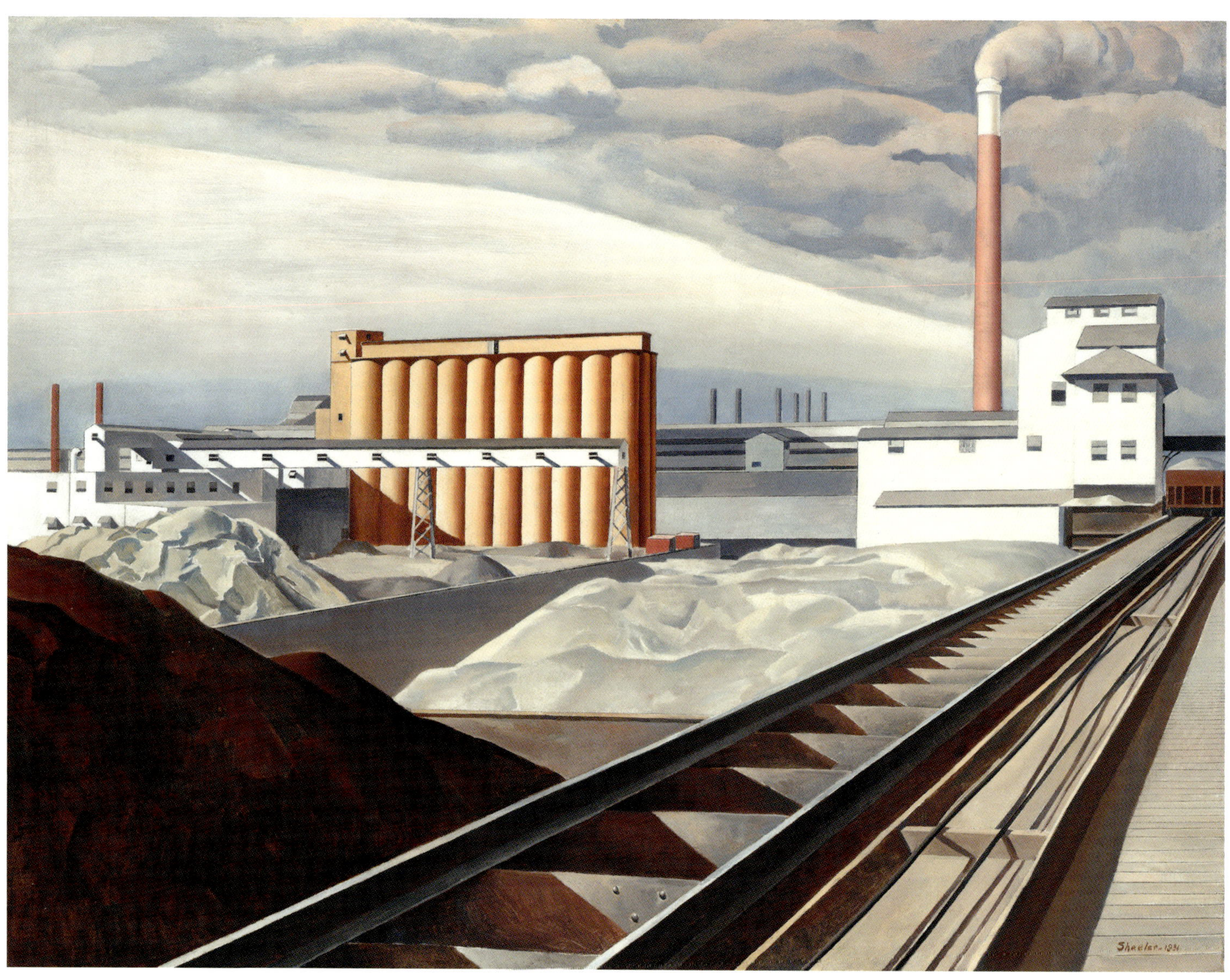

Fig. 23

Charles Sheeler (American, 1883-1965)
Classic Landscape, 1931
oil on canvas
25 × 32¼ in.
National Gallery of Art, Washington, DC
Collection of Barney A. Ebsworth, 2000.39.2

Rouge complex was more than a square mile in area, included ninety-three separate buildings, and housed over sixteen million square feet of factory floor space. Sheeler considered the immense factory complex "the most thrilling" site he had ever recorded with his camera,[23] and over the next decade, he would produce a half dozen major canvases depicting River Rouge. However, the site Sheeler captured in *Classic Landscape* actually had nothing to do with assembling the Model A. Rather, it depicted a cement plant on the same campus that with typical Ford efficiency produced a salable product from some residue of the automobile manufacturing process.[24]

The same year that he photographed the River Rouge plant, Sheeler had been part of the "Artists Committee" that helped organize the Machine-Age Exposition in New York, a project international in scope that nonetheless sought to advance America's leadership in areas of technological development. The two-week exhibition ranged across a variety of industries, but most countries, the United States included, focused on modernist architecture, feats of engineering, industrial design (IBM showcased its coffee mill and meat slicer), and painting and sculpture. In his essay for the catalogue, Louis Lozowick expressed the powerful inspiration that the Machine Age offered the visual artist:

> The dominant trend in America of today … is towards order and organization, which find their outward sign and symbol in the rigid geometry of the American city: in the verticals of its smoke stacks, in the parallels of its car tracks, the squares of its streets, the cubes of its

factories, the arc of its bridges, the cylinders of its gas tanks.[25]

Lozowick could have just as easily referenced the "parallels" of train tracks, but in a showcase of all things mechanized, standardized, soaring, infinitely repeatable, and most importantly new, there was simply no place for an old-fashioned industry such as the American railways. The rails were as conspicuously absent from the 1927 Machine-Age Exposition as they had been abundantly present as recently as the 1893 World's Columbian Exposition in Chicago.

In painting *Classic Landscape* in 1931, Sheeler was more prescient and insightful than he probably could have realized at the time. A set of neatly aligned railroad tracks leads into and dominates the right half of the composition, as shadows zigzag across the ties in a repeating pattern. Representing only a small part of the ninety miles of track within the River Rouge complex, Sheeler's rails are in service to the automotive industry (even if only its cement plant), already nudging the railways into a much less prominent place in the transportation hierarchy. Railway executives in the late 1920s were more than aware of the threat that automobile manufacturing posed. But they were also more than a thousand separate companies, and staging anything like an industry response was slow, if in fact it ever occurred. By late October 1929, two years after the Machine-Age Exposition in New York and two years before Sheeler painted his masterpiece, the American stock market crashed, setting off the Great Depression, and railroad traffic in the United States all but collapsed.

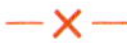

On August 4, 1927, Jimmie Rodgers (fig. 24) entered a Bristol, Tennessee, studio and, accompanied only by his guitar, recorded "Ben Dewberry's Final Run," a railroad-tragedy story-song about an engineer who favored speed over safety. Although Rodgers did not write the tune, the persuasive authenticity of his vocal styling made the song his own. Over the next two years, Rodgers returned to studios in Camden, New Jersey; Atlanta, Georgia; and Dallas, Texas, recording "The Brakeman's Blues," "I'm Lonely and Blue," "Waiting for a Train," and "Train Whistle Blues," all of which were his own compositions. As his following grew, he also began to bill himself to audiences in the Southeast and in Texas as the "Singing Brakeman," playing on the fact that he had once been an employee of the Southern Railway and the New Orleans & Northeastern line.

Rodgers was not the first musician to translate traditional blues structures into popular song, but his canny recordings of the late 1920s and early 1930s were unquestionably the first to find plausible links between migration, homesickness, loneliness, and the American railroad. His hugely popular "Blue Yodels," three of which were later and more familiarly known as "T for Texas," "California Blues," and "Muleskinner Blues," all expressed a sense of yearning or described loss or escape sometimes facilitated by hopping a train. Perhaps most poignantly, in "Waiting for a Train," Rodgers captured the palpable sense of loneliness felt by someone flat broke and just trying to get back to more familiar ground when he crooned: "I'm a thousand miles away from home, just waiting for a train."[26]

The success of Jimmie Rodgers continued to grow even after the start of the Great Depression,

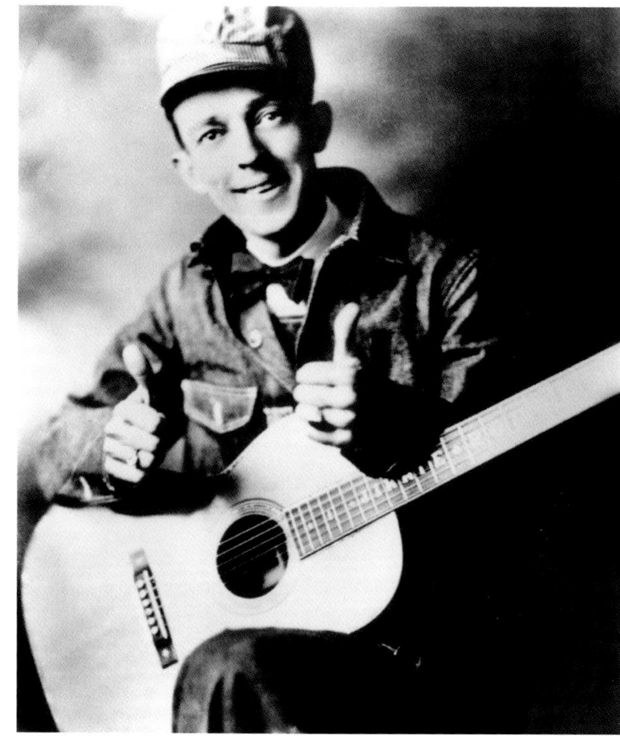

Fig. 24

Blues Guitarist James Charles "Jimmie" Rodgers (1897-1933), ca. 1925.

as did America's appetite for train songs. Literally hundreds were recorded in the 1920s and 1930s alone by dozens of artists, from country musicians to blues players to big bands. But few could match the popularity or the sales of Jimmie Rodgers. In the Columbia Pictures short *The Singing Brakeman* of 1930, Rodgers, in brakeman's garb, serenades two women early in the morning at the Railroad Eating House while waiting to start his shift on the Extra West at 10:15. The short film only increased his appeal, and his song selection (two were actually requests by the women) deepened the association between Rodgers and the railroad. He sang "Waiting for a Train," followed by a maudlin ballad called "Daddy and Home," about trying to get back to family, and "Blue Yodel No. 1."

The songs of Jimmie Rodgers fueled even more interest in a particular vision of the rails as less about points of connection than as a catalyst for separation, isolation, and loneliness. Charles T. Bowling was born in Quitman, Texas, a small town east of Dallas, and became a late addition to the group of artists known as the Dallas Nine. In 1936, Bowling painted *Church at the Crossroads* (cat. 24), a white, rural, one-room chapel that not only sat at the dusty corner of two lonely intersecting roads, as the title of the work implies, but backed up to a set of railroad tracks as well. The setting of Bowling's painting is desolate, but even in the stark Texas landscape the church is still a meeting house. The spirit of community is further reinforced by the electric lines (and perhaps telephone service) that connect the church to the outside world, and a house across the road and another on the horizon, where members of the congregation may live. Even the tracks in the road running alongside the church

suggest that someone has traveled by recently. The same year Bowling completed *Church at the Crossroads*, he sent it to the vast Texas Centennial Exposition, where it hung in the first room of the Texas Painting section.[27]

As a young painter, Charles L. Goeller had attracted attention when one of his still-life paintings was featured in a 1930 exhibition of forty-six artists under the age of thirty-five at the still relatively new Museum of Modern Art in New York.[28] Goeller continued to try to establish himself, moving to New York sometime in the early 1930s, seeking commercial gallery interest, and participating in another museum show at the Whitney in 1936.[29] Goeller had difficulty finding his footing as an artist. A native of Newark, he made attempts to penetrate the New York art world, but he ultimately left the city and returned to New Jersey, where he worked in his family's iron business. Later in Goeller's relatively short life he commented on the mood of his work, which the Newark *Sunday News* described as filled with "wistful loneliness" and a "haunting, disquieting aspect."[30] Goeller's *Factory Yard* (cat. 25) of about 1938 may or may not have represented the family business, but in either event, it captures a plant that may have been rendered out of commission by the economic struggles still playing out during the late years of the Great Depression. A large pile of sand has begun to spread from disuse and now covers much of the railroad tracks that once carried raw materials in and finished products out of the yard.[31]

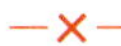

American railways finally responded to the challenges of both twentieth-century competition and the overall perception of the industry as

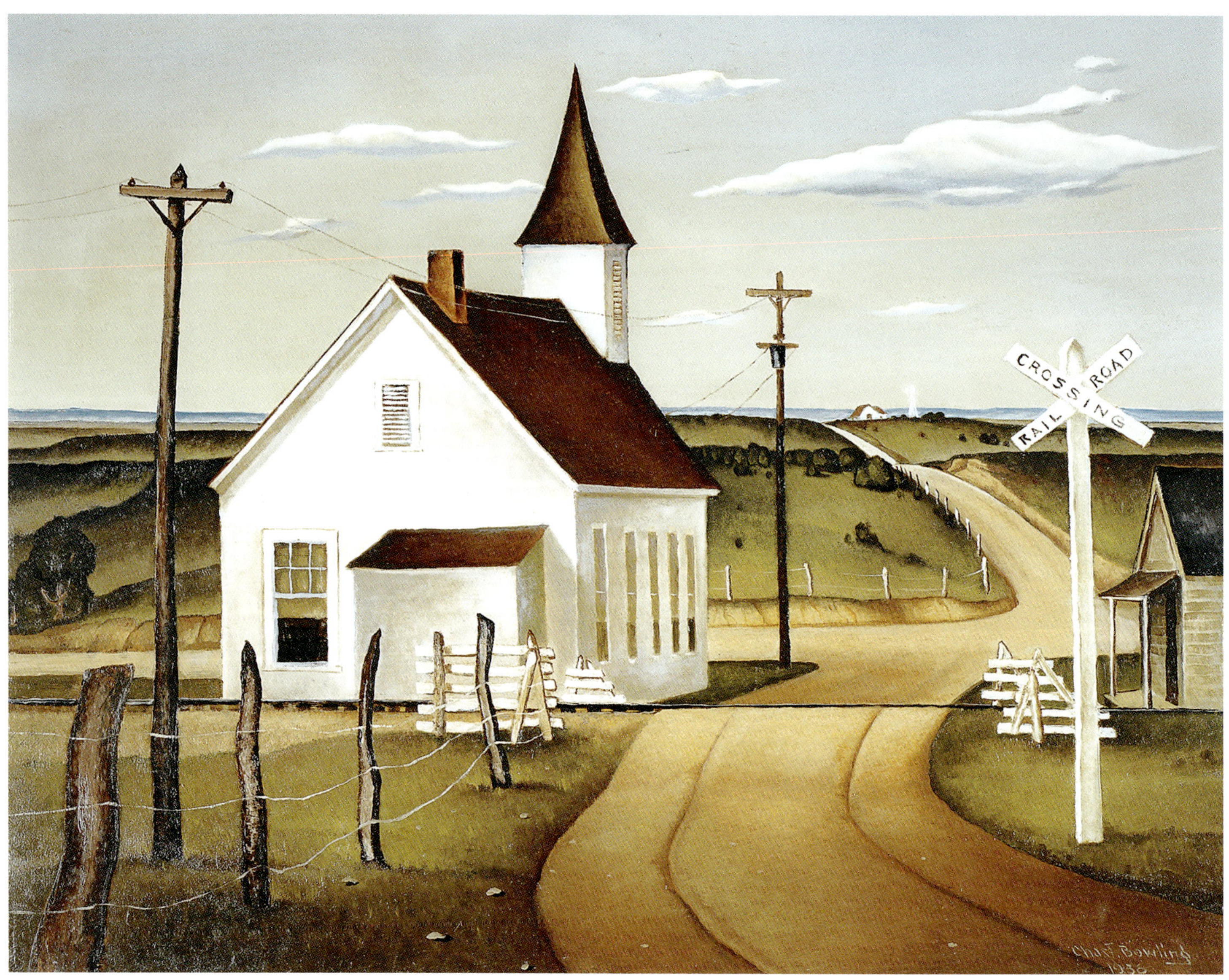

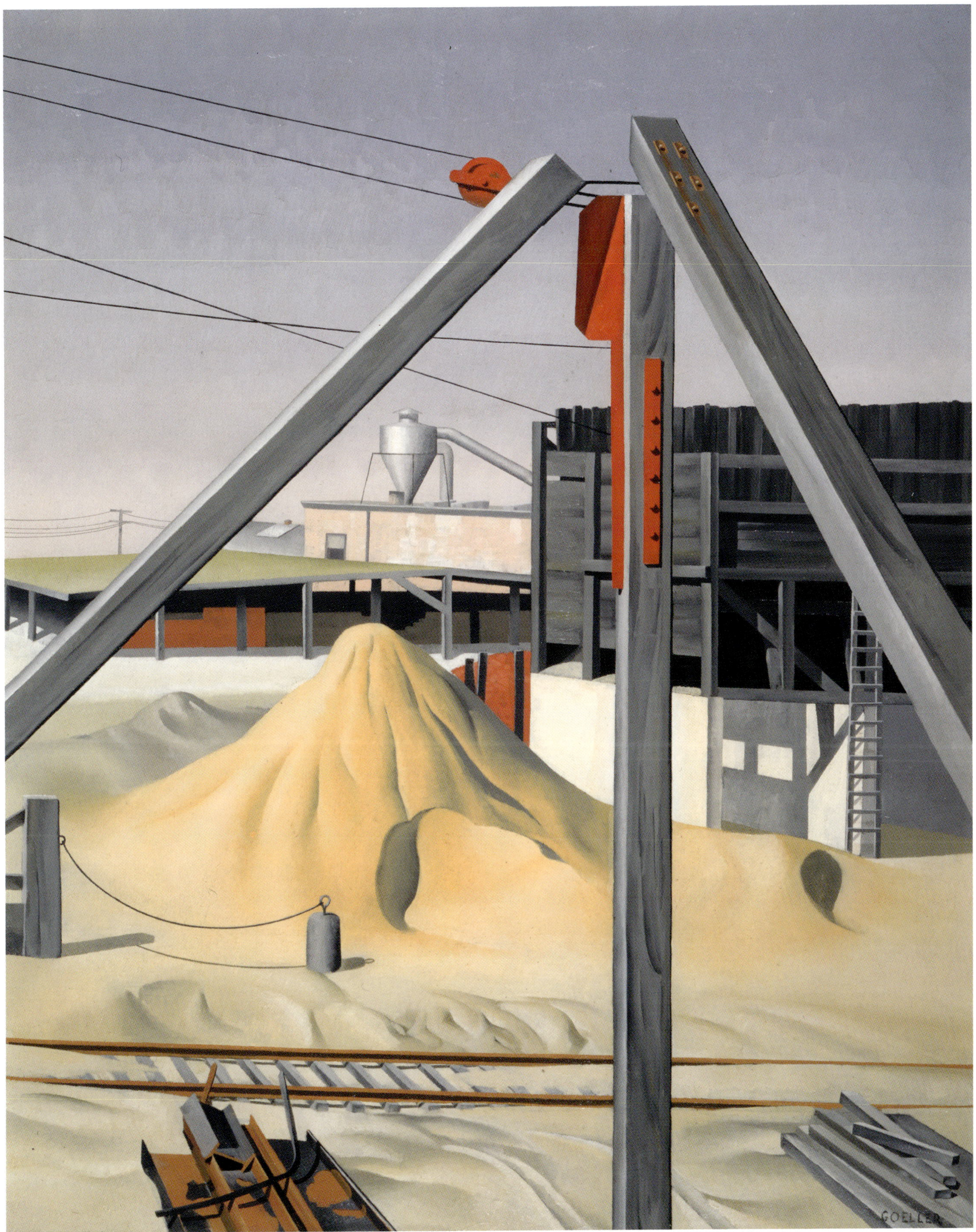

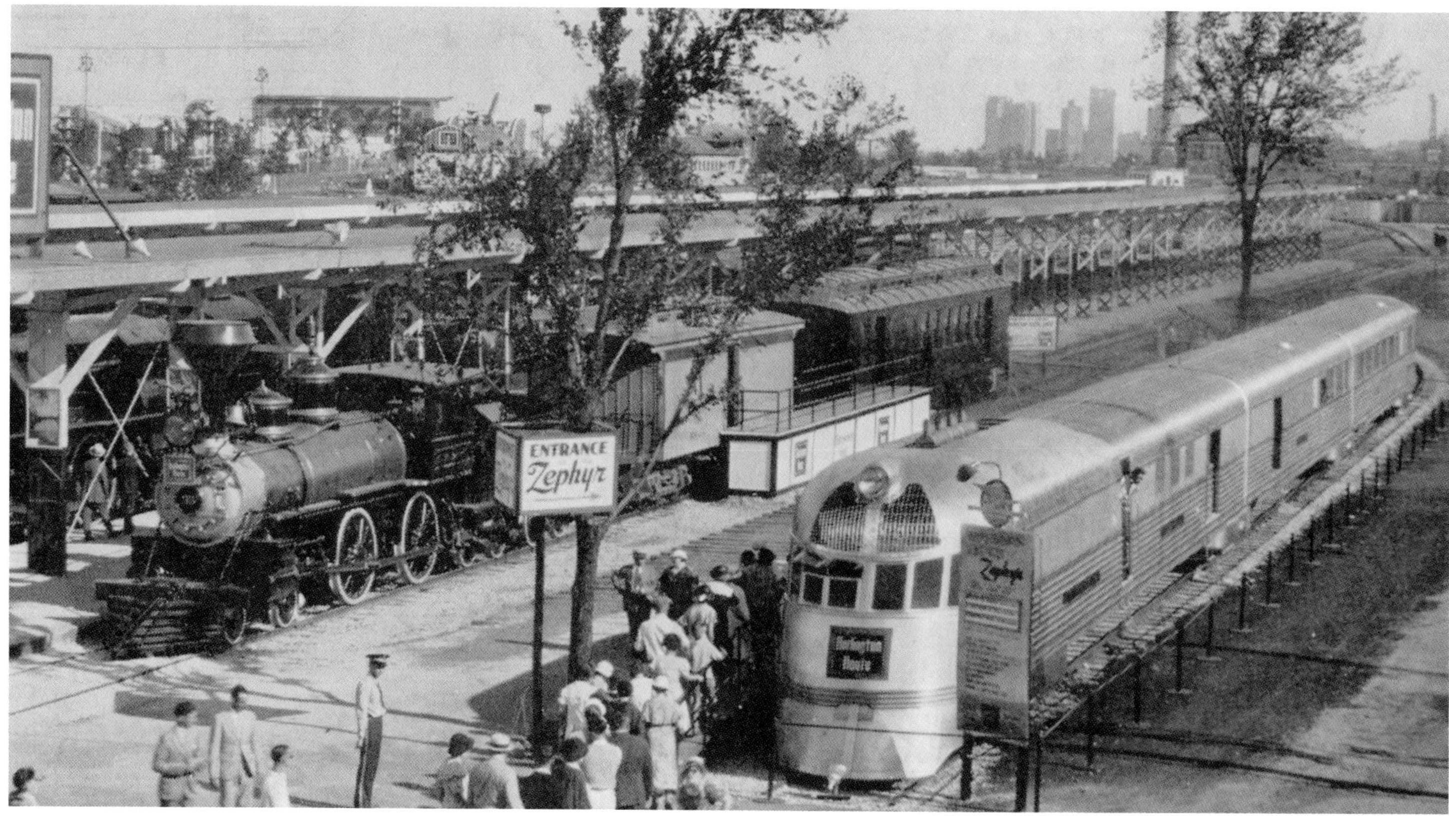

Fig. 25

The Burlington Zephyr at a Century
of Progress Exposition, 1934.

Museum of Science and Industry,
Chicago, USA

something old fashioned and ultimately rooted in the past. On May 26, 1934, the Burlington Zephyr made its debut at the Century of Progress World's Fair in Chicago (fig. 25). The Zephyr made a dramatic entry, having just completed a record-breaking trip from Denver to Chicago's Union Station in a little over thirteen hours; the previous fastest time was twenty-six hours. Along with Union Pacific's M10000, which debuted almost simultaneously, the Zephyr was designed with streamlining in mind, reducing drag and making increased speed possible (on the trip from Denver, the Zephyr reached a top speed of 112 miles per hour). After the short trip from Union Station to the lakefront, where the World's Fair was held, the Zephyr was thronged by crowds who came pouring out of the viewing stands to get a closer look.[32] It was almost as if the Chicago audience had been waiting for the railroad to do something, anything, and it finally had.

Streamlining brought American railways back into the vanguard of modernist design and technology. Borrowing from airplane design and the relatively new field of aerodynamics, and shrewdly hiring talented architects, industrial designers, and artists to update the look and feel of passenger cars, club cars, dining cars, furnishings, and other accoutrements, the railways enjoyed a comeback of sorts in the late 1930s.[33] That return to relevance was further bolstered a few years later, in 1941, by the United States' entry into World War II. The American railways, having learned from painful experience during World War I, became a crucial resource in the newest war effort. Between 1941 and 1945, American railway lines transported 90 percent of all army and navy freight and nearly all military personnel within the United States, including the operation of nearly 114,000 troop trains.[34]

With gasoline and rubber rationing taking a toll on the automobile industry during the war years, Americans again looked to the railroads as a means of connecting families before departing soldiers shipped off to training camps and eventually to the war itself. America's railways invested billions in diesel locomotives and infrastructure during the early 1940s and ultimately proved far more efficient and effective at managing the industry than the federal government had been just over twenty years earlier.[35]

Not everyone's experience of the rails was positive during the 1940s, however. Trains also moved Japanese-Americans from their homes, mostly on the West Coast, to internment camps as far east as Jerome and Rohwer, Arkansas. Among those held at the Jerome War Relocation Center were the painter Henry Sugimoto and his wife and young daughter, starting in October 1942. In his painting of the following year, *When can we go home?* (cat. 26), Sugimoto portrays his wife and daughter, the child wearing a red dress with sailor stylings, in a compressed landscape of two distinct worlds. One captures the civilization the Sugimoto family wished to return to and the other describes the grim internment camp itself.

At the upper right of *When can we go home?*, the barracks where the Sugimotos may have been housed and the watch tower from which they were routinely observed loom against a dark sky and are separated by a bolt of lightning; on the left, an Art Deco suspension bridge and skyscraper seem to speak to future possibilities. The little girl points upward to the left side of the composition and presumably poses the title question to her mother. The mother reaches down to comfort her daughter, as a rattlesnake is coiled just behind her and may reference the treachery that Sugimoto felt for any so-called civilizing force that would incarcerate his own family and many others. The child points to a locomotive with smoke billowing from its stack. The train would indeed eventually bring the Sugimotos home, just as it had brought them from Hanford, California, to Arkansas. Jerome and Rohwer were selected as sites for relocation camps because the federal government owned land near both towns and because of their proximity to railway lines.[36]

Edward Hopper was capable of finding the loneliness in almost any subject he painted. But somehow his depictions of the railroad, where strangers turn inward and try to maintain their

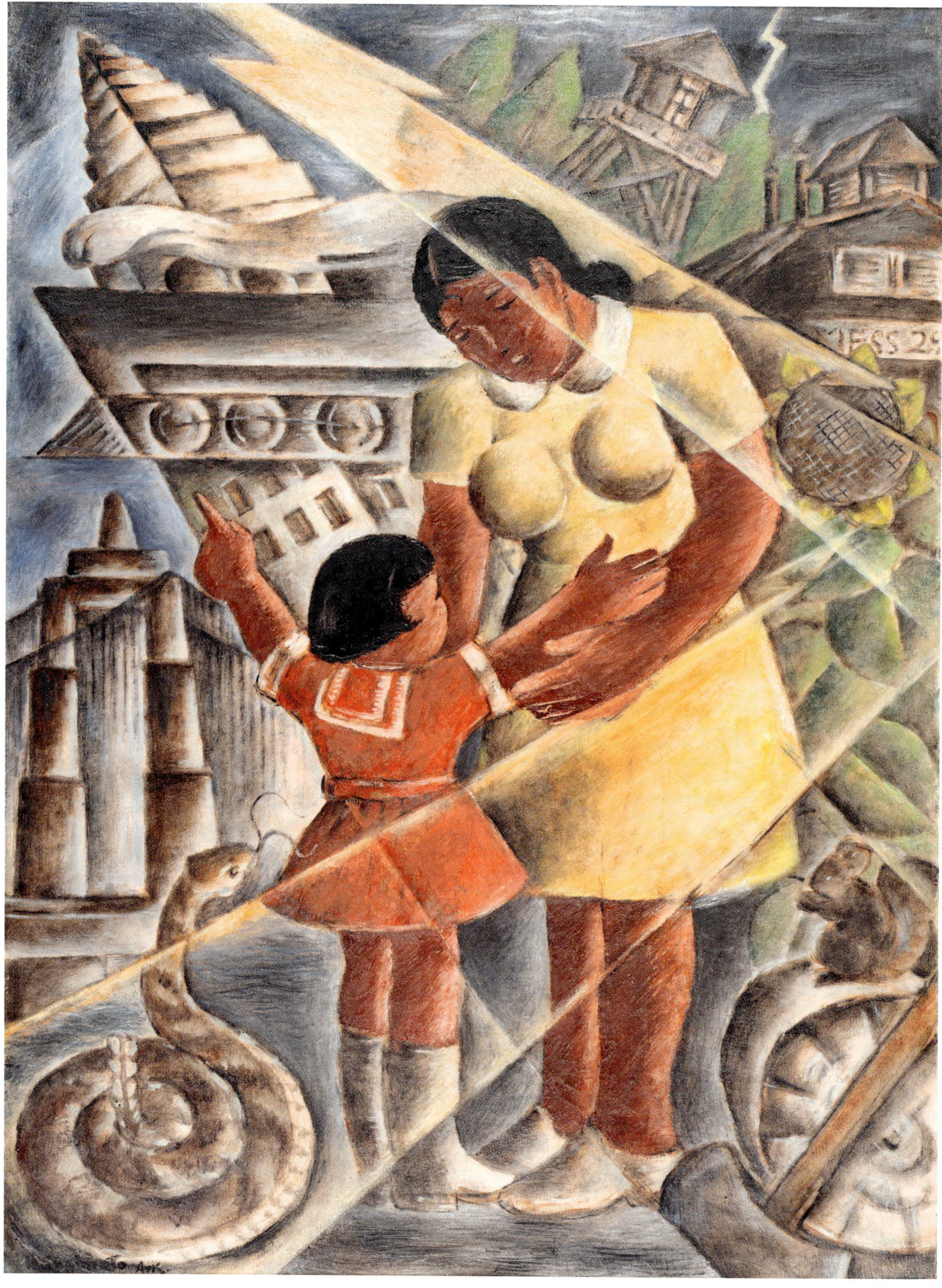

anonymity, were perhaps the most effective in establishing feelings of isolation. Hopper painted *Approaching a City* (cat. 26a) in early February 1946, not long after the war ended. His wife Jo noted in her diary that Hopper had been "going up town … & has found something to start on."[37] The artist had traveled as far north from his Washington Square home as Carnegie Hill, in Manhattan's Upper West Side. He positioned himself on the east side of Park Avenue between 97th and 98th Streets, where the train tracks enter a tunnel and continue underground to Grand Central Station. Hopper later told an interviewer:

> I've always been interested in approaching a big city by train; and I can't exactly describe the sensations. But they're entirely human and perhaps have nothing to do with esthetics. There is a certain fear and anxiety, and a great visual interest in the things that one sees coming into the city.[38]

While there certainly are interesting things to see when entering almost any major town by rail, in *Approaching a City*, Hopper's chosen subject was anything but arresting at first glance. Two sets of railroad tracks spread across the lower quarter of the canvas simply disappear into a tunnel. A stone retaining wall, simplified by the artist to more closely resemble poured concrete, hides the southbound lanes of Park Avenue while three or possibly four multistory buildings block all but a small wedge of sky. Lonely almost to the point of bleakness, Hopper's view of railroad tracks disappearing into darkness is nonetheless highly suggestive. Experiencing a city for the first time from below, and seeing its infrastructure and subterranean nature in a way that could really only be known from the window of a train, lends an associative power to the work that might not be obvious on the surface.

Hopper implied that *Approaching a City* was assembled from "improvised memories pieced together." But the drawings he produced as studies for the final painting indicate that the work was more carefully planned than he let on. The artist's curious characterization may have been designed to obscure one possible meaning of the picture. Trains entering railway tunnels had been used by film directors as symbols of sexuality at least as early as 1899, when G. A. Smith produced *A Kiss in the Tunnel*, and with similar effect much nearer to the date of Hopper's painting in *Brief Encounter*, David Lean's 1945 film based on a Noël Coward play. The missing train in *Approaching a City* may have been informed, as Hopper claimed, by "improvised memories," quite possibly recollections about his own complicated relationship with Jo.[39]

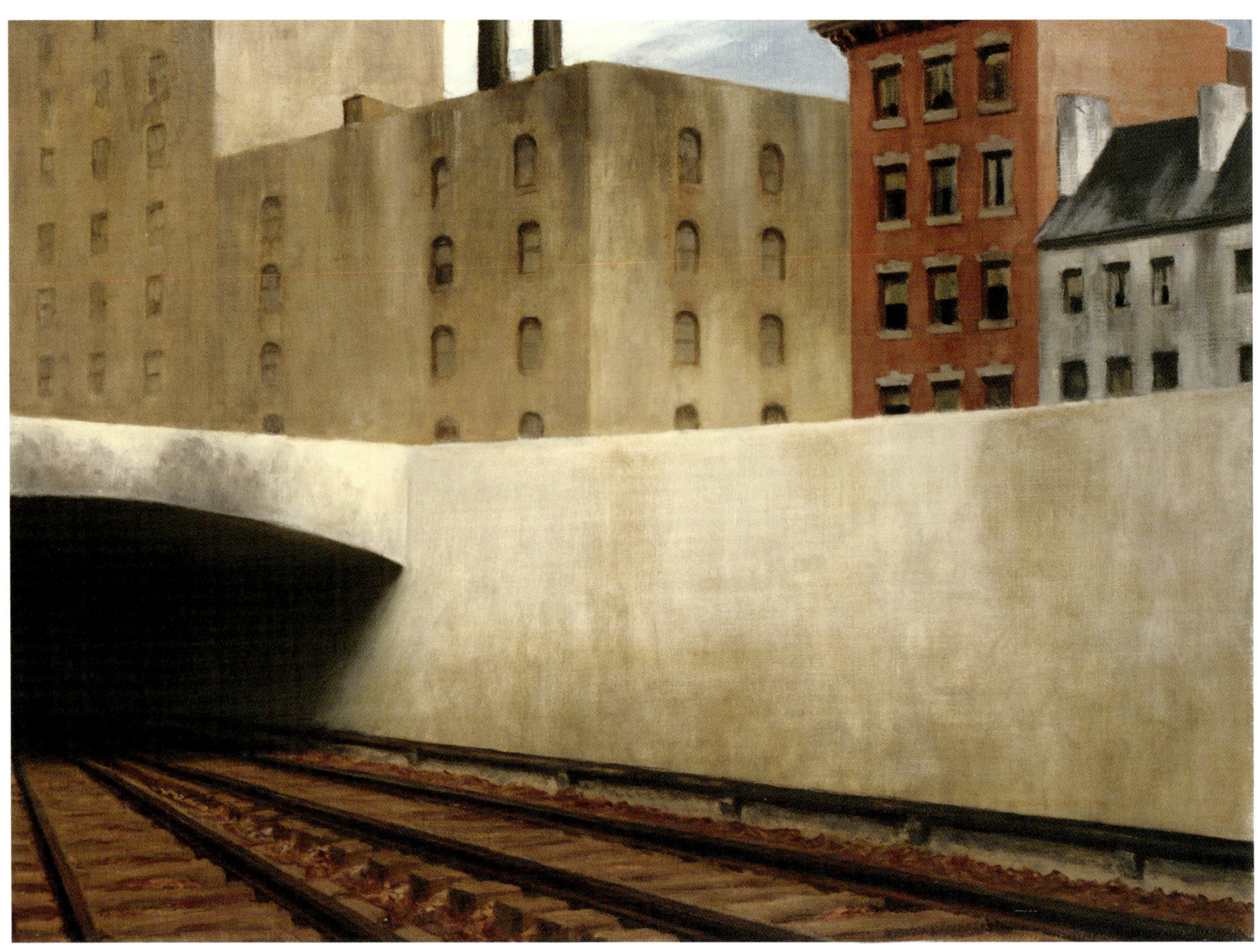

Cat. 26a

Edward Hopper (American, 1882–1967)
Approaching a City, 1946
oil on canvas
27⅛ × 36 in.
The Phillips Collection, Washington, DC
Acquired 1947, 0923

The surprising adaptability of the American railroad and its ability to conjure or manifest meaning was even put to use by postwar painters working in the Surrealist style. Kay Sage came by her Surrealism in Europe before the war and through her marriage to the French artist Yves Tanguy.[40] Her *Unusual Thursday* (cat. 27) of 1951 includes a railroad bridge across one of her typical dreamscapes, leading either to nowhere or to infinity or perhaps both. Similarly, Carroll Cloar's appetite for the railroad, stations, tracks, and trains as subjects for his paintings were filtered through his memories of growing up in Earle, Arkansas. But they are also tinged by a sense of strangeness and the distortion revealed as more and more time passes since those remembered experiences occurred. In Cloar's *The Red Caboose (Where the Southern Cross the Yellow Dog)* (cat. 28), two cars and a caboose sit on largely idle and barely visible siding tracks, the grass growing tall between the ties.[41]

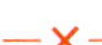

During the first half of the twentieth century, America's railways adapted to the pressures and opportunities of a rapidly changing age. The industry was largely tamed by the federal government in the first two decades of the century, especially during World War I; they saw their leadership in the transportation sector challenged by new advances in the automotive and aeronautics fields in the 1920s and 1930s; and they learned from bitter experience as the United States found itself at war once again in the 1940s. All the while, a kind of nostalgia began to inform the nation's perception of trains and all that came with them. For artists, the rails began to embody and deliver a different iconography, one that spoke more to nostalgia and loneliness than to speed and strength. That change in perception—and the outpouring of paintings, songs, poems, and films about the rails that followed—recast the railroad in a more sympathetic light than the industry had ever known. And the rails endured.

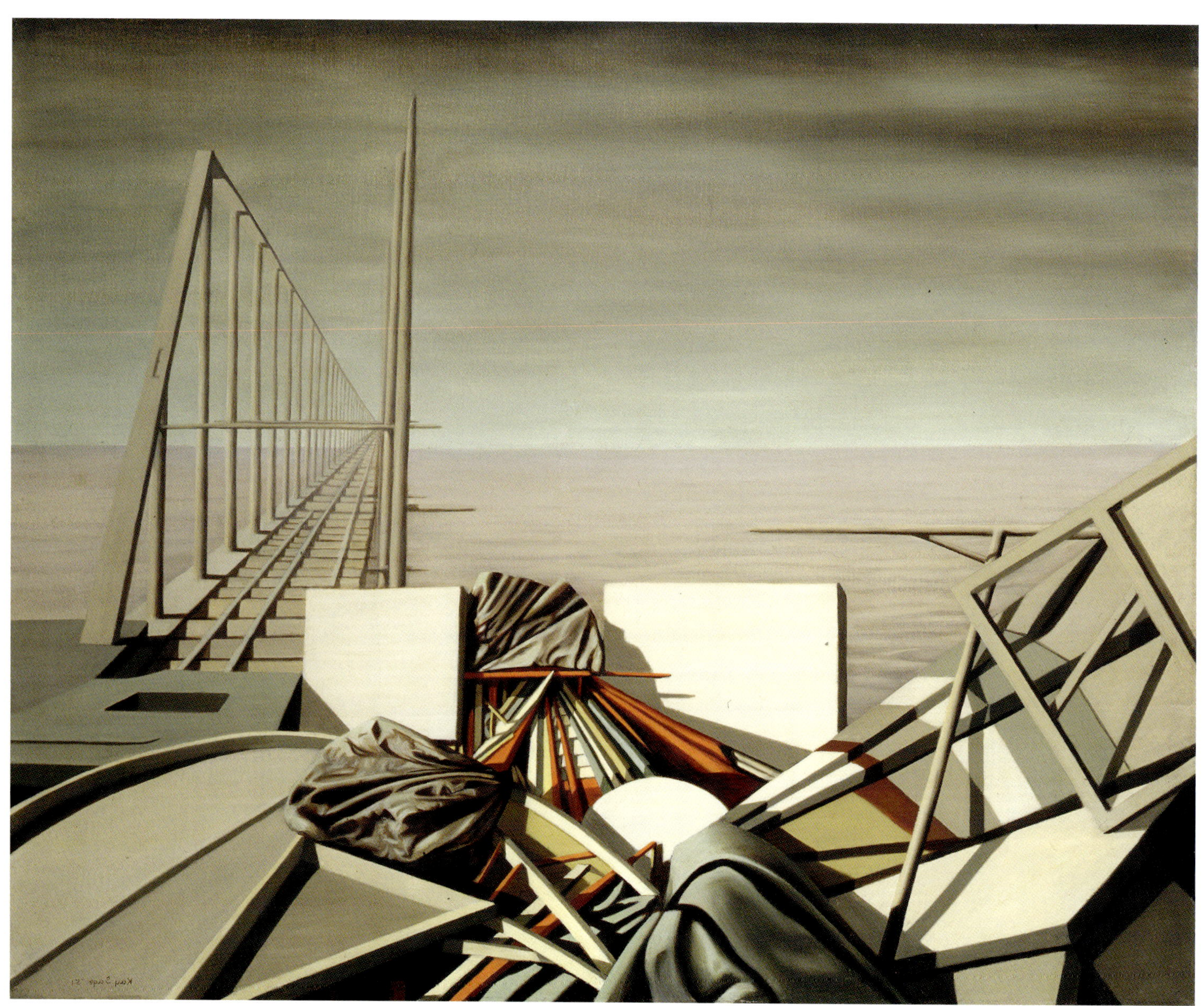

Cat. 27

Kay Sage (American, 1898-1963)
Unusual Thursday, 1951
oil on canvas
31¾ × 38¾ in.
New Britain Museum of American Art
Gift of Mrs. Naum Gabo, 1978.90

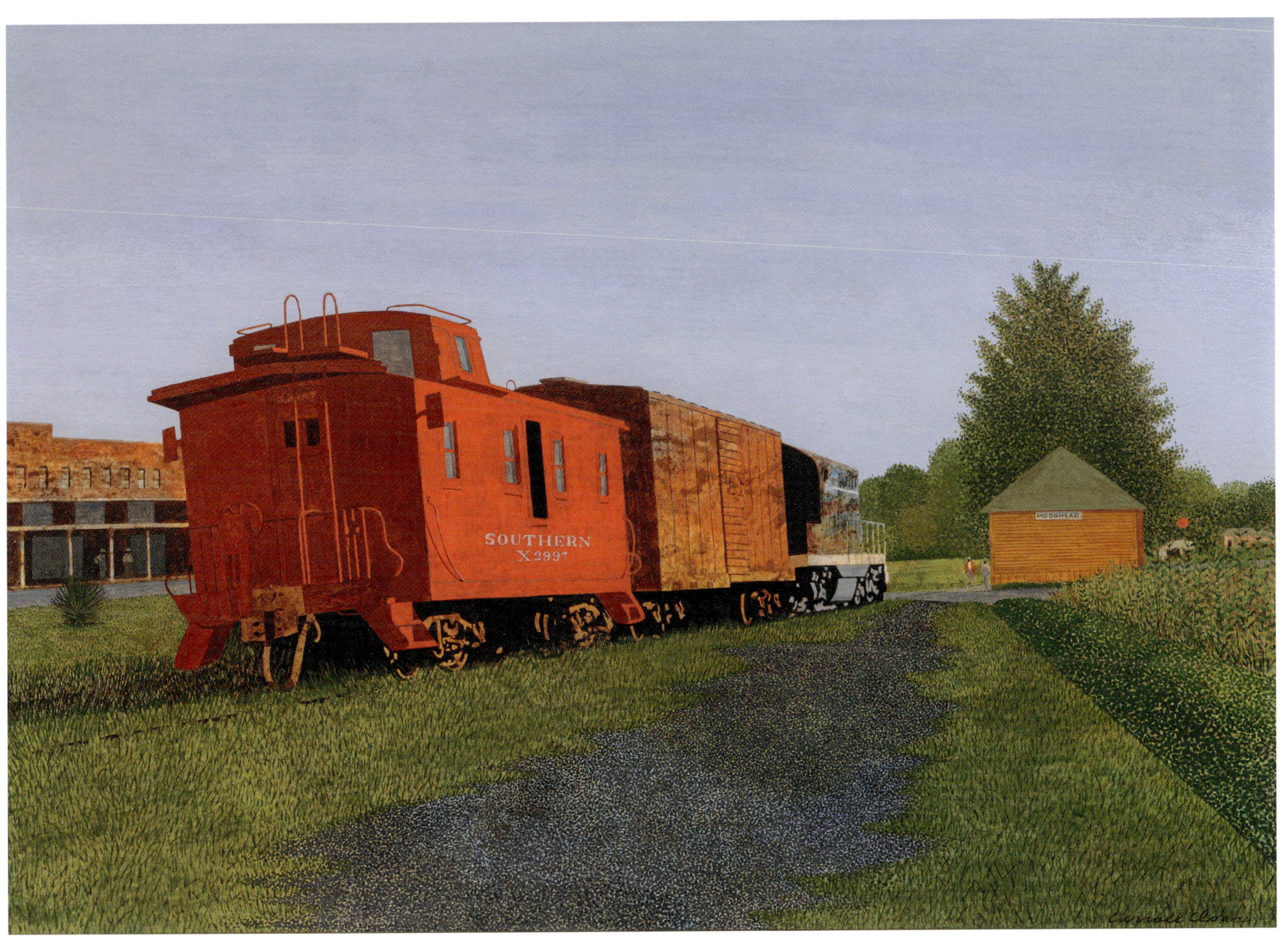

Cat. 28

Carroll Cloar (American, 1913–1993)
The Red Caboose, 1964
Casein tempera on Masonite
22½ × 31½ in.
Private collection

Endnotes

1   See Slason Thompson, *A Short History of American Railways: Covering Ten Decades* (New York and London: D. Appleton & Company, 1925), 366-90.

2   Charles T. Morrissey, "More Than Embers of Sentiment: Railroad Nostalgia and Oral History Memories of the 1920s and 1930s," *Public Historian* 15, no. 3 (Summer 1993): 29.

3   Richard White, *Railroaded: The Transcontinentals and the Making of Modern America* (New York and London: W. W. Norton & Company, 2011), 511-13.

4   "When You Come North," *Chicago Defender*, May 30, 1925, reprinted in *A Movement in Every Direction: A Great Migration Critical Reader*, ed. Jessica Bell Brown (New Haven and London: Yale University Press, 2022), 82.

5   Little known today, Hugo Robus gave up painting not long after producing *Train in Motion*, and was a popular and successful sculptor from the 1920s until his death in 1964. The most comprehensive work on Robus is Roberta Tarbell, *Hugo Robus (1885-1964)*, exh. cat. (Washington, DC: Published for the National Collection of Fine Arts by the Smithsonian Institution Press, 1980). An article on Robus in *Picture Scope* magazine in 1958 suggested that "Robus' appeal according to many will live forever." See "Sculpture Set to Music," *Picture Scope* 7, no. 1 (November 1958): 95.

6   See Arnold Rampersad, "Introduction," in Langston Hughes, *The Big Sea: An Autobiography* (New York: Hill and Wang, 1993), xxi. The poem was first published in *The Crisis*, the official organ of the National Association for the Advancement of Colored People, in June 1921.

7   Langston Hughes, *The Weary Blues* (New York: Alfred A. Knopf, 1926).

8   Langston Hughes, *Fine Clothes to the Jew* (New York: Alfred A. Knopf, 1927), 24.

9   See the very useful chronology by Ben Glenn II in Ruth E. Fine, *John Marin*, exh. cat. (New York: Abbeville Press, 1990), 289-90. The publication accompanied an extraordinary exhibition of Marin's work at the National Gallery of Art, Washington, DC, entitled *Selections and Transformations: The Art of John Marin*, held from January 28 until April 15, 1990.

10   Quoted in Fine, *John Marin*, 119.

11   "A Great Grain Elevator," *New York Times*, September 11, 1901, 3.

12   "Explosion Wrecks Big Grain Elevator," *New York Times*, July 16, 1915, 18.

13   Georgia O'Keeffe to Alfred Stieglitz, Canyon, Texas, September 4, 1916; and Georgia O'Keeffe to Anita Pollitzer, Canyon, Texas, September 11, 1916; in Jack Cowart, Juan Hamilton, and Sarah Greenough, *Georgia O'Keeffe: Art and Letters*, exh. cat. (Washington, DC: National Gallery of Art, 1987), 155, 156-57.

14   See, for example, *Colonel W. F. Cody: An Autobiography of Buffalo Bill* (New York: Rinehart & Company, 1920). See also Chauncey M. Depew, *My Memories of Eighty Years* (New York: C. Scribner & Sons, 1924). Depew was an attorney who worked for Cornelius Vanderbilt and eventually led the New York Central Railroad System. See also J. A. L. Waddell, *Memoirs and Addresses of Two Decades* (Easton, PA: Mack Printing Company, 1928). Dr. Waddell was a consulting engineer who designed more than a thousand railroad bridges.

15   Thompson, *A Short History of American Railways*.

16   Henry Adams, *Thomas Hart Benton: An American Original* (New York: Alfred A. Knopf, 1989), 10-12.

17   Thomas Hart Benton, *An Artist in America*, 4th ed. (Columbia: University of Missouri Press, 1983), 71. Benton wrote: "As soon as I was able to get loose from my mother's skirts, I followed the boys of Neosho to the railroad station and watched with the yearning loafers of the town the evening passenger roll in." Benton writes at some length about trains in his autobiography.

18   Adams, *Thomas Hart Benton*, 134.

19   Adams, 137.

20   Quoted in Karen Tsujimoto, *Images of American Precisionist Painting and Modern Photography*, exh. cat. (Seattle: Published for the San Francisco Museum of Modern Art by University of Washington Press, 1982), 71.

21   See Alexander Nemerov, *To Make a World: George Ault and 1940s America*, exh. cat. (New Haven, CT: Yale University Press, 1911), 35, 131-33.

22   J. K., "Further Comment on Art Exhibitions," *New York Times*, November 25, 1928, 13.

23   Sheeler to Walter Arensberg, October 25, 1927, quoted in Theodore E. Stebbins Jr. and Norman Keyes Jr., *Charles Sheeler: The Photographs*, exh. cat. (Boston: Little, Brown, 1987), 25.

24   David L. Lewis, *The Public Image of Henry Ford: An American Folk Hero and His Company* (Detroit: Wayne State University Press, 1976), 160. See also *Classic Landscape* in the National Gallery of Art's excellent online catalogue, accessed September 10, 2023, https://www.nga.gov/collection/art-object-page.105596.html, for a discussion of the Sheeler painting in their collection and comprehensive research the gallery staff has produced.

25   Louis Lozowick, "The Americanization of Art," in *Machine-Age Exposition: Catalogue*, exh. cat. (New York, 1927), 18. Lozowick was himself a gifted painter and printmaker.

26   See Nolan Porterfield, *Jimmie Rodgers: The Life and Times of America's Blue Yodeler* (Urbana: University of Illinois Press, 1979), 107-21, 390-99, 430-35.

27   Bowling's *Church at the Crossroads* is described in a catalogue entry by Drew Kane in *Coming Home: American Paintings, 1930-1950, from the Schoen Collection*, exh. cat. (Athens: Georgia Museum of Art, 2003), 76-77. See also *The Centennial Exposition: Catalogue of the Exhibition of Paintings, Sculptures, Graphic Arts*, exh. cat. (Dallas: Dallas Museum of Fine Arts, 1936), 76, no. 6, https://texashistory.unt.edu/ark:/67531/metapth183290/.

28   *46 Painters and Sculptors under 35 Years of Age*, Museum of Modern Art, New York, April 11- 27, 1930, https://www.moma.org/calendar/exhibitions/2025.

29   For Goeller's participation in the Whitney exhibition, see "Contemporary Art on View Next Week," *New York Times*, October 29, 1936, 22.

30   The *Newark Sunday News* article appeared on June 28, 1953, just two years before Goeller died. The article is referenced in Gail Stavitsky's essay in *Emotion Expressed through Precision: The Art of Charles Goeller*, exh. cat. (New York: Franklin Riehlman Fine Art, 2003).

31   Discussions of Goeller's work are rare, but see Ann Prentice Wagner, *1934: A New Deal for Artists*, exh. cat. (Washington, DC: Smithsonian American Art Museum in association with D Giles Limited, 2009), 112-13.

32   See Richard Guy Wilson, *The Machine Age in America, 1918-1941* (New York: Harry N. Abrams, 1986), 136-44.

33   Wilson, 136-37. The theatre and industrial designer Norman Bel Geddes contributed a great deal to the new look of trains in the 1930s. The painter Walt Kuhn designed club car interiors for Union Pacific at the request of Averell Harriman. Kuhn was represented in New York by the gallerist Marie Harriman, Averell's wife. See my entry for Kuhn's *Woman in Vest* in *American Made: Paintings and Sculpture from the DeMell Jacobsen Collection*, ed. Elizabeth B. Heuer and Jonathan Stuhlman, exh. cat. (Lewes, UK: D Giles Limited, 2022), 325.

34 See the Association of American Railroads, "Chronology of America's Freight Railroads," accessed September 6, 2023, https://www.aar.org/chronology-of-americas-freight-railroads/.

35 John Heitman, *The Automobile and American Life*, 2nd ed. (Jefferson, NC: McFarland & Co., 2018), 128–29.

36 Kristine Kim, *Henry Sugimoto: Painting and American Experience*, exh. cat. (Los Angeles: Japanese American National Museum; Berkeley, CA: Heyday, 2001), 55–59, 76–77.

37 Quoted in Gail Levin, *Edward Hopper: An Intimate Biography* (New York: Alfred A. Knopf, 1995), 388.

38 Quoted in Levin, 388.

39 Levin, 388. See also three studies for *Approaching a City* in the collection of the Whitney Museum of American Art (70.184, 70.185a–b, and 70.869), https://whitney.org/collection/works. Of course, Alfred Hitchcock would later famously adopt the motif of a train entering a tunnel in the final sequence of *North by Northwest* in 1959. Gail Levin, the great authority on the life and work of Edward Hopper, would dispute my reading of *Approaching a City*. In her discussion of the painting in *The Railroad and American Art: Representations of Technological Change*, eds. Susan Danly and Leo Marx (Cambridge: Massachusetts Institute of Technology, 1988), 177-78, Levin called any allusion to sexuality in Hopper's railroad paintings "unconscious," noting that the painter was sixty-four years old in 1946, and "his own energy was much diminished." Perhaps so, but I stand by my reading.

40 On Kay Sage, see Stephen Robeson Miller and Jonathan Stuhlman, *Double Solitaire: The Surreal Worlds of Kay Sage and Yves Tanguy*, exh. cat. (Charlotte: Mint Museum, 2011), 82 (plate 29).

41 On Carroll Cloar, see Stanton Thomas, *The Crossroads of Memory: Carroll Cloar and the American South*, exh. cat. (Little Rock: Arkansas Art Center, 2014), 11-12, 101-2, 111-12.

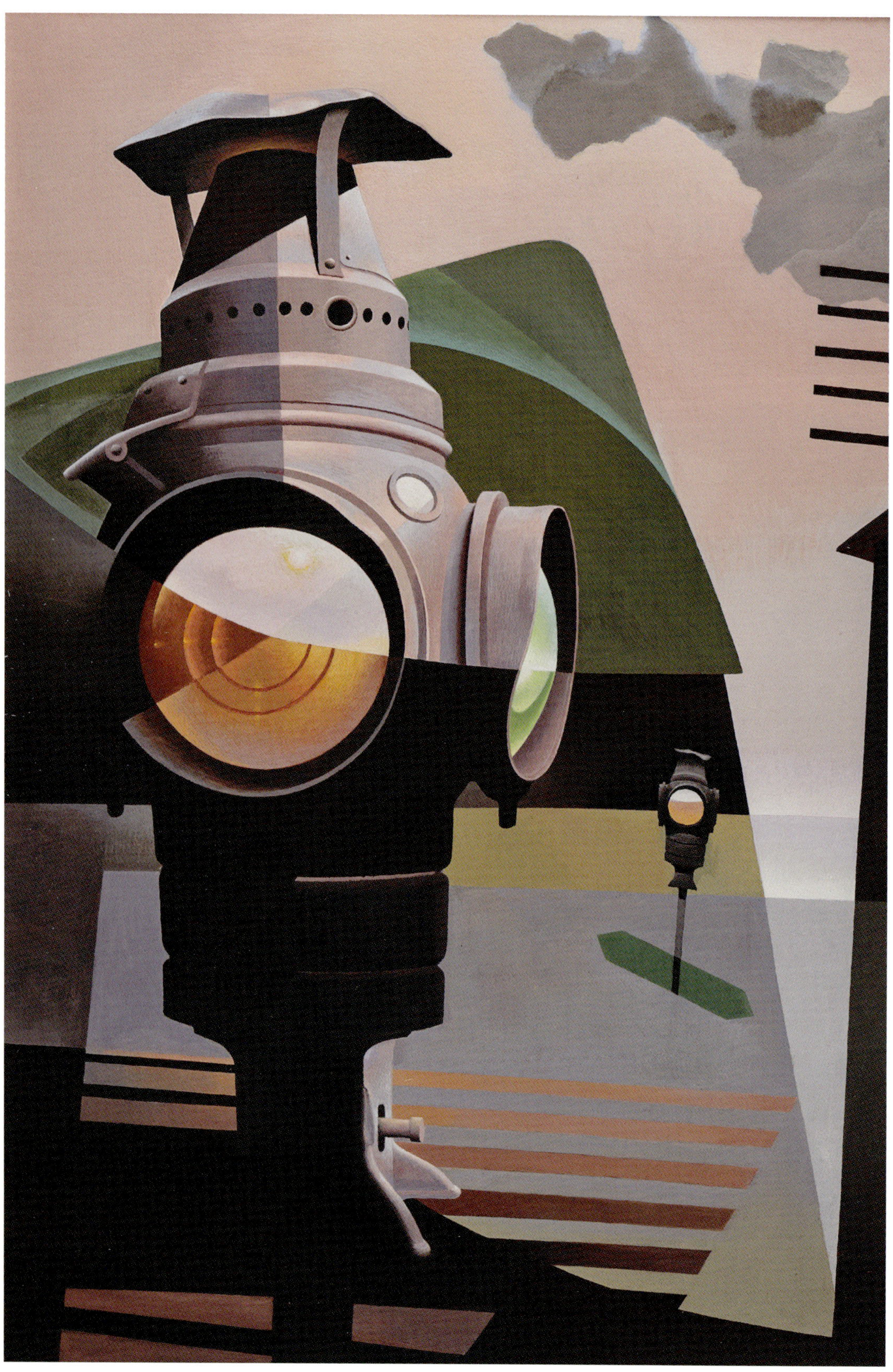

Cat. 29

William Charles Libby (American, 1919–1982)
Lanterns, 1945

tempera on board
27⅛ × 17¾ in.

Carnegie Museum of Art, Pittsburgh

Gift of Mr. and Mrs. James H. Beal, 63.1.5

Cat. 30

Joseph Stella (American, 1877–1946)
Man in the Elevated (Train), 1916

oil, wire, and collage on glass
14¼ × 14¾ in.

Mildred Lane Kemper Art Museum,
Washington University in St. Louis

University purchase, Kende Sale Fund,
1946. WU 3806

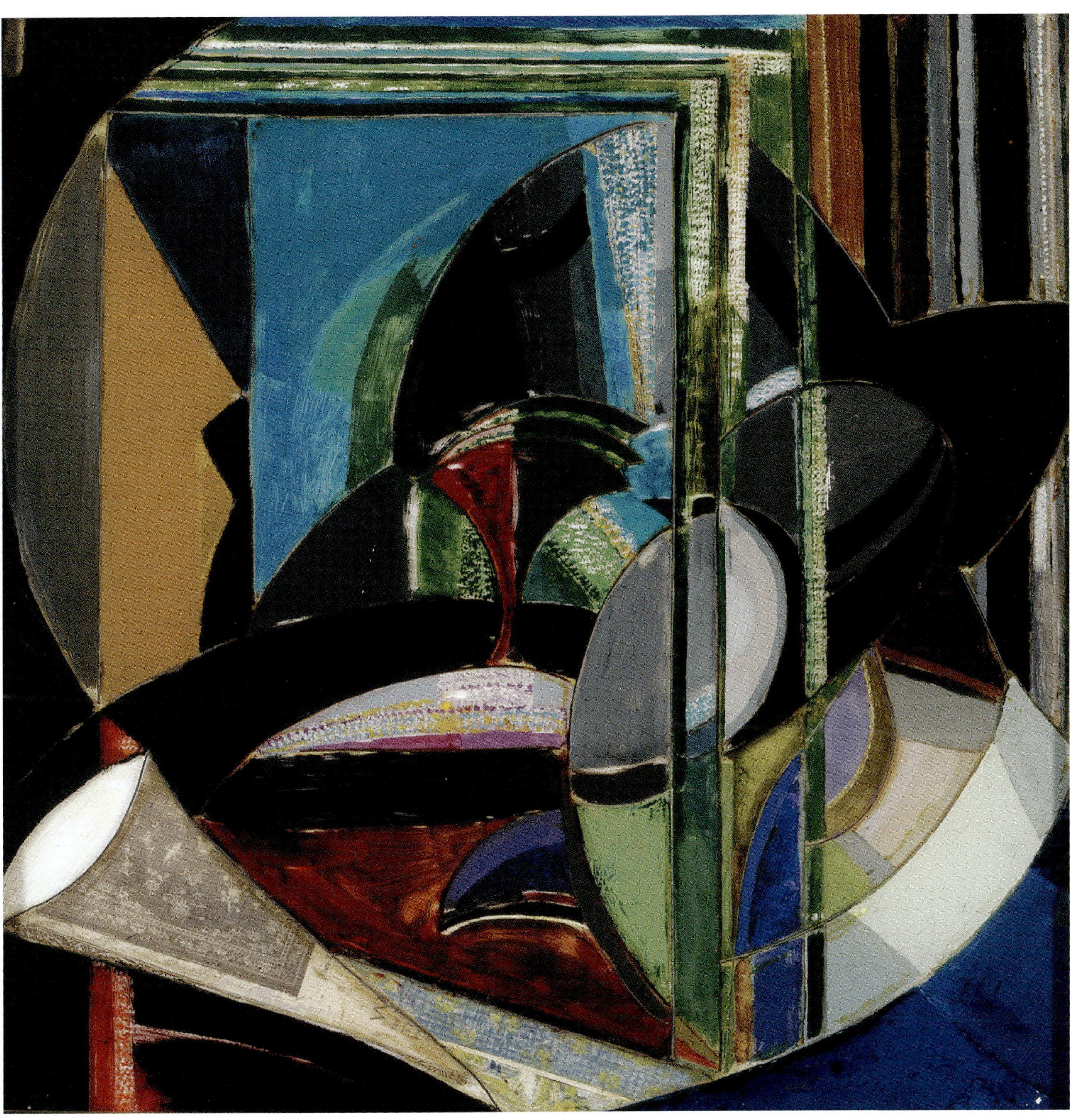

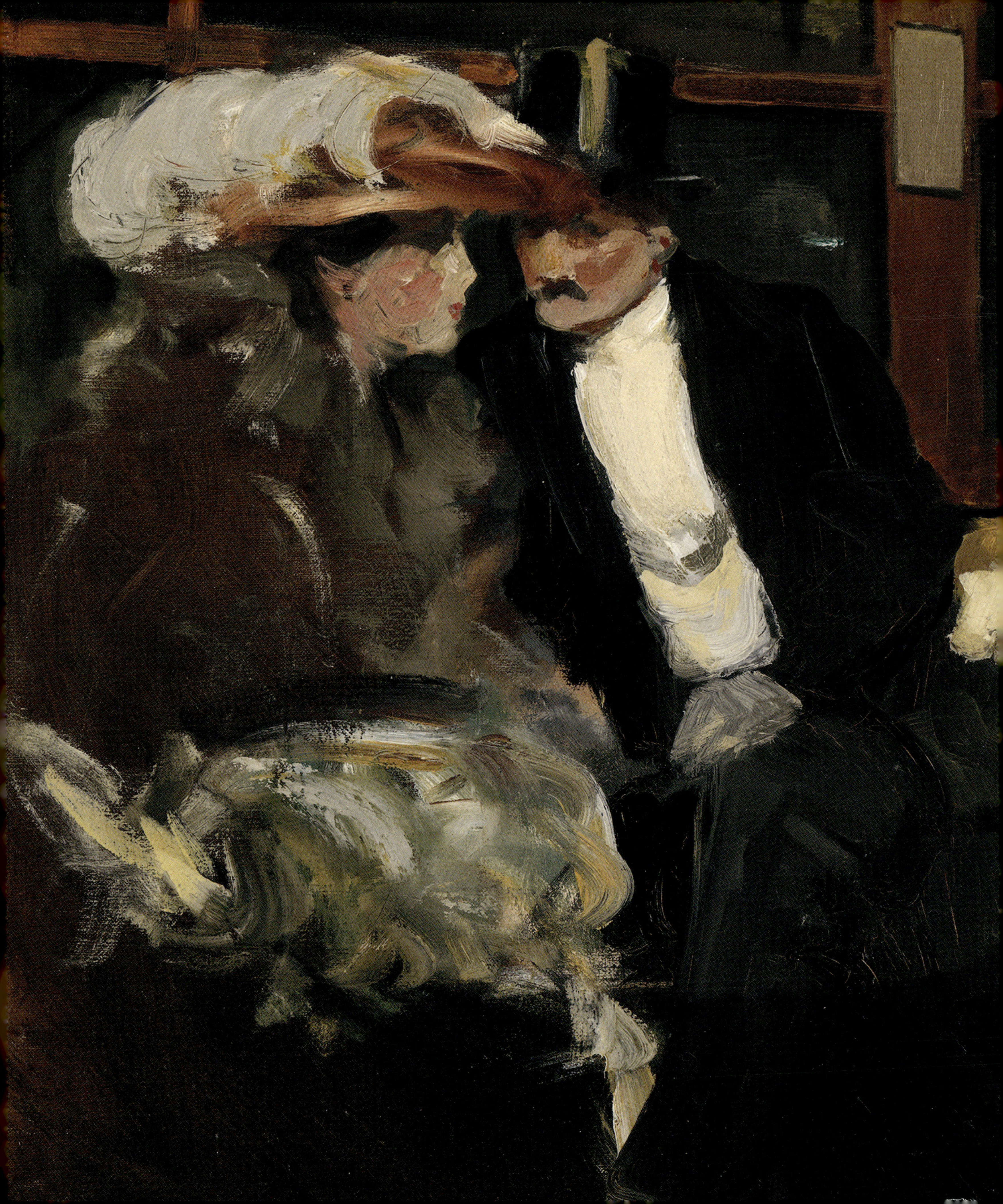

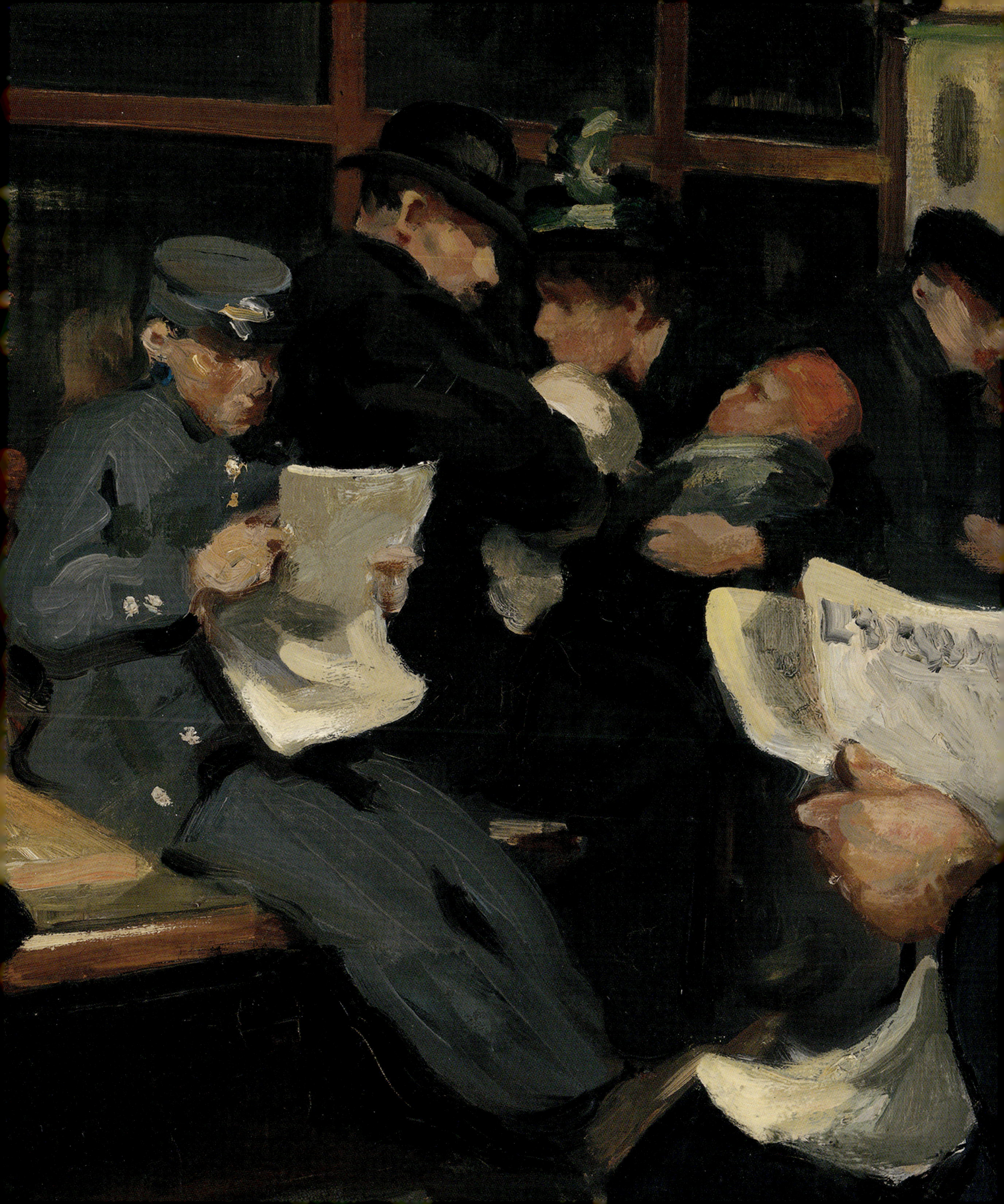

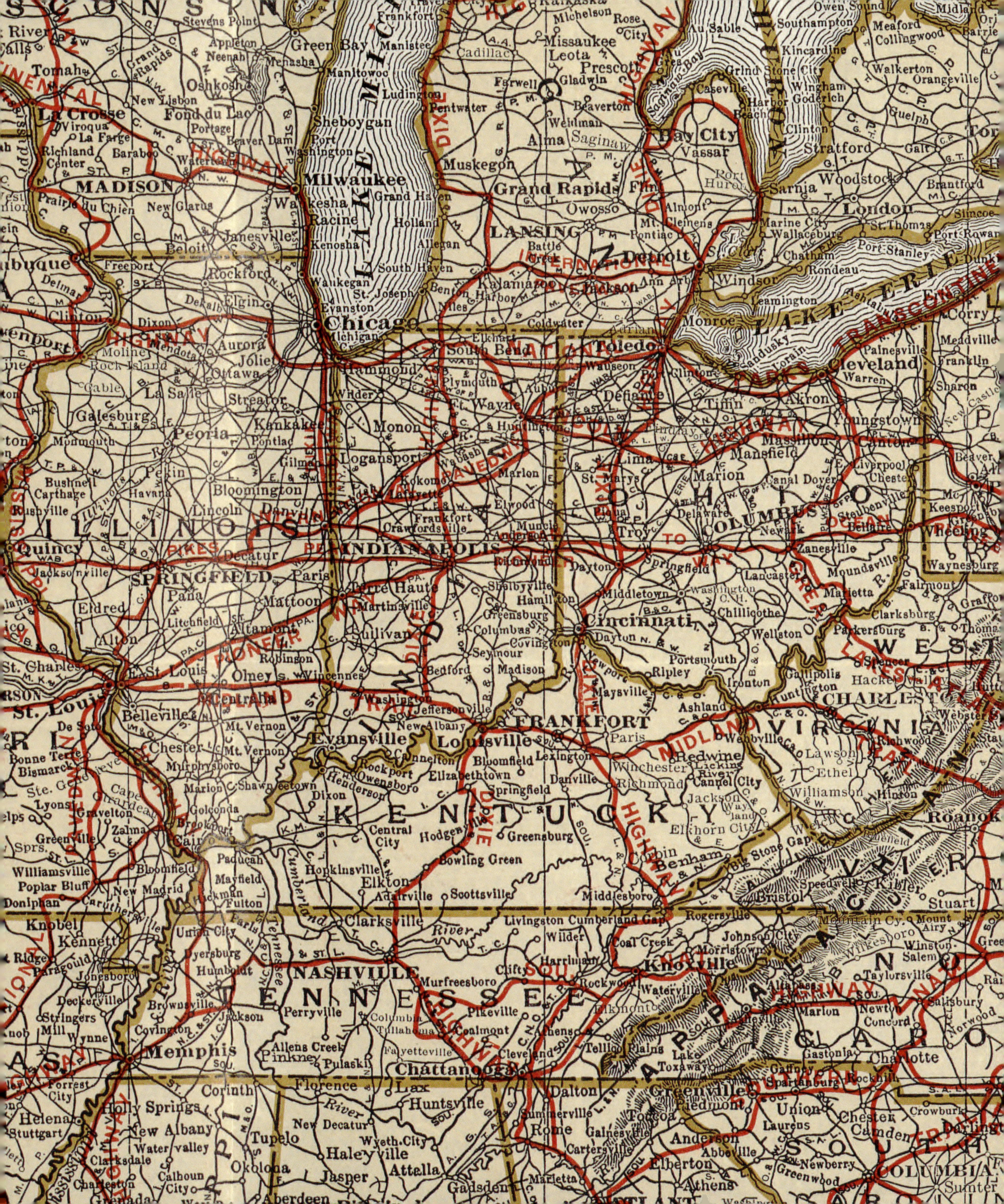
WISCONSIN
ILLINOIS
OHIO
KENTUCKY
TENNESSEE
WEST VIRGINIA
VIRGINIA
LAKE MICHIGAN
LAKE ERIE
MADISON
La Crosse
Milwaukee
Green Bay
Grand Rapids
LANSING
Detroit
Toledo
Cleveland
Chicago
Rockford
Peoria
Bloomington
SPRINGFIELD
Quincy
INDIANAPOLIS
Terre Haute
COLUMBUS
Cincinnati
Dayton
Evansville
Louisville
FRANKFORT
Lexington
Paducah
NASHVILLE
Memphis
Chattanooga
Knoxville
Bay City
Saginaw
Muskegon
Kalamazoo
South Bend
Fort Wayne
Marion
Mansfield
Akron
Youngstown
Wheeling
Charleston
Roanoke
DIXIE HIGHWAY
NATIONAL HIGHWAY
LINCOLN HIGHWAY
PIKES PEAK OCEAN TO OCEAN HIGHWAY
DIXIE BEE LINE
MIDLAND TRAIL
APPALACHIAN

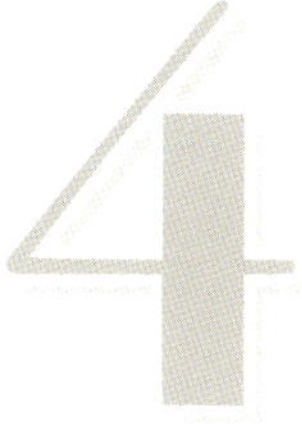

PASSENGERS ALL

People on the Train in American Art, 1900-1950

Thomas Denenberg

RAIL TRAVEL SETS THE STAGE FOR THEODORE DREISER'S *Sister Carrie*. Published to great controversy in 1900, the book has long been regarded as the author's magnum opus and a landmark of literary realism. A new-model novel, the frank and gritty narrative raises the curtain on evolving notions of gender, class, and social mobility at the turn of the century. As a text, *Sister Carrie* dramatically animates our understanding of the impact of the railroad on American culture and provides a concordance to closely read the efforts of twentieth-century painters looking at people on the train.

Drawing on Victorian conventions of propriety, Dreiser initially frames the book as a morality play. We meet Caroline Meeber, "Sister Carrie" to her family, on page one as she boards a train to Chicago from her small town in Wisconsin, setting out for the city like so many before and after her, drawn to the "gleam of a thousand lights" in the bustling metropolis.[1] Carrie has barely started her journey when she attracts the attention of a smooth-talking, well-dressed traveling salesman bent on seduction.

When a young woman leaves home, writes Dreiser, she either "falls into saving hands … or she rapidly assumes the cosmopolitan standard of virtue."[2] Had Dreiser written for an earlier generation, we can well imagine the downward spiral to follow: Carrie, a fallen woman, would see out her days in ever-increasing depravation, succumbing at a young age. Dreiser, however, transcends nineteenth-century sentimentality to forge a tale for the coming era. As the train leaves the station, her would-be seducer leans over, placing his elbows on the back of her seat to offer blandishments. Naive yet preternaturally sure of herself, Carrie parries the rake's overtures while preserving her options, and so begins a very different sort of narrative. Although a second philanderer soon appears and tricks Carrie into going on the lam in a series of late-night train rides—first to Detroit and then, chased by private detectives, overnight to Montreal, and eventually down the line to New York City—Dreiser proceeds to flip the script, for in this elaborate bildungsroman it is Carrie who ends up a star of

Rand McNally and Company, *Rand McNally New Official Railroad Map of the United States and Southern Canada* (detail), 1920.

Library of Congress Geography and Map Division, Washington, DC

the Broadway stage, while her corrupter ends his days in a flophouse.

Set on the rails, *Sister Carrie* is a tale for a nation of change. The United States, once a social economy of rural communities, had grown into an urban, industrial nation by the turn of the century. Modernity transformed the country into a heterogeneous culture of consumption marked by large cities peopled by immigrants from around the world. Dreiser, well aware of these currents of change, recognized the railroad as an agent and a driving force. As Elissa Gurman has written, trains not only provided the rhetorical device Dreiser used to change scenes in his novel but also offered a new way of looking at American culture. In "mechanical determinism," she writes, "actions are determined not solely by free will, or even by biology, but by a combination of these forces and those of the technological–economic system" brought about by the railroad.[3] Although earlier writers such as Henry David Thoreau and Nathanial Hawthorne sounded the alarm, depicting the railroad as a sinister force, Dreiser gave agency to his female protagonist, allowing her to lose little by dint of inappropriate relationships and gain much in her desire for fine things. In fact, for Carrie and her generation, the geographic mobility and social fluidity provided by the railroad heralded life in the modern era.

America Underground

Dreiser's novel arrived on the American scene at a pivotal moment as, time and time again, railroads and especially the subway provided the setting for painters exploring the drama of the modern city. Subterranean mass transportation entered the popular imagination in 1863 with the advent of the London Underground, followed by advancements around the globe, including in New York, a city of almost 3.5 million in 1900. Samuel J. Woolf captured the frisson of riding the city's new subway system in his 1909-10 painting *The Under World* (cat. 31). Opened in 1904, the Interborough Rapid Transit Company, or IRT, offered an alternative to earlier elevated rail systems and accommodation for all strata of New York society, from the immigrant family at right to the uniformed messenger boy reading the newspaper in the center. Within twenty years, the IRT connected Manhattan to the outer boroughs as never before (fig. 26). The painting's theatrical focus, however, is at stage left, where a man in evening dress leans over to whisper confidences to a woman dressed as a fashion plate, complete with a fur collar and plumed hat. Employing a brushy realism, Woolf concretizes what Dreiser had earlier imagined in *Sister Carrie*: a place where class, ethnicity, and gender roles slipped earlier bounds of gentility and were redefined in the new public space of the passenger car.

New York City, by the time Woolf took up his brush, had long been considered suspect by most—dangerous by many—even as it served as muse to myriad creative visions. Heterogeneity itself became the stock in trade of writers, painters, and photographers offering a cornucopia of imagery that, as often as not, became a literal gallery of class, racial, and ethnic stereotypes. Walter Pach's 1919 painting *The Subway* (cat. 32) draws on social themes explored earlier by Woolf but with ever-increasing awareness of European styles of painting made popular by critical reaction to the 1913 Armory Show. Pach, who helped organize and contributed to the landmark Armory Show, creates a vortex-

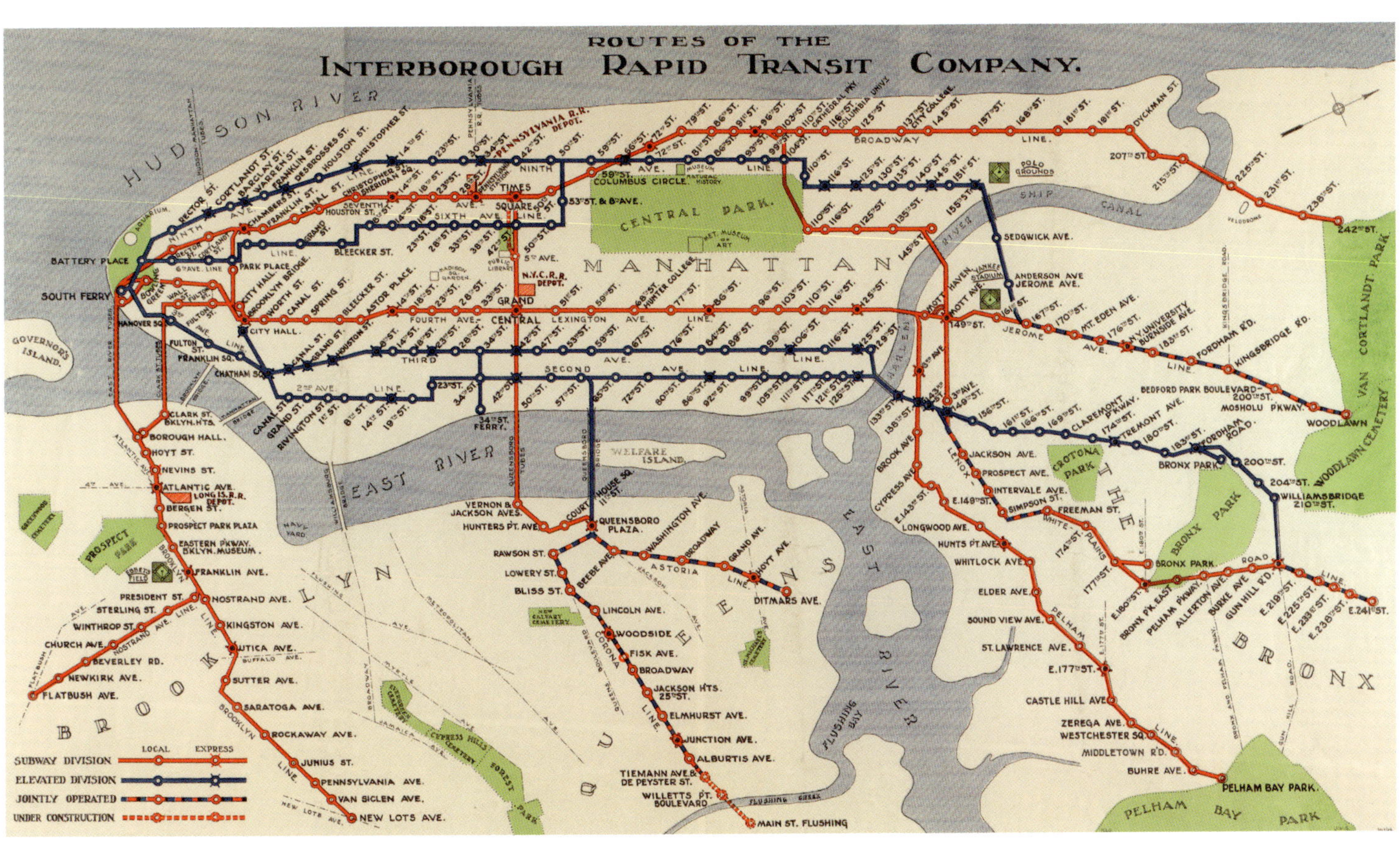

Fig. 26

Routes of the Interborough Rapid Transit Company, 1924.

Library of Congress Geography and Map Division, Washington, DC

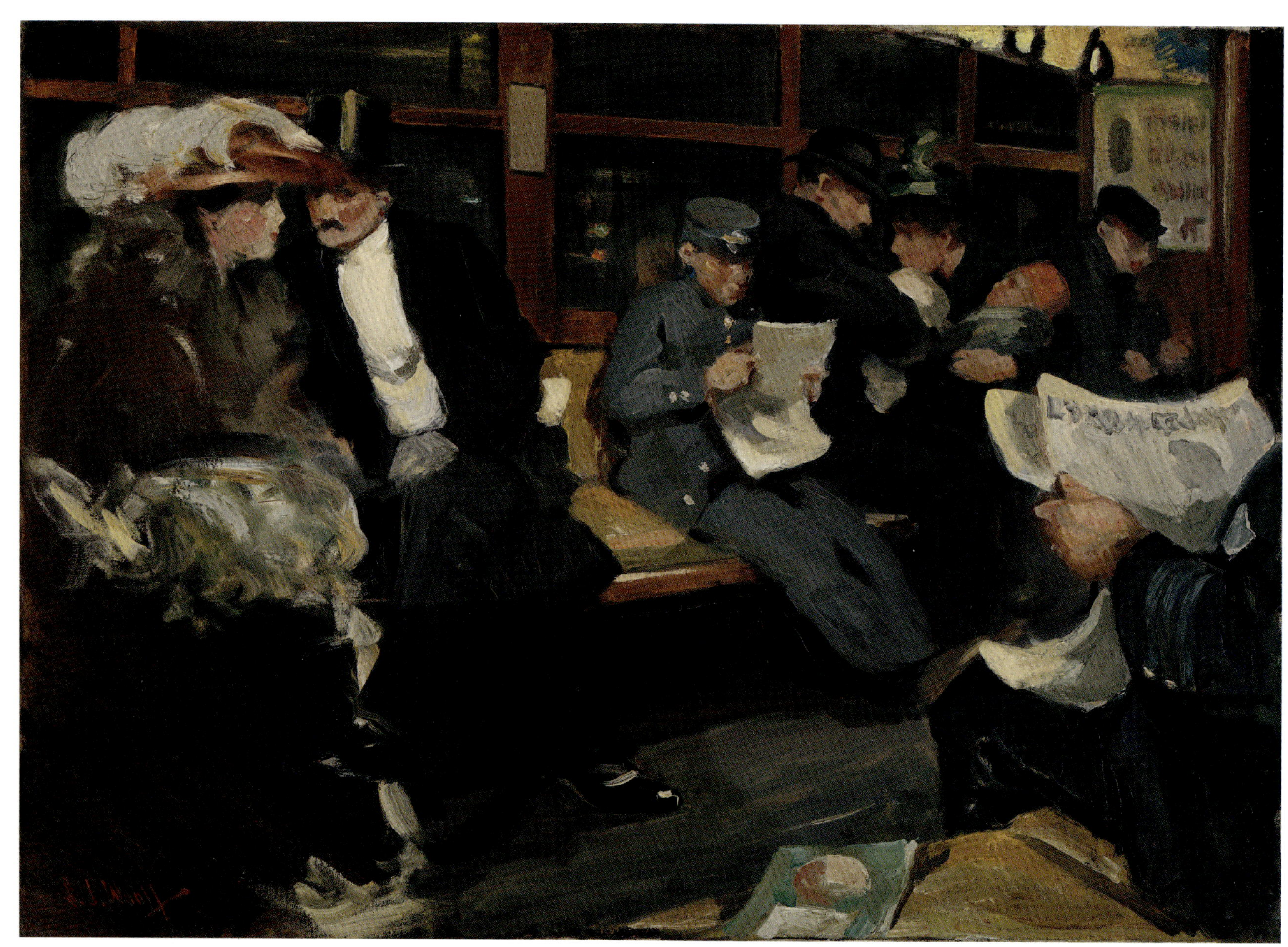

Cat. 31

Samuel J. Woolf (American, 1880-1948)
The Under World, ca. 1909-10

oil on canvas
22½ × 30½ in.

Virginia Museum of Fine Arts, Richmond

Funds provided by a private Richmond foundation, 95.101

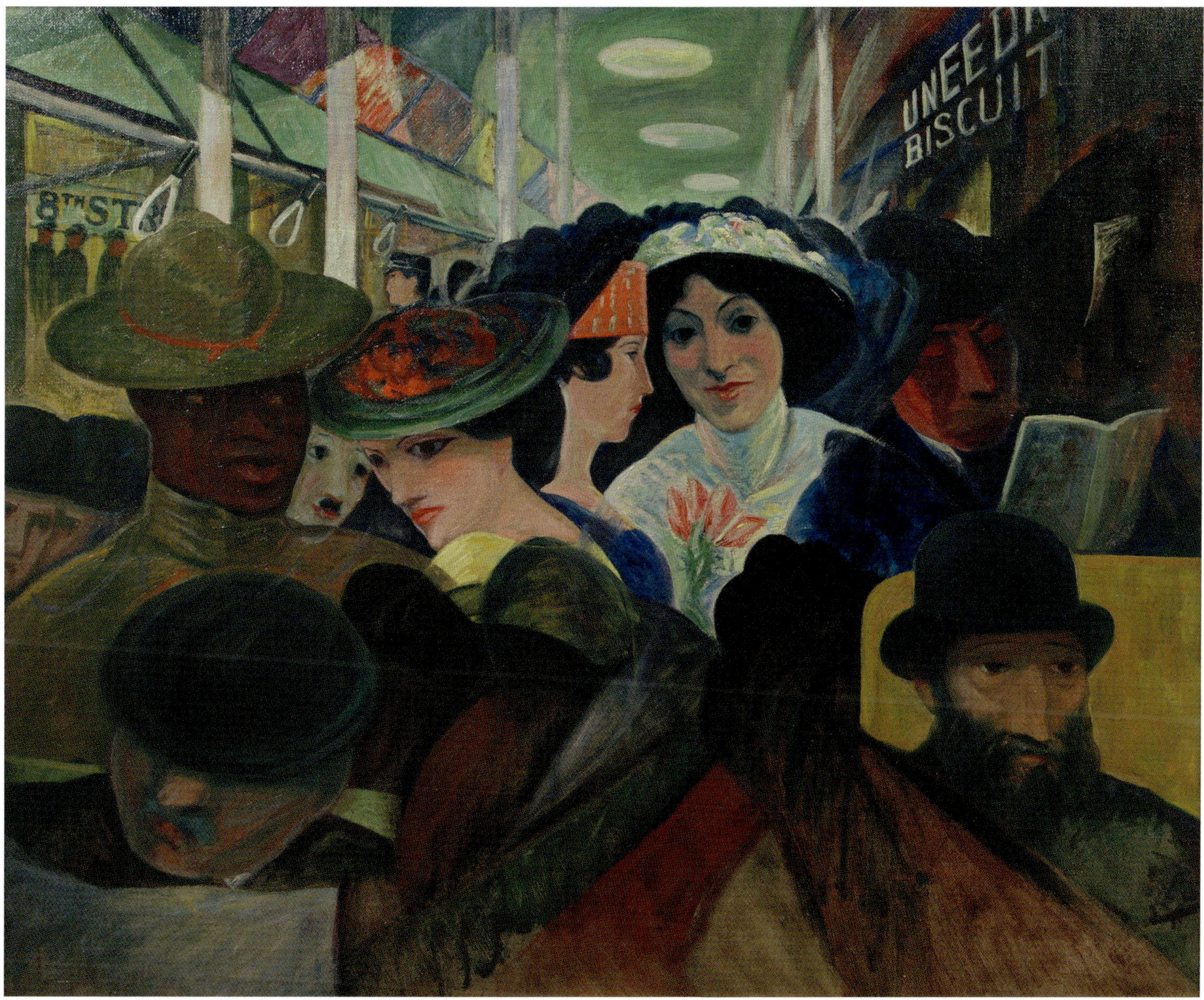

Walter Pach (American, 1883–1958)
The Subway, 1919
oil on canvas
26 × 31 in.
Saint Louis Art Museum
Gift of John and Susan Horseman, in honor of
Melissa Wolfe, Curator of American Art, 106:2019

like scene in *The Subway* wherein the very car of the train has decomposed, leaving the passengers exposed to the rush of arrivals at the 8th Street station. The artist's inside-out sleight of hand places the viewer directly in the hustle and bustle of Lower Manhattan.

Pach's melting pot trades in caricature to provide a document of urban life in the boom following World War I. Remembered today as a critic, curator, and modernist activist, Pach served as a bridge between avant-garde circles in New York and Europe. In *The Subway* he takes the viewer on a ride through New York, cataloguing racial and ethnic stereotypes along the way, all under the corporate banner of UNEEDA BISCUIT, one of the most recognizable brand names in the world at the time. The newspaper, omnipresent in subway scenes, sets the stage at lower left, read intently by a figure in a round workingman's cap. The narrative picks up pace as our eye moves clockwise. The next character is a Black artilleryman, a telling choice on the part of the artist. Pach was an early and earnest supporter of African American artists, and it seems significant that he elected to prominently depict a man of color in uniform, making eye contact with the well-dressed woman to his left. She is one of three women who provide the fulcrum around which the scene swings, all flamboyantly displaying the milliner's art and dramatically representing new roles played by women in the public sphere. The central figure is in white, once a time-honored symbol of constancy and virtue but by 1919 readily recognized as the costume of the suffragette. The Nineteenth Amendment, which granted women the right to vote, dominated conversation the year Pach painted *The Subway*, passing into law on June 4, 1919.

The shadowy figure at right lends complexity and a significant psychological burden to the painting. Pach includes a caricature of an Eastern European, legible as Jewish by his heavy beard, bowler hat, and hooked nose. Whereas Woolf depicted the immigrants in *The Under World* as a sympathetic family group, Pach's single figure is an abject stereotype. Pach's own biography—he was himself a secular Jew—may explain his inclusion of the figure. As Lynn Dumenil has written, a principal distinction within this diverse and complex community was between new and old immigrants.[4] By the third quarter of the nineteenth century, Jews from German-speaking countries had been in the United States long enough to assimilate and achieve professional stature and financial prosperity. Pach's father and uncle, for example, were proprietors of one of New York's premier photography studios. The racist caricature at the lower right becomes a subplot in the painting, a reminder that antisemitism reached an apogee in the 1920s in the United States and that the trope of the melting pot obscures a great deal of nuance while providing an organizing myth for the nation.

Waiting for the Future

Boston, the fifth-largest city in the United States at the turn of the twentieth century, is invariably framed in terms of filial piety to its Puritan origins. New England authors such as Hawthorne and the "schoolhouse poets," Henry Wadsworth Longfellow and John Greenleaf Whittier, set the stage in the nineteenth century with works that helped define New England as a region of rectitude and quiescence. Painters like Edmund Tarbell, immersed in this literary culture, reinforced historical sensibility at every turn.[5] Influenced as much by seventeenth-century Dutch interiors as by the radical themes and techniques of French Impressionism, Tarbell and his followers developed a signature style that coalesced into the Boston school. Dubbed "Tarbellites" in 1897 by the critic Sadakichi Hartmann, the Boston school promulgated a vision of an idealized "old" New England that placed a premium on a timeless genealogical imagination.[6] Tarbell, of old Yankee descent himself, leveraged his lineage to become an arbiter of taste, defining a look for Boston's Brahmin class, whether on Beacon Hill or an island in Maine during the summer. He came to critical acclaim by composing domestic interiors featuring the well-to-do performing their identities among such historical mnemonics as ancestral silver, porcelain, and hoary seventeenth-century furniture.

In the Station Waiting Room, Boston of 1915 (cat. 33) is thus an unusual departure for Tarbell. Light fascinated him, and his manipulation of sun and shade provoked critical reaction throughout his career. "The effect of sunlight falling on figures … has seldom been represented with greater force and accuracy," declared a satisfied reviewer in the *Boston Evening Transcript* in 1890.[7] Shafts of heavenly illumination pick out a family in the middle distance, calling our attention to a mother and child waiting patiently while a couple of swells sporting boater hats jog by, late for their train in a visual cliché painted to great success by Norman Rockwell forty years later in *Crestwood Commuter Station* (cat. 44) of 1946. Tarbell's waiting room lacks Rockwell's sense of playfulness, but his is a space that also places modernity in contest with tradition. In foregrounding three female sitters in white summer dresses, Tarbell assures the viewer

that technology marches forward and cities grow, but traditional female virtues are a constant in Boston. Tarbell would live until 1938, old enough to see such assumptions challenged and updated by "New Women," individuals who increasingly took on roles out of the home and closely resemble Carrie Meeber's latter-day nonfiction sisters.[8]

Tarbell's vision of an idealized Puritan city ultimately proved to be an overtly narrow construction. Waves of immigration made Boston an ethnically heterogeneous city by the time John Francis "Honey Fitz" Fitzgerald became mayor in 1906 and an Irish political dynasty began that continues to this day with the Kennedy family. Often overlooked is Boston's rich African American history, including Black participation in the maritime trades in the nineteenth century. Allan Rohan Crite, born in New Jersey and raised in Boston, studied at the School of the Museum of Fine Arts, and later earned his degree through Harvard University Extension School. He worked as a draftsman and technical illustrator for the Boston Naval Shipyard while executing a series of "neighborhood paintings" on his own time. Later in life he explained his intention to depict a "real Negro" rather than a "Harlem" or "jazz Negro," figures that he held were white representations of the African American community.[9] *The Carstop* of 1940 (cat. 34) reflects that goal, depicting an intersection in the South End of Boston where the bus line, street cars, and the MBTA, known as the "T," then Boston's elevated railroad, come together to form a vibrant crossroads at the Northampton Street Station. Crite's creative work remained underappreciated for decades, with his paintings gleaning sustained critical attention only late in the artist's life. His work

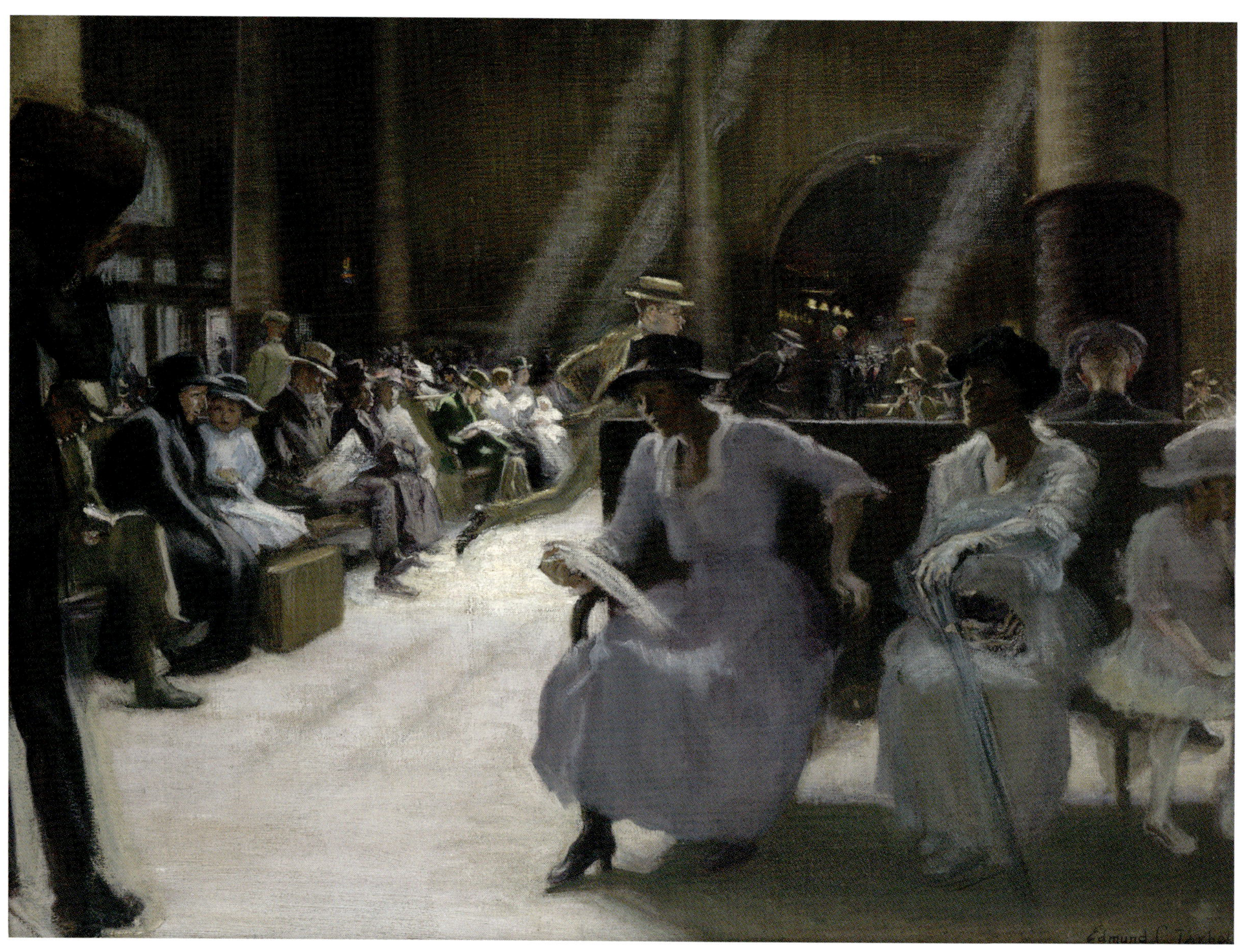

Cat. 33

Edmund Charles Tarbell (American, 1862-1934)
In the Station Waiting Room, Boston, ca. 1915
oil on canvas
24⅜ × 32 in.
Crocker Art Museum
Gift of Dr. Joseph R. Fazzano, 1956.7

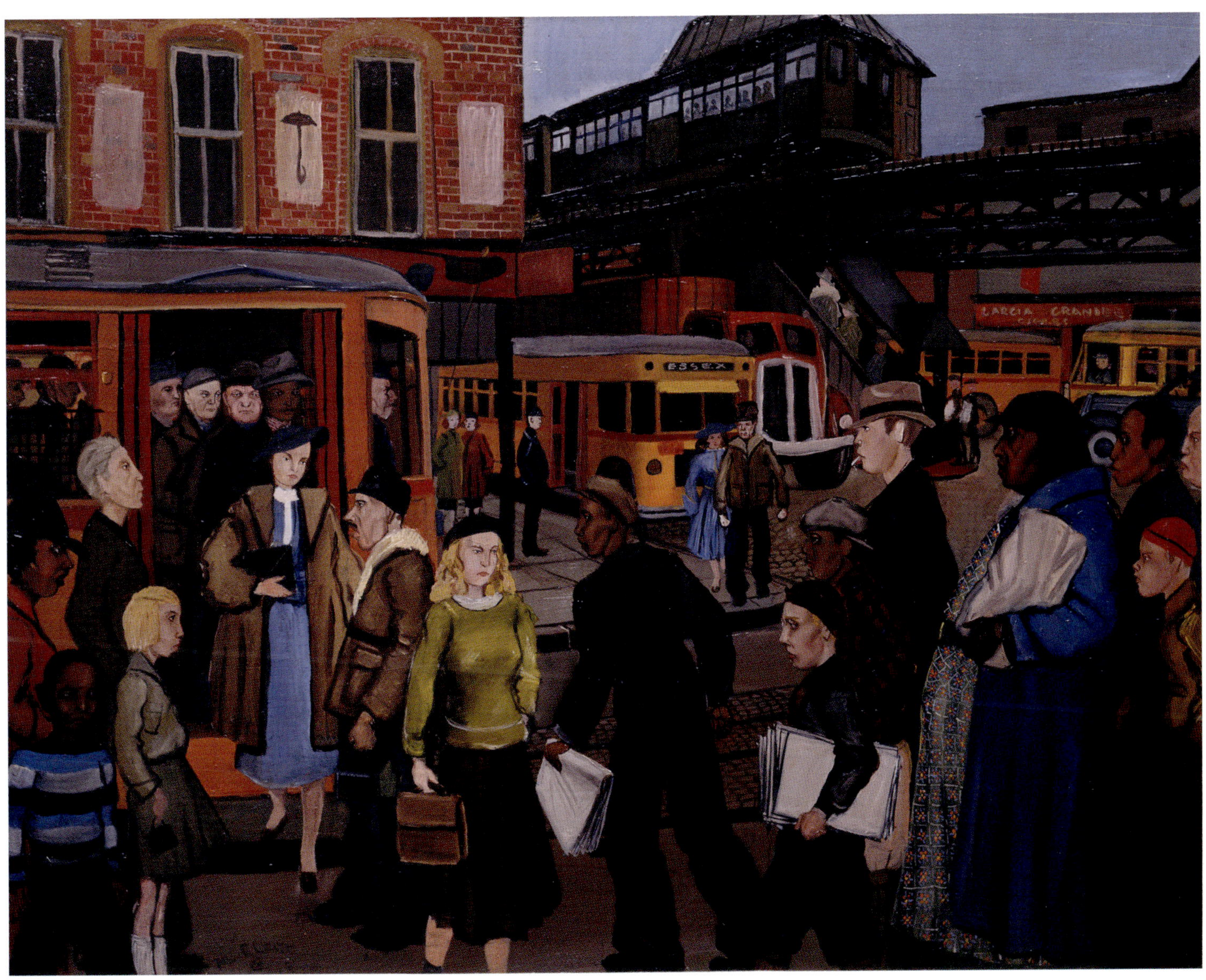

Cat. 34

Allan Rohan Crite (American, 1910–2007)
The Carstop, 1940
oil on canvas
37¼ × 31¼ in.
Boston Athenaeum
UR75

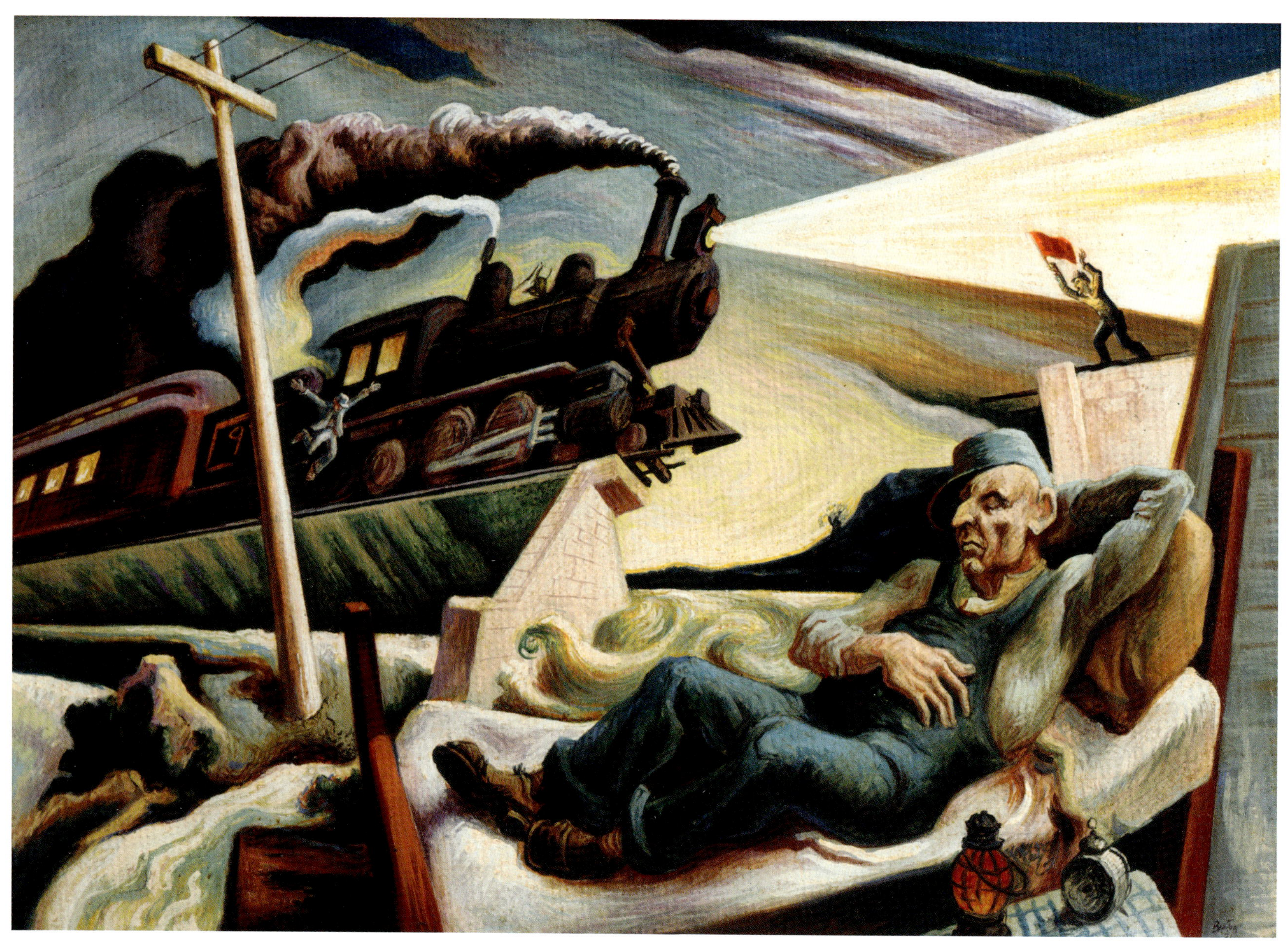

Cat. 35

Thomas Hart Benton (American, 1889–1975)
Engineer's Dream, 1931
oil on panel
29⅞ × 41¾ in.
Memphis Brooks Museum of Art
Eugenia Buxton Whitnel Funds, 75.1

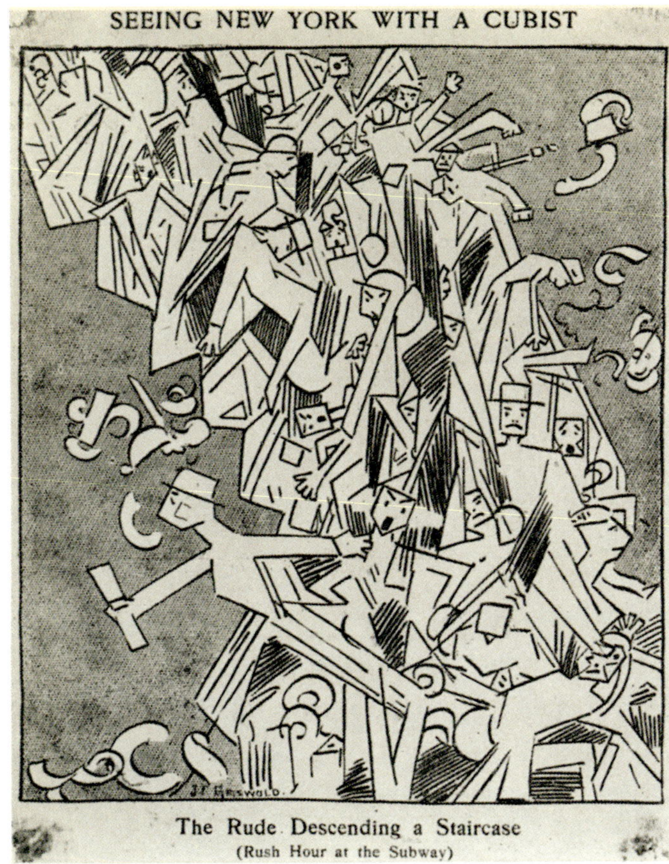

Fig. 27

J. F. Griswold
*The Rude Descending a Staircase
(Rush Hour at the Subway)*, cartoon from
the *New York Evening Sun*, March 20, 1913

The Granger Historical Picture Archive

is now celebrated as a rare lens through which to view Boston's neighborhoods before urban renewal changed the social topography of the "city upon a hill" in the 1960s and 1970s.

Social Realism on the Rails

Modernism in the visual arts, writes Bruce Robertson, was never solely a "Manhattan project" or simply about a lockstep march toward abstraction, as the critic Clement Greenberg would have us understand in the 1950s.[10] Painters such as Thomas Hart Benton, an artist trained in New York and Paris, eschewed abstraction for a sinuous, exaggerated realism that rendered the American scene as if in a dream state.[11] Indeed, Benton's *Engineer's Dream* of 1931 (cat. 35), despite the bright, illustrative palette and comic pose of the railway worker at right, is clearly the stuff of nightmare. An engineer, asleep in his bed, conjures a steam locomotive, canted as if caught by

camera or projected on a movie screen, speeding to the precipice of a washed-out bridge while a forlorn figure is caught in the blinding sweep of the headlamp, frantically waving a red signal flag. The diminutive engineer—presumably the sleeping protagonist—has leapt from the controls to an uncertain fate. The painting is fittingly symbolic of economic conditions in the United States two years into the Great Depression.

Benton, often derided by the intelligentsia as a Regionalist pandering to middlebrow sensibilities, found his *bête noire* in the person of Stuart Davis, an early advocate for abstract representation. According to Davis and his cronies, Benton was a rube at best and a racist at worst for the way he exaggerated African American bodies in a series of highly publicized murals executed for New York's New School for Social Research and the nascent Whitney Museum of American Art in the 1930s. Benton, however, gave as good as he got, decrying Davis and his ilk as marching in a "crazy parade" of Cubism, Futurism, Dadaism, and Surrealism, movements that he called so "deliberately unintelligible that it was no longer news when a picture was hung upside down."[12] Benton's gratuitous humor followed a long tradition of ridiculing modernist modes and styles. Indeed, two decades earlier, the Armory Show provided fodder for the pundits in 1913 when the *New York Evening Sun* included a cartoon *The Rude Descending a Staircase (Rush Hour at the Subway)*, a satire of Marcel Duchamp's Cubist *Nude Descending a Staircase* from the exhibition (fig. 27). The parody lampooned advancements in art with improvements in transportation, taking a dim view of both. Such thinking persisted for decades—

witness John Sloan's *Subway Stairs* of 1926 where
the crush of humanity offers a prurient variation on
the theme (fig. 28). Although New York-based critics
derided Benton's stylized midwestern scenes,
along with those of other painters such as Grant
Wood and John Steuart Curry, as middlebrow, they
proved to be engaging, accessible, and multivalent,
and frequently offered a subversive critique of
mainstream American culture, often pitting past
against present.

Trains captivated Benton. "My first pictures were
of railroad trains," he wrote later in life:

Engines were the most impressive things to come
into my childhood. To go down to the depot and
see them come in, belching black smoke with their
big headlights shining and their bells ringing and
pistons clanking, gave me a feeling of stupendous
drama, which I have not lost to this day.[13]

The Wreck of the Ole '97 (cat. 36) stands as
perhaps the apogee of Benton's many railroad
scenes. Painted in 1943 in egg tempera, a precise
and highly traditional medium popular with other
artists, most famously Andrew Wyeth, the work
depicts a famous rail disaster: on September 27,
1903, the Southern Railway mail train, Fast Mail
Number 97, derailed at the Stillhouse Trestle near
Danville, Virginia, killing eleven on board. Benton's
narrative makes use of a time-honored cliché—the
iron horse fulminating darkly as it roars past a white
horse and wagon—but it clearly hit home during
the Depression and subsequent world conflict.
The accident itself resonated in popular culture,
amplified as the subject of a ballad recorded in
1924 and subsequently reinterpreted so many times

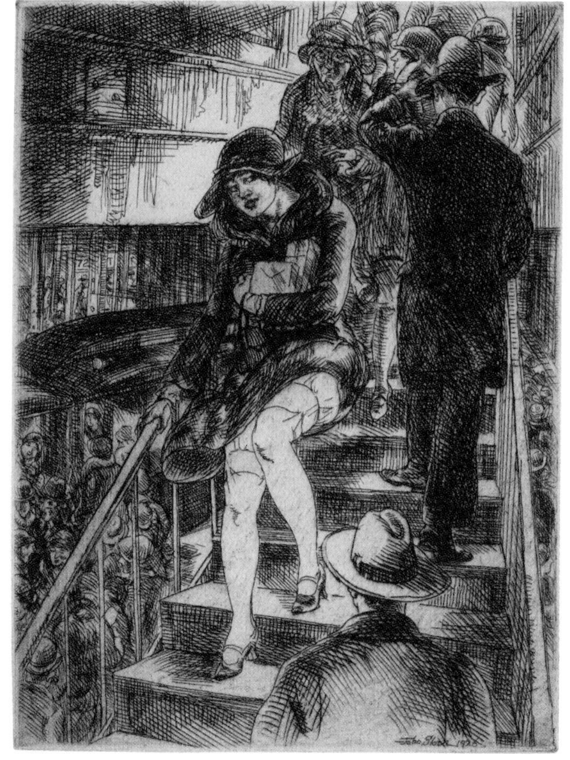

Fig. 28

John Sloan (American, 1871-1951)
Subway Stairs, 1926
etching
10$\frac{13}{16}$ × 8$\frac{7}{16}$ in.
The Metropolitan Museum
of Art, New York
Gift of Mrs. Harry Payne
Whitney, 1926, 26.30.158

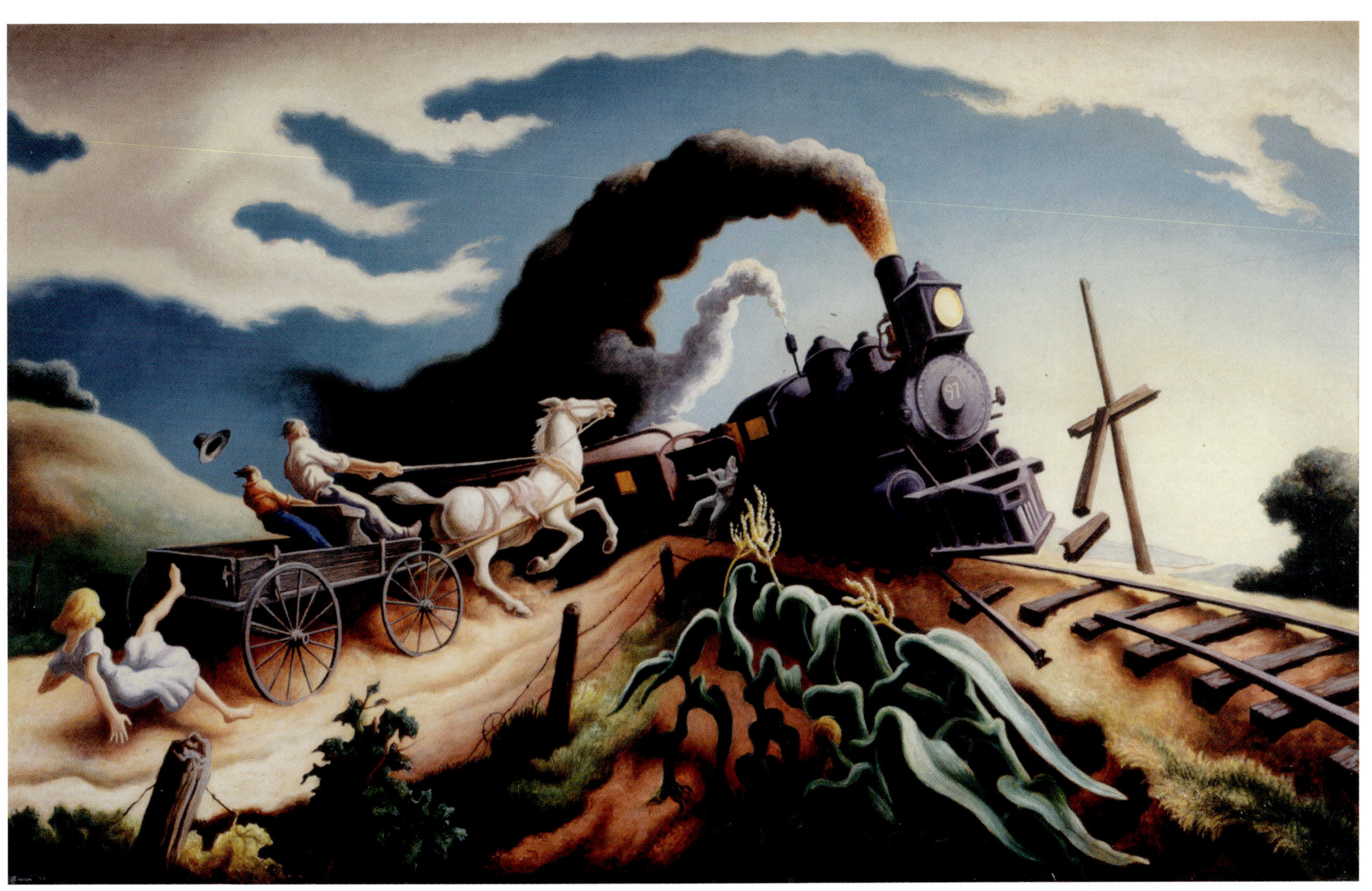

Cat. 36

Thomas Hart Benton (American, 1889-1975)
The Wreck of the Ole '97, 1943

egg tempera on gessoed Masonite
28½ × 44½ in.

Hunter Museum of American Art,
Chattanooga, Tennessee

Gift of the Benwood Foundation, 1976.3.2

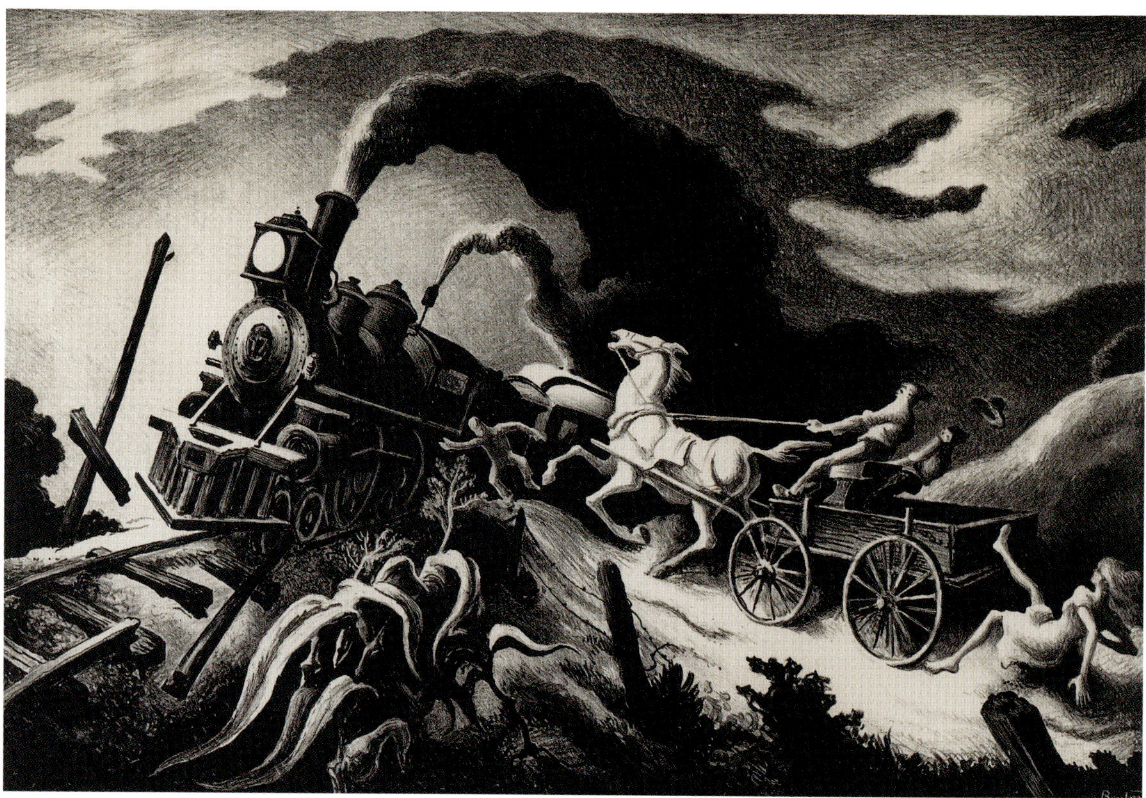

**Thomas Hart Benton
(American, 1889–1975)**
Wreck of the Ol' '97, 1944

lithograph
12⅞ × 17 in.

Minneapolis Institute of Art

Gift of Richard L. Hillstrom in
memory of his parents, Martin
and Alma Hillstrom, P. 85.62

that it is often credited as being the first country song to sell one million copies. Tale, song, painting, and ultimately print: the image achieved wider distribution than many of Benton's efforts when it was published as a lithograph in 1944 (fig. 29). The publisher, Associated American Artists in New York, provided a way for artists to earn income during the financial crises of the 1930s and 1940s by selling prints to middle-class consumers.[14]

Working on the Railroad

The stock market crash in the fall of 1929 heralded unprecedented economic suffering and social unrest in the United States. Reginald Marsh, otherwise a child of privilege, frequently took up the cause of the working poor in his art and became known for scenes of impoverished people and burlesque performers in New York City. His *Gathering the Mail* of 1934 (cat. 37), however, depicts a railroad postal worker posed in heroic fashion, employing a mail hook and catcher pouch to gather mail on the fly. The US Postal Service employed Railroad Post Offices (or RPOs) throughout the continental United States in the early twentieth century as a systemized and integrated method of moving letters, eventually developing a standardized layout for these special railcars. The RPO engendered communication and commerce in far-flung corners of the country. In the depths of the economic crisis, various branches of the federal government, especially the Works Progress Administration (WPA), commissioned artists to create work that heroized labor to provide economic support for creatives while influencing public policy through soft power. Marsh's contributions included a series of railway murals, including a high-profile example that depicts sorting the mail at Pennsylvania Station in New York. In this way the Roosevelt administration reinforced popular understanding of the stabilizing role of centralized government at a time of fundamental political uncertainty.

Imagery such as *Gathering the Mail* provided subtle visual reinforcement of a fundamental change in the American attitude toward both the

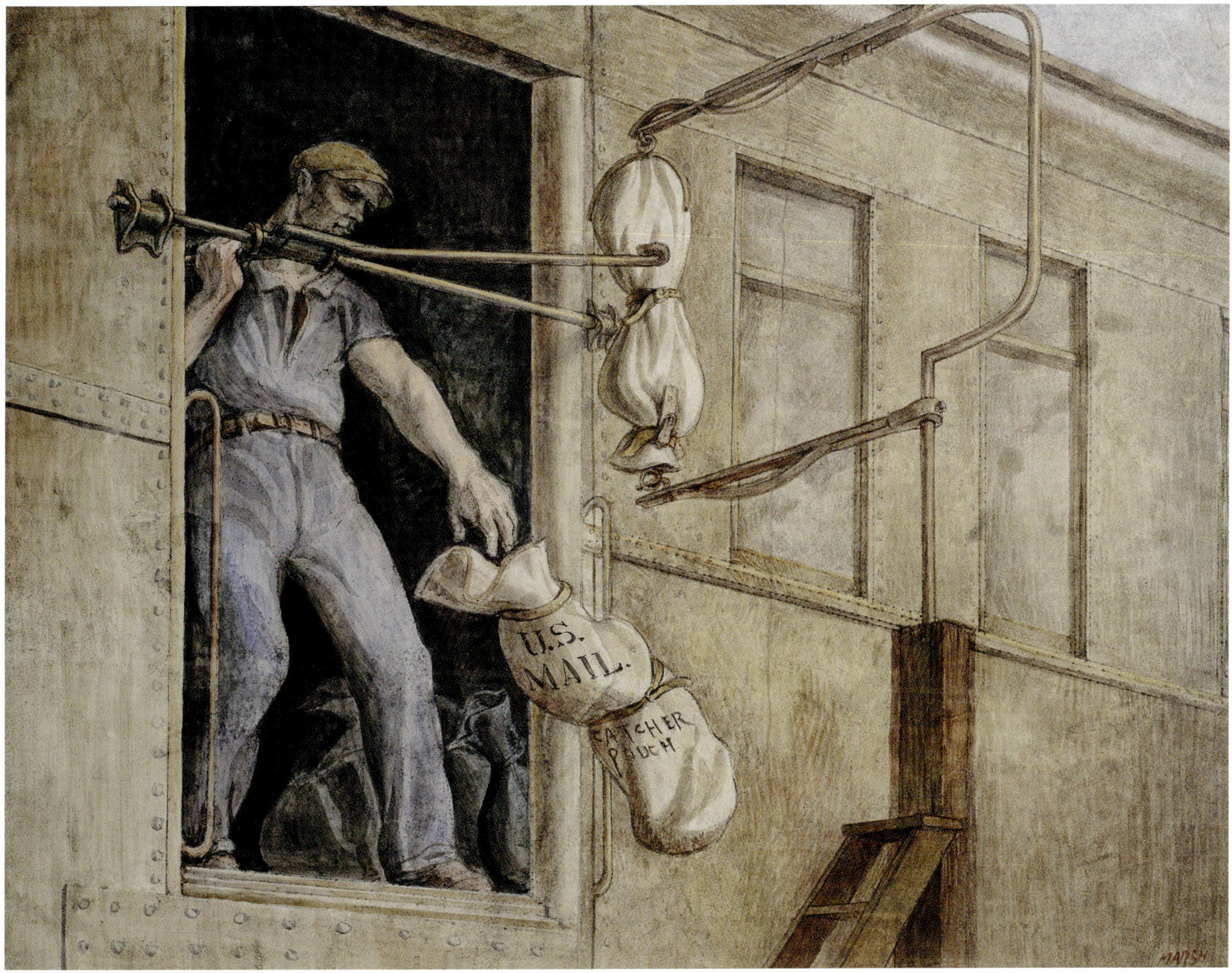

Reginald Marsh (American, 1898-1954)
Gathering the Mail, 1934
fresco on cement
37⅝ × 47¾ in.

Palmer Museum of Art at Penn State

Purchased with funds provided by the
Friends of the Palmer Museum of Art, 85.3

free market and big government during the Great Depression. Indeed, the railroad industry itself was so damaged by fiscal mismanagement by 1933 that President Franklin D. Roosevelt was compelled to bail it out. The Emergency Railroad Transportation Act was among the fifteen key pieces of legislation enacted during his first one hundred days in office, an unprecedented series of laws regulating the devastated United States economy. A railroad "czar" would now ensure cooperation between individual railway lines and their attendant labor unions, or else all concerned would face the threat of executive fiat.

The valorization of labor organized the creative culture of the Great Depression, especially among artists influenced by the so-called Ashcan school, whose practitioners often took workers and the urban poor as subjects while participating in left-leaning conversations about the future of a capitalist nation. Harry Gottlieb's *Dixie Cups* of 1936-37 (cat. 38) is one such painting, a stark representation of the monumental glowing red railcars used in the production of steel, steaming in the cold air, and painted in the darkest days of economic crisis. Belying their innocent-sounding sobriquet, these "dixie cups" contained slag, a byproduct of the steel industry, and transported the red-hot waste from blast furnaces in cities such as Cleveland, Detroit, and Bethlehem to immense dumps prone to leaching toxic materials. Massive conical vessels designed to withstand the harshest of conditions, these specialized railcars shared little in common with the ephemeral paper Dixie cups that sprang up in public washrooms as part of a public health effort aimed at curbing the 1918 influenza epidemic.

Like Gottlieb, Joe Jones encodes his 1939 painting *All the Live Long Day* (cat. 39) with a title referencing popular culture, but in quoting the well-known and time-honored work song "I've Been Working on the Railroad" he also weaves a political reference into the scene. Jones, termed a "proletarian artist" by the critic Thomas Craven and an avowed member of the Marxist John Reed Club, creates a layered visual narrative.[15] While framing his painting with the complex geometry of a large switchyard, populated by boxcars on the horizon, he leaves no doubt that the focus of the work is the thirteen men toiling to lay the heavy and awkward steel rails. The rhythm of the scene is amplified by the popular song, a traditional tune from the mid-nineteenth century originally published in a collegiate songbook by Princeton University in 1894.[16] Popular in minstrel shows and later bowdlerized as nursery rhymes, such music found new relevance during the Depression when various federal agencies such as the WPA sought to catalogue and record examples of African American field hollers and work chants. Jones's painting captures the moment when the work gang syncopates and synchronizes their efforts and becomes as if one to perform difficult labor under onerous circumstances.

Palmer Hayden also concretized a well-known folk song—but to a very different end—when he painted *His Hammer in His Hand* (cat. 40), one of twelve canvases in the *Ballad of John Henry* series executed between 1944 and 1947. Hayden, born in Virginia of African descent, studied at Cooper Union and Columbia University before living in Paris for five years, returning to the United States during the depths of the Depression. Securing employment with the WPA, Hayden frequently explored the

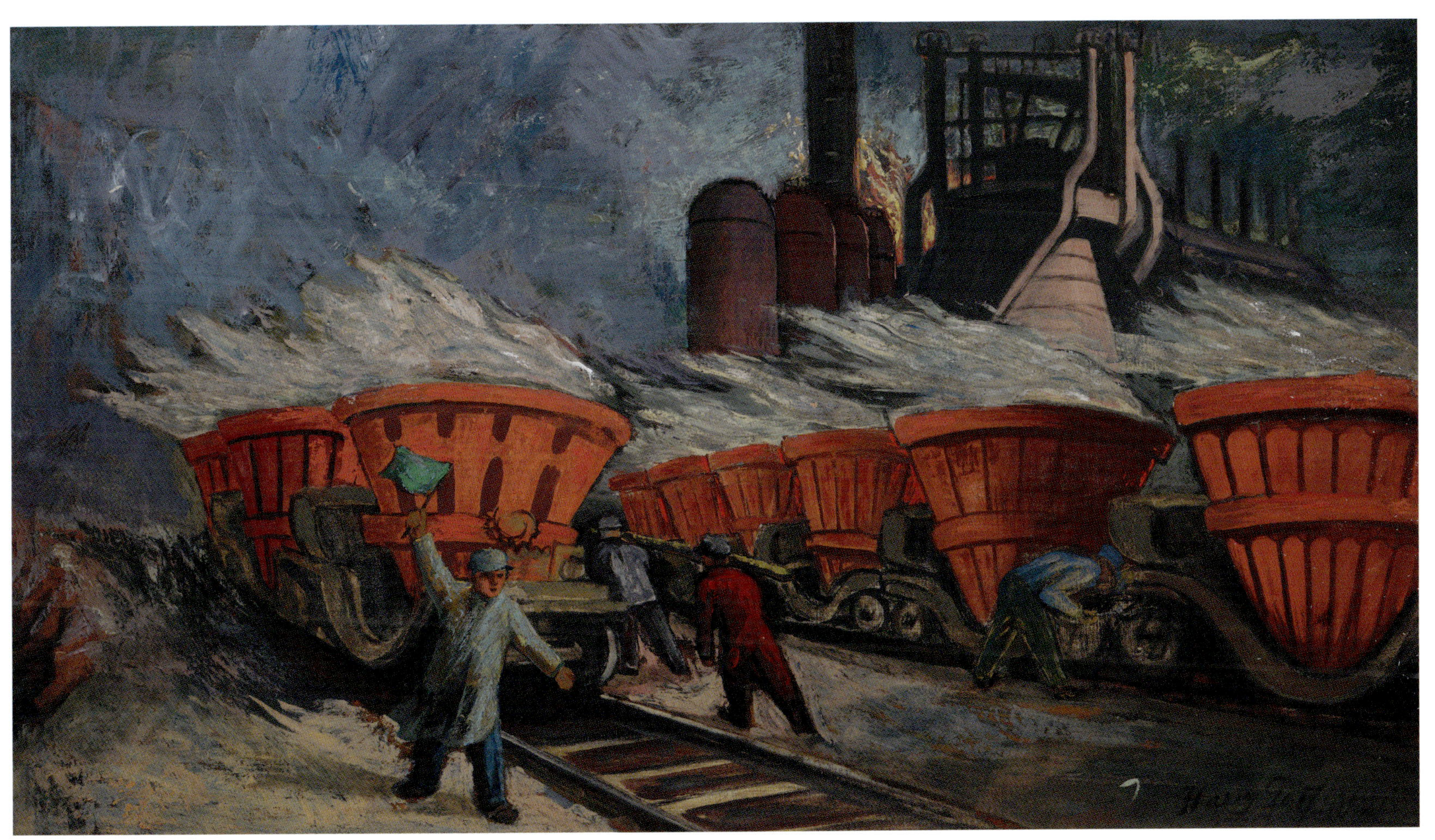

Cat. 38

Harry Gottlieb (American, 1895–1992)
Dixie Cups, 1936–37

oil on canvas
24⅛ × 41 in.

Wichita Art Museum

Museum purchase, Friends of the Wichita Art
Museum, Director's Discretionary Fund, 1982.42

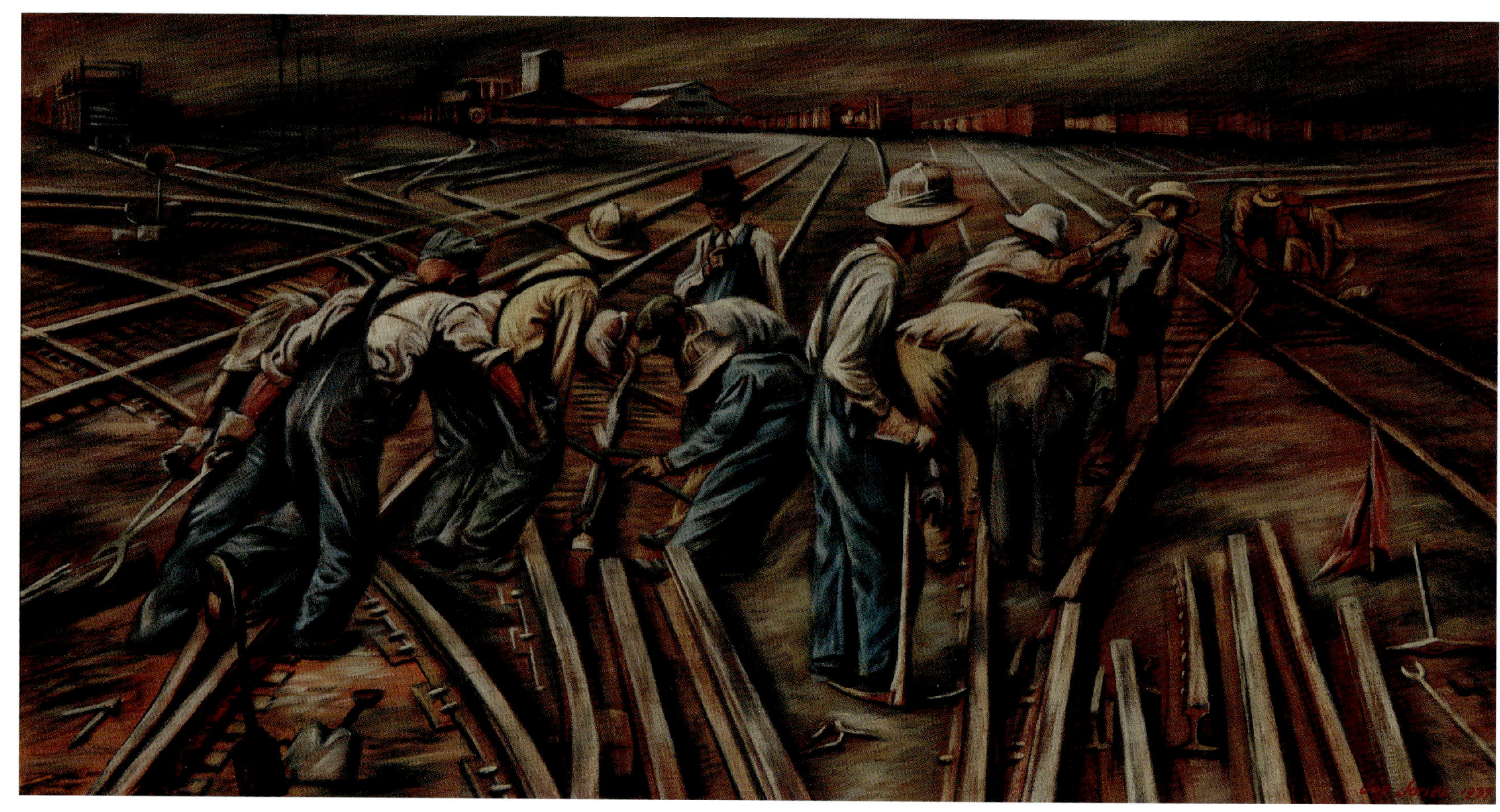

Cat. 39

Joe Jones (American, 1909-1963)
All the Live Long Day, 1939
oil on paper mounted on board
16 × 29⅝ in.
Art Gallery of Hamilton
Gift of Mr. Herman H. Levy, O.B.E., 1961

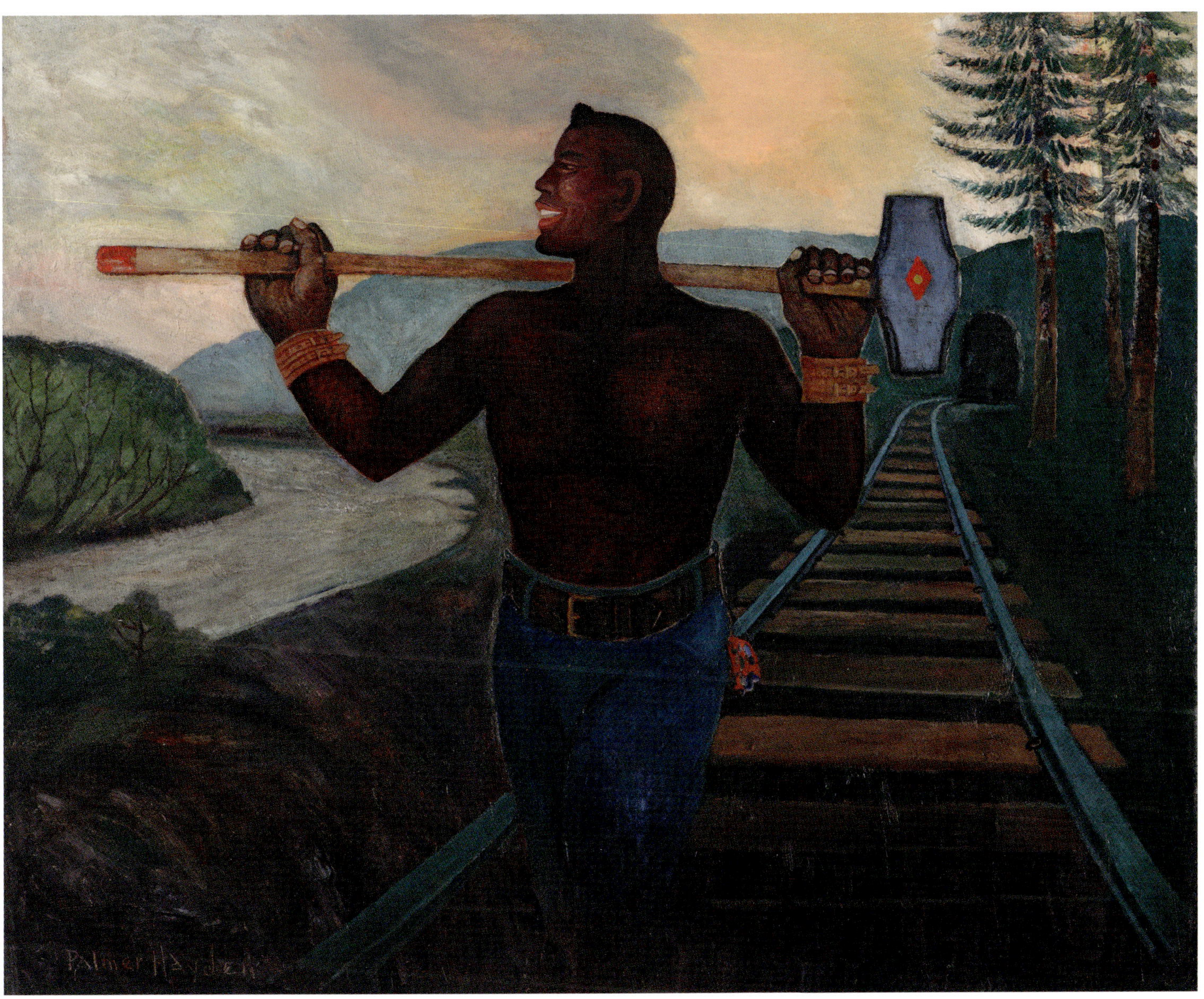

Cat. 40

Palmer C. Hayden (American, 1890-1973)
His Hammer in His Hand, from the
Ballad of John Henry series, ca. 1944-47

oil on canvas
27 × 33 in.

Museum of African American Art, Los Angeles

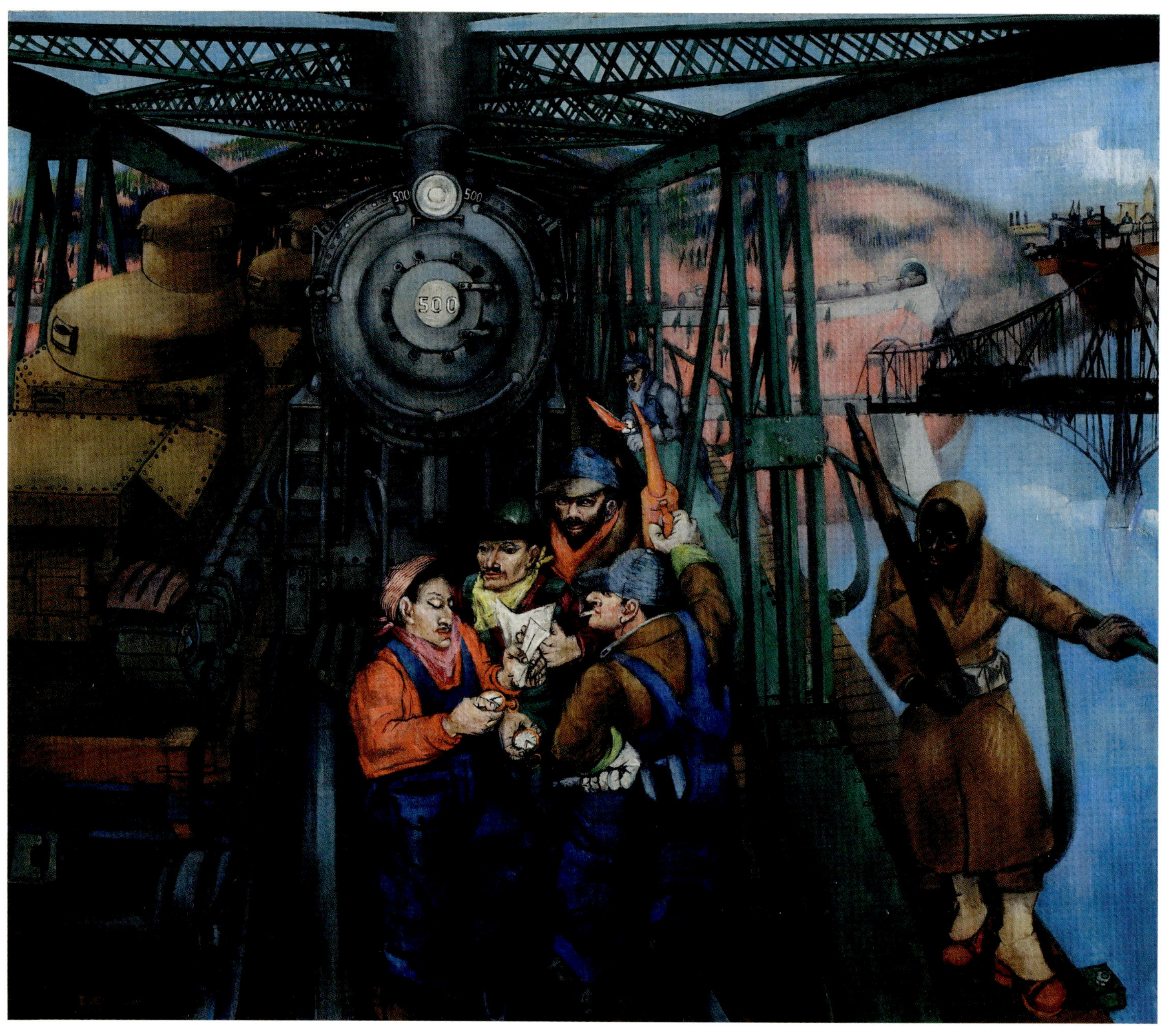

African American experience in his paintings, which drew an ambivalent critical response for employing racist stereotypes such as exaggerated features and child-like pastimes.[17] Unlike these crude caricatures, however, *His Hammer in His Hand* celebrates the folk hero John Henry, the well-known "steel-driving man" who bested a pneumatic drill before laying down his life, a parable of man versus machine and the dignity of labor in the face of modernity. "A man ain't nothing but a man," declares one verse of the song, "but before I let your steam drill beat me down, I'd die with a hammer in my hand, Lord, Lord, I'd die with a hammer in my hand." In Hayden's painting, John Henry is depicted as handsome, triumphant, and smiling while walking from the tunnel he personally carved to lay the tracks that march off the canvas.

While Hayden fleetingly offered the promise of a new day with *His Hammer in His Hand*, Philip Evergood's *Wheels of Victory* from 1944 (cat. 41) served to remind viewers that the country remained deeply conflicted when it came to questions of race. The painting offers a seemingly simple narrative. Two trains cross on a steel bridge, with the locomotive facing the viewer crossing paths with a light tank on a flat car, perhaps leaving a factory and on its way to the theater of war. Five men, all white, confer in the foreground, checking their pocket watches and regarding important papers, possibly the manifest for their shipment. The figure on the right, however, provides the moral center of the composition. Harking back to Walter Pach's Black soldier in *The Subway*, Evergood has included an African American sentry, silently witnessing the fraternity of railway workers as he guards the bridge and secures the future of a country that will exclude him from economic opportunity at every turn.

Modern Life and Detachment

Jacob Lawrence achieved acclaim as a young artist for *The Migration Series* of 1940–41. An exploration of the dramatic demographic shift of African American workers from the rural South to northern cities between the wars, railroad imagery figured prominently in the series as the prime mover of the Great Migration, what W. E. B. DuBois called "social evolution working itself out before our eyes."[18] Edith Halpert of the Downtown Gallery famously brokered the sale of *The Migration Series* to the Museum of Modern Art and the Phillips Collection in 1942, placing half of the sixty-panel series with each institution. Halpert, whose stable of artists included such luminaries as Stuart Davis, Marsden Hartley, Edward Hopper, Georgia O'Keeffe, and Charles Sheeler, and ensured that Lawrence joined this pantheon of early modernists in the popular imagination while the painter himself served in the US Coast Guard.

Lawrence's *Subway—Home from Work (In the Evening the Mother and Father Come Home from Work)* (cat. 42), painted during the middle of World War II in 1943, shares a theme with Crite's *The Carstop*, but it also demonstrates Lawrence's deep immersion in modernist circles, particularly in its formal, Cubist composition and pervasive atmosphere of cool detachment.[19] A study in shapes, two subway entrances separated by a broad, empty avenue become classical temples through which purposeful figures silently go about their business. The absence of automobiles reminds us that gas rationing is in effect, while the somber palette evens out the gouache, making the evening scene mellow despite the sharp geometry of figures emerging from underground. The title also hints at conditions during the war, as both mother and father are working out of the home, replacing those at the front and providing labor for factories running around the clock in service of the war effort.[20] The circumstances would have been no surprise to those African Americans who came from the South to northern cities, as the privations of a segregated society had long required women to labor alongside men.

The end of World War II brought about a massive, dramatic shift in American culture. Soldiers returned home, prosperity beckoned, and the United States briefly stood uncontested on the world stage. Louise Rönnebeck's 1945 painting *End of Summer* (cat. 43) captures the moment as two young women—mother and daughter perhaps—curl up and sleep, the leather valise at their feet hinting at the end of a vacation. Rönnebeck, best known as a muralist, creates an elliptical work by rendering her subjects unconscious and intertwined. While she captures the sleepy, waning days of the season, she also hints at the dark new truths that accompanied a peace brought about by the United States' deployment of two atom bombs over Japan in August of 1945. At the end of summer, 1945, the war is over, but the world will never be the same for innocents sleeping on a train, creating a composition of red, white, and blue.

Four short years separate Norman Rockwell's *Crestwood Commuter Station* of 1946 (cat. 44) and George Tooker's unsettling subterranean 1950 drama *The Subway* (cat. 45). At first glance, myriad differences separate the works. The former is jocular to the point of being arch, an engaging outdoor suburban scene; the latter is an existential drama that could only take place in the hermetic, urban underground. When placed in conversation, the two paintings graphically demonstrate the impact of the railroad on twentieth-century American visual culture.

Crestwood Commuter Station is a seemingly simple narrative that served as the cover illustration for the *Saturday Evening Post* of November 16, 1946 (fig. 30). The painting, as with all of Rockwell's efforts, repays close examination. In *Crestwood Commuter Station* the artist offers a soothing view of middle-class life to a nation still reckoning with the trauma of the recent world war. Rockwell essentializes an identifiable and humorous narrative of the "American Dream," an ideal shared throughout the country and fixed along lines of gender, class, and race.[21] A row of commuters neatly lines the station platform, engaged in the individual and communal act of reading multiple copies of the same newspaper. A few latecomers rush to catch the arriving train, each stopping by the newsboy,

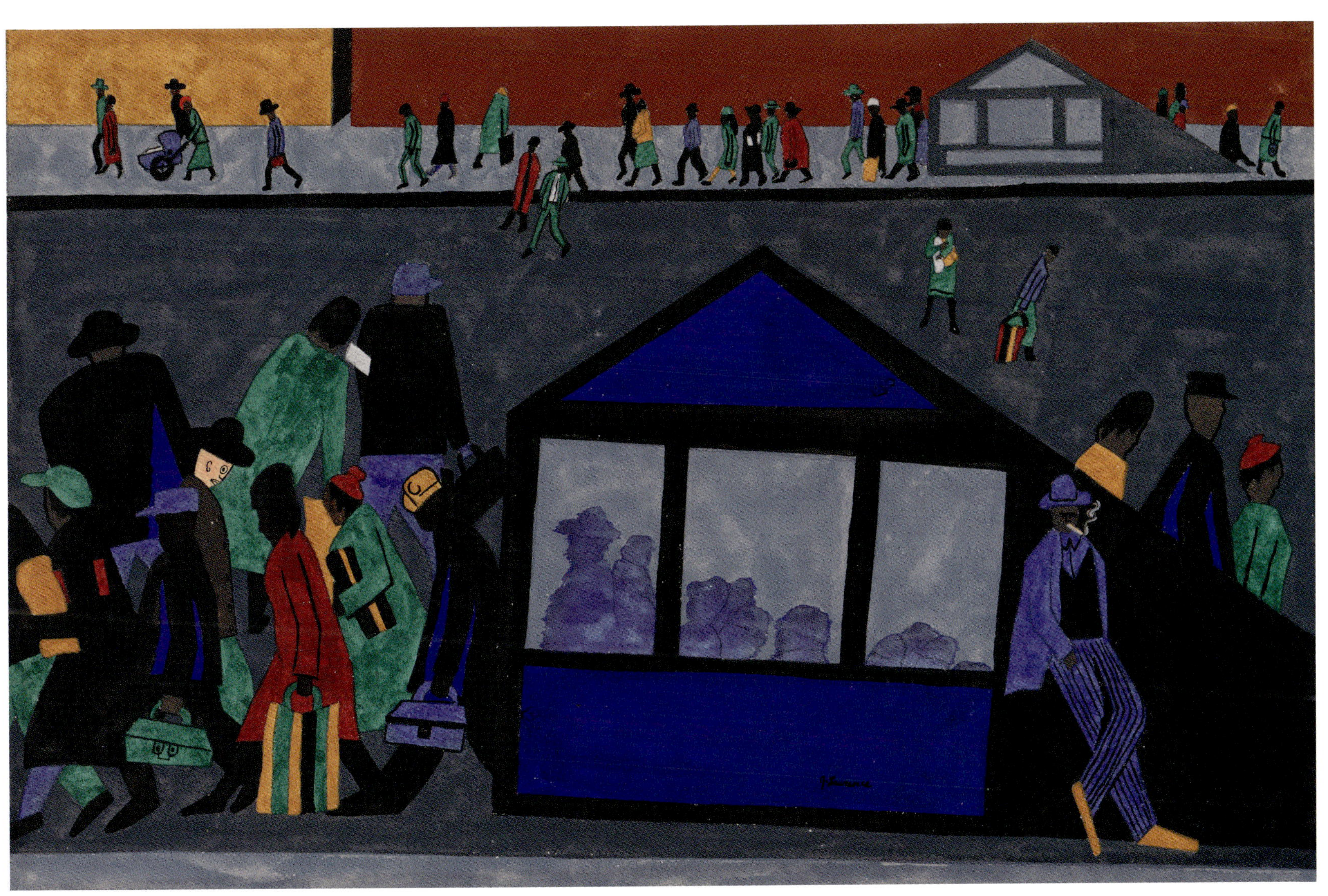

Cat. 42

Jacob Lawrence (American, 1917-2000)
Subway–Home from Work (In the Evening the Mother and Father Come Home from Work), 1943
gouache on paper
14⅜ × 21¾ in.
Virginia Museum of Fine Arts, Richmond
Gift of the Alexander Shilling Fund, 44.18.1

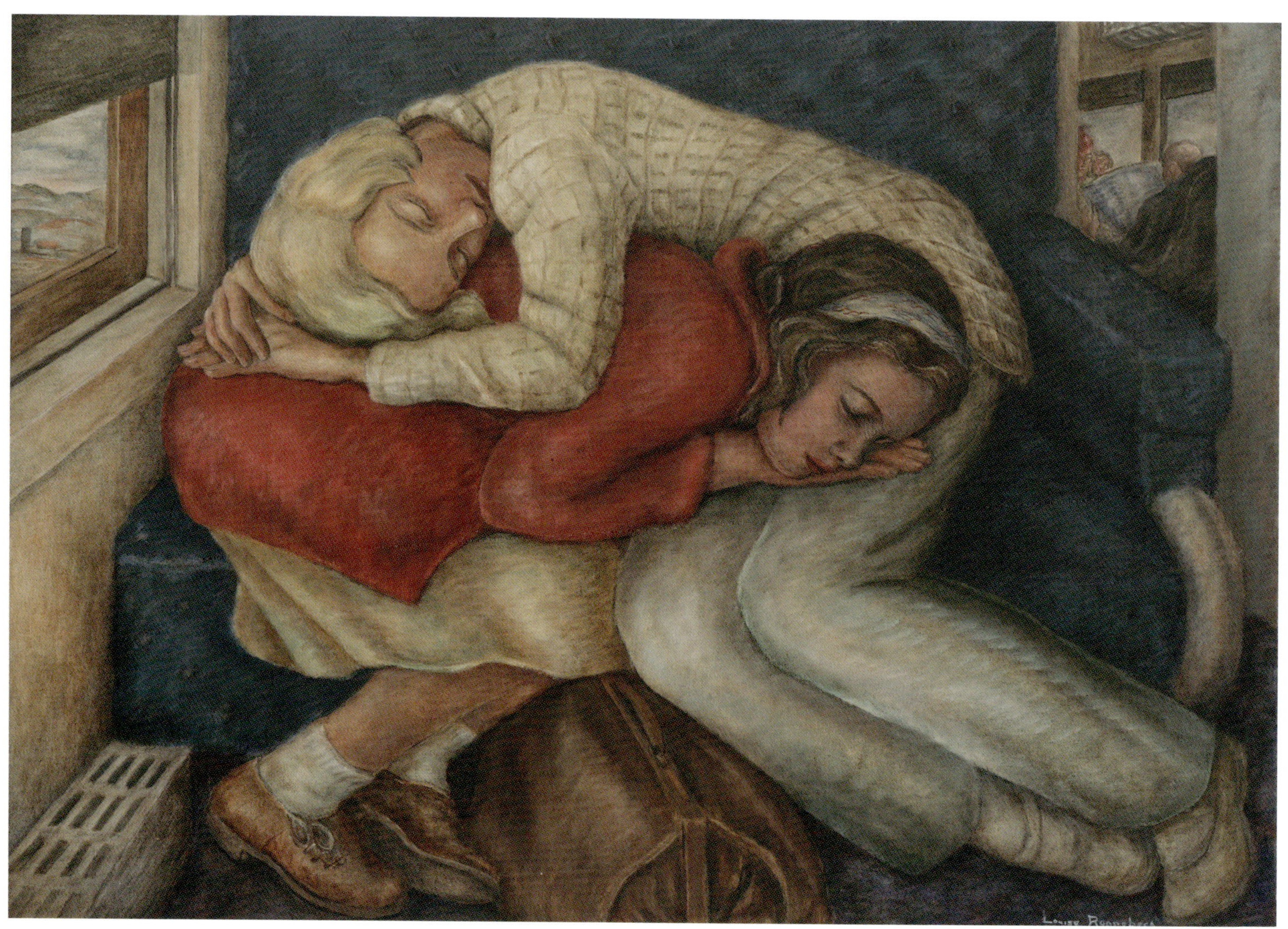

Cat. 43
**Louise Emerson Rönnebeck
(American, 1901-1980)**
End of Summer, 1945
oil/tempera on canvas
26 × 36¼ in.
Private collection

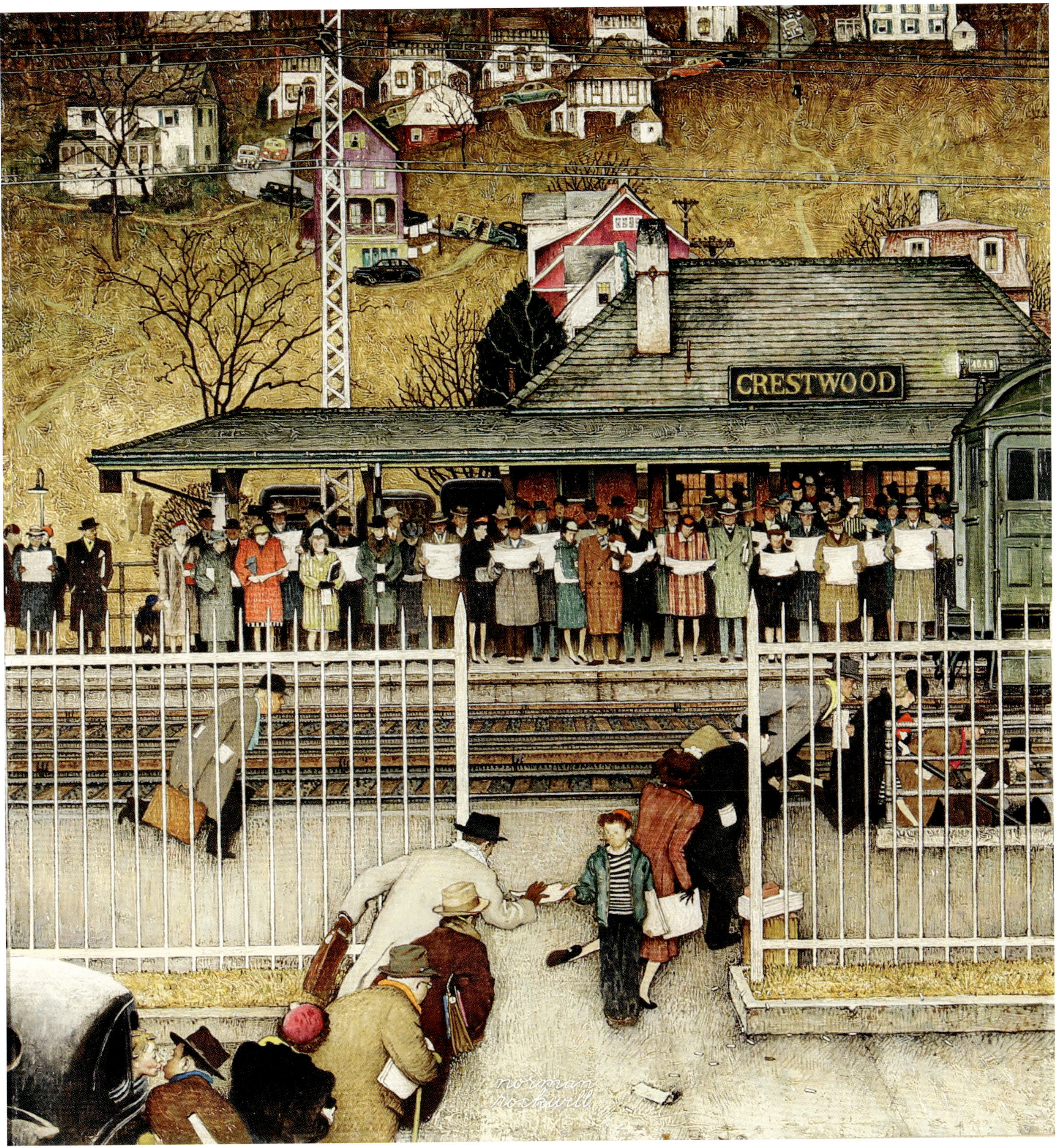
CRESTWOOD

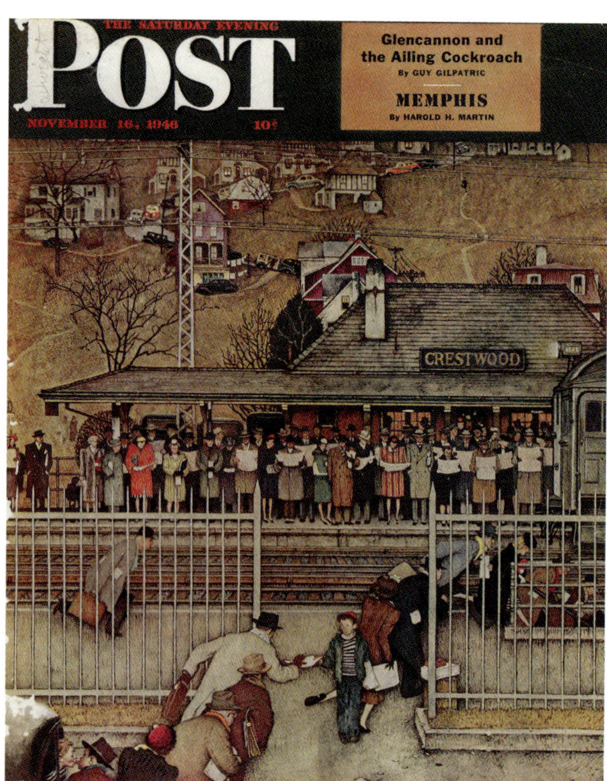

Fig. 30

Cover of the *Saturday Evening Post* featuring Norman Rockwell's *Crestwood Commuter Station*, November 16, 1946.

The Curtis Publishing Company, Philadelphia, Pennsylvania

dashing through a tunnel under the tracks and adding comic relief to the scene.

Like so many of Rockwell's efforts, *Crestwood Commuter Station* is a master class in formal composition. A white fence reinforces a sense of order in the already tidy composition, offering symbolic protection to the viewer—the train, after all, is on the other side of the barrier. A diagonal queue of bustling passengers zigzag through the fence, mirrored by a row of tranquil suburban houses ascending the hill, just offstage from the morning drama. Crestwood served Tuckahoe, New York, indicating a throng on the way to Grand Central Station in Manhattan. Despite this geographic specificity, Rockwell conjures a scene repeated every morning throughout the country. Men (and a handful of well-dressed women) are on their way to work in the city from an idealized commuter suburb. With a wink and a nod, Rockwell assures us all is well in America.

In 1950, George Tooker begged to differ. His chilling painting *The Subway* (cat. 45) distills the alienation and anxiety of the Cold War.[22] The work shares a surprising number of formal attributes with Rockwell's effort, with a turnstile-barred entryway and railing substituted for the neat iron fence bisecting *Crestwood Commuter Station*. A line of businessmen in phone booths mimics Rockwell's ziggurat composition, emphasized by Tooker's flat, universal way of lighting his scenes. In Tooker's drama, however, it is a woman—the only one in the painting—who takes center stage. Well-dressed but guarded, her countenance is haunted. "I was thinking of the large modern city as a kind of limbo," wrote Tooker. "The subway seemed a good place to represent a denial of the sense and the negation of life itself … being underground with a great weight overhead was important."[23] Painted one year after the Soviet Union tested a nuclear weapon, Tooker's vision is a stark reminder that subways now serve as bomb shelters.

Forty years after Samuel Woolf painted *The Under World*, a pictorial novel of manners hinting at dangerous liaisons made possible by the mixing of classes underground, Tooker takes the same theme as his own and renders it terrifying. The warmth of the immigrant family has been replaced by icy stares from a phalanx of men in trench coats, once the uniform of the soldier and now the garb of the office worker. The newspapers, once ubiquitous, are conspicuously absent. All sense of community has fallen away. It is as if the woman in Tooker's subway station is Carrie Meeber's granddaughter—a college graduate, approaching middle age, working in a midtown office—now realizing that the trains her grandmother rode into the modern era have left her, fifty years hence, as vulnerable as Carrie setting off on her journey.

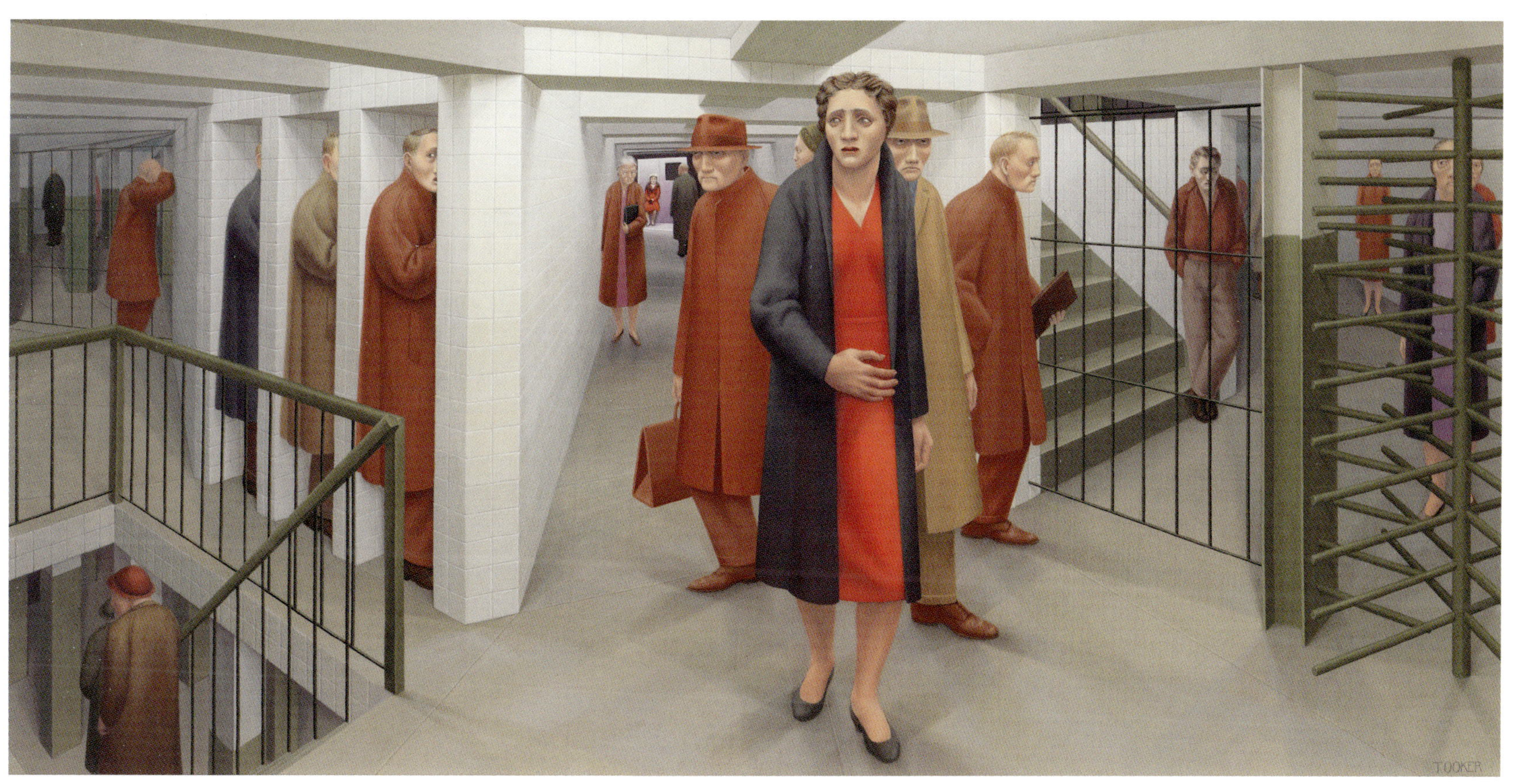

Cat. 45

George Tooker (American, 1920–2011)
The Subway, 1950

tempera on composition board
18½ × 36½ in.

Whitney Museum of American Art, New York

Purchase, with funds from the Juliana Force
Purchase Award, 50.23

Endnotes

1   Theodore Dreiser, *Sister Carrie* (1900; New York: W. W. Norton & Company, 2006), 2.

2   Dreiser, 1.

3   Elissa Gurman, "Onward, Onward: *Sister Carrie* and the Railroad," *Canadian Review of American Studies* 47, no. 2 (Summer 2017): 199–218.

4   Lynn Dumenil, *Modern Temper: American Culture and Society in the 1920s* (New York: Hill & Wang, 1995), 260.

5   Trevor J. Fairbrother, *The Bostonians: Painters of an Elegant Age, 1870–1930*, exh. cat. (Boston: Museum of Fine Arts, 1986).

6   Laurene Buckley, *Edmond C. Tarbell: Poet of Domesticity* (New York: Hudson Hills Press, 2002), 45.

7   "The Fine Arts," *Boston Evening Transcript*, December 30, 1890, 6.

8   For more on the New Woman, see Martha H. Patterson, ed., *The American New Woman Revisited: A Reader, 1894–1930* (New Brunswick, NJ: Rutgers University Press, 2008).

9   Judith K. Maxwell, "Allan Rohan Crite," in *Picturing Old New England: Image and Memory*, ed. William H. Truettner and Roger B. Stein, exh. cat. (New Haven: Yale University Press in association with the National Museum of American Art, 1999), 205.

10   Bruce Robertson, "Yankee Modernism," in Truettner and Stein, *Picturing Old New England*, 171. For more on Greenberg, see Caroline A. Jones, *Eyesight Alone: Clement Greenberg's Modernism and the Bureaucratization of the Senses* (Chicago: University of Chicago Press, 2005).

11   For more on Benton, see Henry Adams, *Thomas Hart Benton: An American Original*, exh. cat. (New York: Alfred A. Knopf, 1989).

12   Judith Barter, ed., *America After the Fall: Painting in the 1930s*, exh. cat. (New Haven, CT: Yale University Press in association with the Art Institute of Chicago, 2016), 33.

13   Thomas Hart Benton, *An Artist in America*, new and rev. ed. (Kansas City, MO: University of Kansas City Press, 1951), 13.

14   Erika Doss, "Catering to Consumerism: Associated American Artists and the Marketing of Modern Art, 1934–1958," *Winterthur Portfolio* 26, no. 2/3 (Summer/Autumn 1991), 143–67.

15   Thomas Craven, ed., *A Treasury of American Prints* (New York: Simon & Schuster, 1939), pl. 59.

16   James J. Fuld, *The Book of World-Famous Music: Classical, Popular, and Folk*, 4th ed. (New York: Dover, 1995), 309.

17   Phoebe Wolfskill, "Caricature and the New Negro in the Work of Archibald Motley Jr. and Palmer Hayden," *Art Bulletin* 91, no. 3 (September 2009): 343–65.

18   DuBois quoted in Leah Dickerman and Elsa Smithgall, *Jacob Lawrence: The Migration Series*, exh. cat. (New York: Museum of Modern Art; Washington, DC: Phillips Collection, 2015), 50.

19   For an excellent exploration of the notion of "cool" in modern painting, see Katherine M. Bourguignon, Lauren Kroiz, and Leo G. Mazow, *America's Cool Modernism: O'Keeffe to Hopper*, exh. cat. (Oxford: Ashmolean Museum, 2018).

20   Isabel Wilkerson, *The Warmth of Other Suns: The Epic Story of America's Great Migration* (New York: Vintage Books, 2010).

21   For more on this moment in American history, see Jim Cullen, *The American Dream: A Short History of an Idea that Shaped a Nation* (Oxford: Oxford University Press, 2003); and Richard Rothstein, *The Color of Law: A Forgotten History of How Our Government Segregated America* (New York: Liveright Publishing Corporation, 2017).

22   Katherine Jane Hauser, "George Tooker, Surveillance, and Cold War Sexual Politics," *GLQ: A Journal of Lesbian and Gay Studies* 11, no. 3 (2005): 391–425.

23   Tooker quoted in Edward Lucie-Smith, *American Realism* (New York: Harry N. Abrams, 1994), 151.

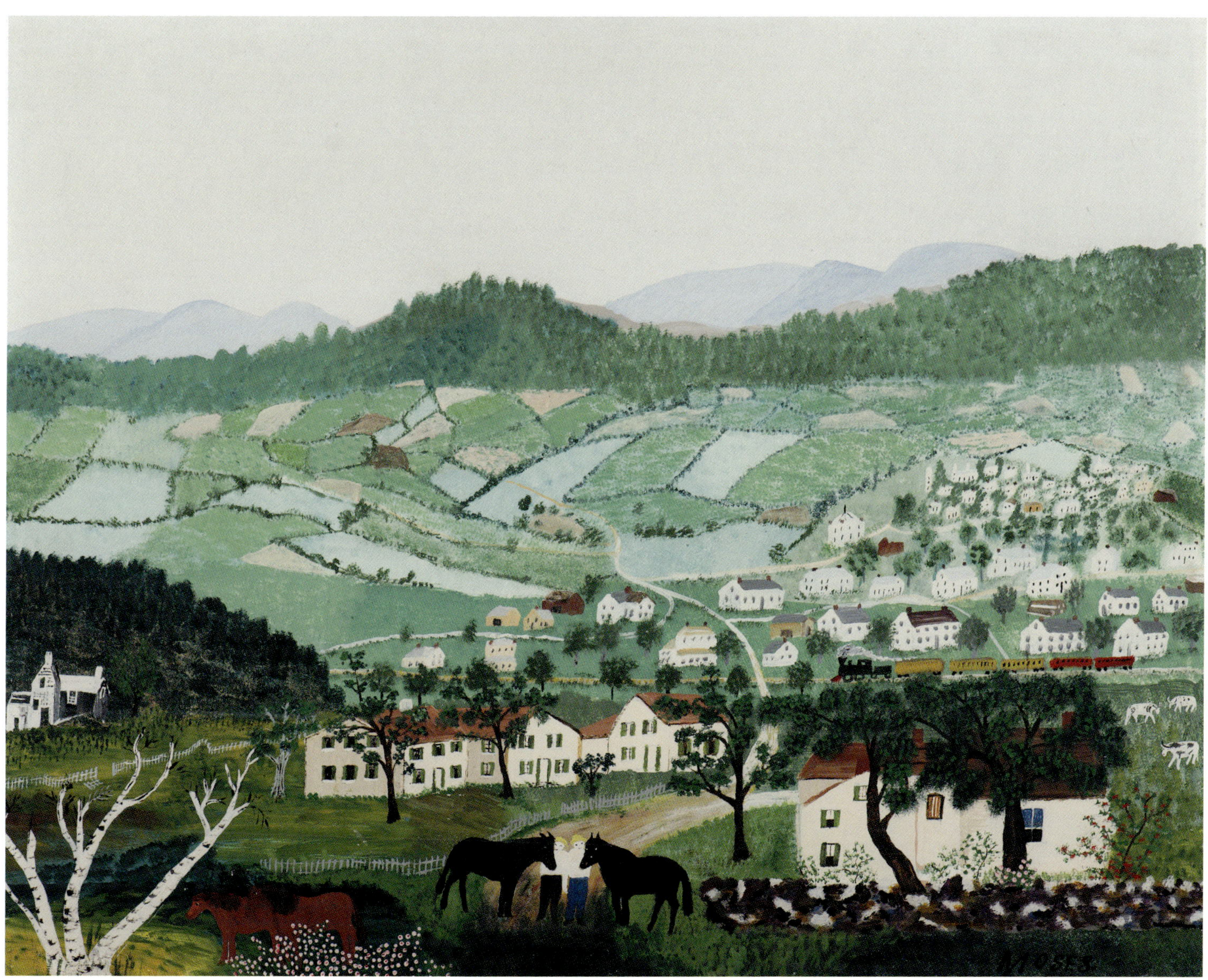

Cat. 46

**Anna Mary Robertson "Grandma"
Moses (American, 1860–1961)**
Cambridge, 1944

oil on Masonite
20¼ × 24⅜ in.

Shelburne Museum

Museum purchase, acquired from
Otto Kallir, 1961–210.1

EXHIBITION CHECKLIST

Thomas Cole
(American, 1801-1848)
River in the Catskills, 1843
oil on canvas
27½ × 40⅜ in.
Museum of Fine Arts, Boston
Gift of Martha C. Karolik for the
M. and M. Karolik Collection of
American Paintings, 1815-1865, 47.1201
Cat. 1

Charles Louis Heyde
(American, 1822-1892)
*Steam Train in North Williston,
Vermont*, 1850
oil on canvas
20⁹⁄₁₆ × 35⁹⁄₁₆ in.
Shelburne Museum
Gift of Edith Hopkins Walker, 1959-49.1
Cat. 2

Theodore Kaufmann
(American, 1814-1896)
Westward the Star of Empire, 1867
oil on canvas
35½ × 55½ in.
Collection of the St. Louis Mercantile
Library at the University of Missouri-
St. Louis
Gift of James E. Yeatman
Cat. 4

Albert Bierstadt
(American, 1830-1902)
View of Donner Lake, California, 1871-72
oil on paper mounted on canvas
29¼ × 21⅞ in.
Fine Arts Museums of San Francisco
Gift of Anna Bennett and Jessie Jonas in
memory of August F. Jonas, Jr., 1984.54
Cat. 5

William Robinson Leigh
(American, 1866-1955)
*The Attempt to Fire the Pennsylvania
Railroad Roundhouse in Pittsburgh, at
Daybreak on Sunday, July 22, 1877*, 1895
oil on canvas on board
28⅜ × 21½ in.
Carnegie Museum of Art, Pittsburgh
Gift of Thomas Mellon Evans, 76.60
Cat. 6

Colin Campbell Cooper
(American, 1856-1937)
Pittsburgh, PA, ca. 1905
oil on canvas
23⅛ × 30¼ in.
The Westmoreland Museum of
American Art
Gift in memory of Alex G. McKenna,
1996.19
Cat. 7

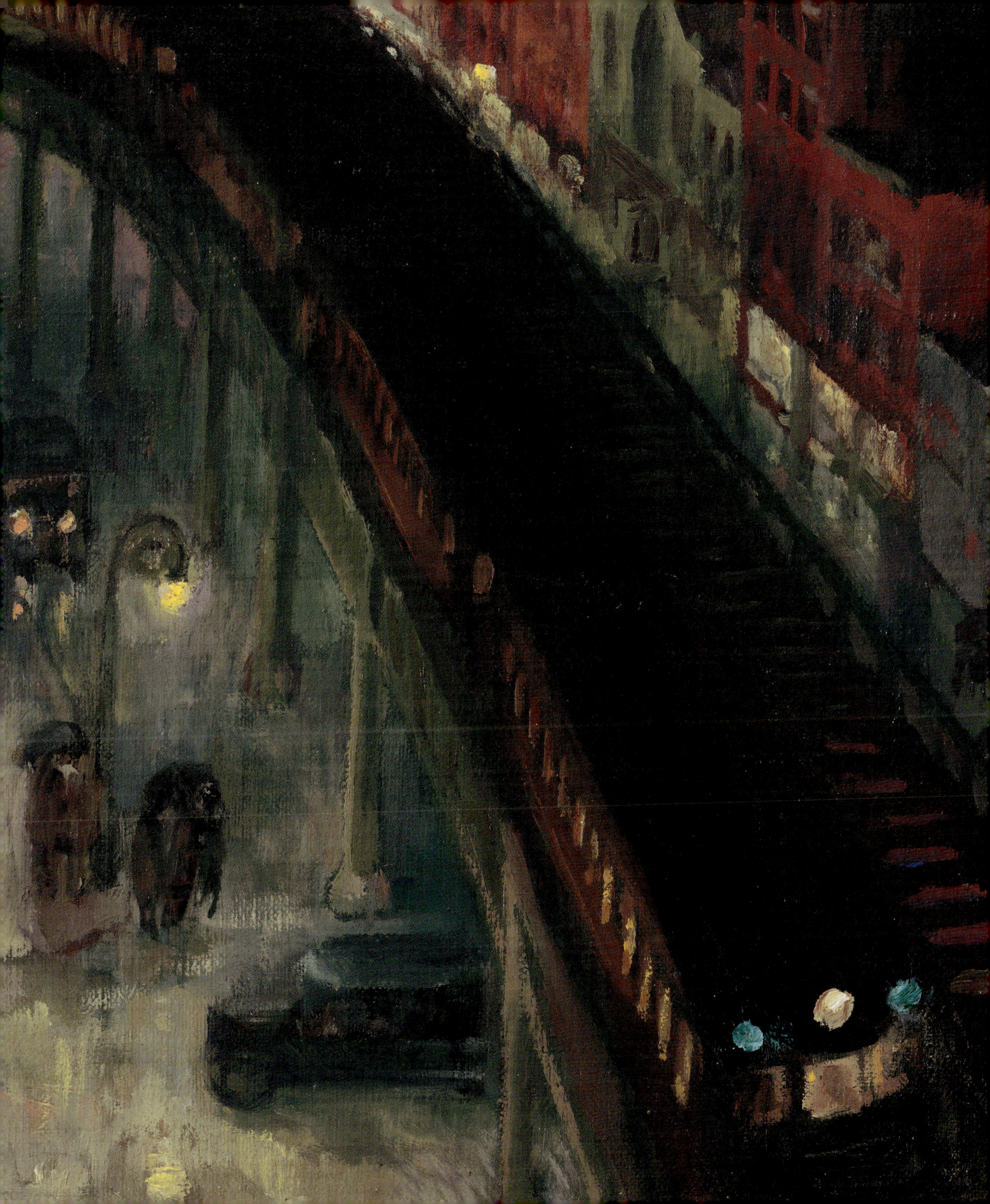

Ernest Lawson
(American, born Canada, 1873-1939)
Excavation–Penn Station, ca. 1906

oil on canvas
18⅛ × 24¼ in.

Collection of the Weisman Art Museum at the University of Minnesota, Minneapolis

Bequest of Hudson D. Walker from the Ione and Hudson D. Walker Collection, 1978.21.845

Cat. 10

Henry Farny
(American, born France, 1847-1916)
Morning of a New Day, 1907

oil on canvas
22 × 32 in.

National Cowboy & Western Heritage Museum, Oklahoma City

Museum Purchase, 1998.72.07

Cat. 3

Samuel J. Woolf
(American, 1880-1948)
The Under World, ca. 1909-10

oil on canvas
22½ × 30½ in.

Virginia Museum of Fine Arts, Richmond

Funds provided by a private Richmond foundation, 95.101

SHELBURNE AND DIXON ONLY

Cat. 31

John Marin
(American, 1870-1953)
Grain Elevator, ca. 1910-15

oil on canvas
16⅜ × 19⅜ in.

Promised Gift to Crystal Bridges Museum of American Art, Bentonville, Arkansas

Cat. 20

John Sloan
(American, 1871-1951)
Six O'Clock, Winter, 1912

oil on canvas
26⅛ × 32 in.

The Phillips Collection, Washington, DC

Acquired 1922

Cat. 11

Leon Kroll
(American, 1884-1974)
Terminal Yards, 1912-13

oil on canvas
46 × 52⅛ in.

Flint Institute of Arts, Flint, Michigan

Gift of Mrs. Arthur Jerome Eddy, 1931.4

Cat. 13

Gifford Beal
(American, 1879-1956)
Freight Yards, 1915

oil on canvas
45 × 57 in.

Collection of the Everson Museum of Art

Museum purchase by the Friends of American Art Fund, PC 15.80

JOSLYN ONLY

Cat. 14

Ernest Lawson
(American, born Canada, 1873-1939)
Washington Bridge, Harlem River, ca. 1915

oil on canvas
20 × 24⅟₁₆ in.

High Museum of Art, Atlanta

J.J. Haverty Collection, 49.38

Cat. 15

Edmund Charles Tarbell
(American, 1862-1934)
In the Station Waiting Room, Boston, ca. 1915

oil on canvas
24⅜ × 32 in.

Crocker Art Museum

Gift of Dr. Joseph R. Fazzano, 1956.7

Cat. 33

Georgia O'Keeffe
(American, 1887-1986)
Train Coming in–Canyon, Texas, 1916

watercolor on paper
9¾ × 8¼ in.

Collection of the Amarillo Museum of Art

Purchased with funds from the National Endowment for the Arts, Amarillo Area Foundation, Amarillo Art Alliance, Fannie Weymouth, Santa Fe Industries Foundation and Mary Fain, AM.1982.1.4

Cat. 21

Joseph Stella
(American, 1877-1946)
Man in the Elevated (Train), 1916
oil, wire, and collage on glass
14¼ × 14¾ in.
Mildred Lane Kemper Art Museum,
Washington University in St. Louis
University purchase, Kende Sale Fund,
1946, WU 3806
Cat. 30 *(not in exhibition)*

Walter Pach
(American, 1883-1958)
The Subway, 1919
oil on canvas
26 × 31 in.
Saint Louis Art Museum
Gift of John and Susan Horseman,
in honor of Melissa Wolfe, Curator of
American Art, 106:2019
DIXON AND JOSLYN ONLY
Cat. 32

Hugo Robus
(American, 1885-1964)
Train in Motion, ca. 1920
oil on canvas mounted on fiberglass
26¼ × 32⅛ in.
Smithsonian American Art Museum
Gift of Mr. and Mrs. Hugo Robus, Jr.,
1978.153.2
Cat. 19 *(not in exhibition)*

John Sloan
(American, 1871-1951)
The City from Greenwich Village, 1922
oil on canvas
26 × 33¾ in.
National Gallery of Art, Washington, DC
Gift of Helen Farr Sloan, 1970.1.1
Cat. 12

Otto Kuhler
(American, born Germany, 1894-1977)
Steel Valley, Pittsburgh, ca. 1925
oil on canvas
45 × 50 in.
The Westmoreland Museum
of American Art
Gift of Mr. Richard M. Scaife, 2004.2
Cat. 8

George Ault
(American, 1891-1948)
From Brooklyn Heights, 1925
oil on canvas
30 × 20 in.
Collection of The Newark
Museum of Art
Purchase, 1928, 28.1802
Cat. 23

Thomas Hart Benton
(American, 1889-1975)
New Mexico (Landscape), 1926
oil and tempera on panel
20 × 26 in.
Denver Art Museum
Funds from Hellen Dill bequest, 1937.2
Cat. 22

Thomas Hart Benton
(American, 1889-1975)
Engineer's Dream, 1931
oil on panel
29⅞ × 41¾ in.
Memphis Brooks Museum of Art
Eugenia Buxton Whitnel Funds, 75.1
Cat. 35

Reginald Marsh
(American, 1898-1954)
Gathering the Mail, 1934
fresco on cement
37⅝ × 47¾ in.
Palmer Museum of Art at Penn State
Purchased with funds provided by the
Friends of the Palmer Museum of Art,
85.3
Cat. 37

Charles T. Bowling
(American, 1891-1985)
Church at the Crossroads, 1936
oil on board
24 × 30 in.
Anonymous, courtesy of the
Dallas Museum of Art
Cat. 24

Harry Gottlieb
(American, 1895-1992)
Dixie Cups, 1936-37
oil on canvas
24⅛ × 41 in.
Wichita Art Museum
Museum purchase, Friends of the
Wichita Art Museum, Director's
Discretionary Fund, 1982.42
Cat. 38

Aaron Bohrod
(American, 1907-1992)
Slag Heaps, 1938

oil on canvas
24 × 30 in.

Sheldon Museum of Art,
University of Nebraska-Lincoln

Allocation of the U.S. Government,
Federal Art Project of the Works
Progress Administration, WPA-106.1943

Cat. 17

Charles Goeller
(American, 1901-1955)
Factory Yard, ca. 1938

oil on canvas
42½ × 33½ in.

Collection of The Newark Museum of Art

Bequest of the artist, 1955, 55.104

Cat. 25

Joe Jones
(American, 1909-1963)
All the Live Long Day, 1939

oil on paper mounted on board
16 × 29⅝ in.

Art Gallery of Hamilton

Gift of Mr. Herman H. Levy, O.B.E., 1961

Cat. 39

Harry Leith-Ross
(American, born Mauritius, 1886-1973)
Tenant's House and Tracks,
ca. late 1930s

oil on canvas
24 × 26 in.

Private collection

Cat. 16

Allan Rohan Crite
(American, 1910-2007)
The Carstop, 1940

oil on canvas
37¼ × 31¼ in.

Boston Athenaeum

UR75

Cat. 34

Thomas Hart Benton
(American, 1889-1975)
The Wreck of the Ole '97, 1943

egg tempera on gessoed Masonite
28½ × 44½ in.

Hunter Museum of American Art,
Chattanooga, Tennessee

Gift of the Benwood Foundation,
1976.3.2

JOSLYN ONLY

Cat. 36

Jacob Lawrence
(American, 1917-2000)
*Subway—Home from Work
(In the Evening the Mother and
Father Come Home from Work)*, 1943

gouache on paper
14⅜ × 21¾ in.

Virginia Museum of Fine Arts, Richmond

Gift of the Alexander Shilling Fund,
44.18.1

Cat. 42

Henry Sugimoto
(American, 1900-1990)
When can we go home?, 1943

oil on canvas
32½ × 23¼ in.

Japanese American National Museum

Gift of Madeleine Sugimoto and Naomi
Tagawa, 92.97.3

Cat. 26

Philip Evergood
(American, 1901-1973)
Wheels of Victory, ca. 1944

oil on panel
37¾ × 42½ in.

Collection of the Weisman Art Museum
at the University of Minnesota,
Minneapolis

Bequest of Hudson D. Walker from the
Ione and Hudson D. Walker Collection,
1978.21.830

Cat. 41

Carl Frederick Gaertner
(American, 1898-1952)
Swamp Spur, 1944

oil on canvas
24 × 40 in.

The John and Susan Horseman
Collection, Courtesy of the
Horseman Foundation

Cat. 18

Anna Mary Robertson "Grandma" Moses
(American, 1860-1961)
Cambridge, 1944
oil on Masonite
20¼ × 24⅜ in.
Shelburne Museum
Museum purchase, acquired from
Otto Kallir, 1961-210.1
Cat. 46

Palmer C. Hayden
(American, 1890-1973)
His Hammer in His Hand, from the
Ballad of John Henry series, ca. 1944-47
oil on canvas
27 × 33 in.
Museum of African American Art,
Los Angeles
Cat. 40

William Charles Libby
(American, 1919-1982)
Lanterns, 1945
tempera on board
27⅛ × 17¾ in.
Carnegie Museum of Art, Pittsburgh
Gift of Mr. and Mrs. James H. Beal,
63.1.5
Cat. 29

Louise Emerson Rönnebeck
(American, 1901-1980)
End of Summer, 1945
oil/tempera on canvas
26 × 36¼ in.
Private collection
Cat. 43

Edward Hopper
(American, 1882-1967)
Approaching a City, 1946
oil on canvas
27⅛ × 36 in.
The Phillips Collection, Washington, DC
Acquired 1947, 0923
Cat. 26a

Norman Rockwell
(American, 1894-1978)
Crestwood Commuter Station, 1946
oil on canvas
22 × 20¾ in.
Private collection
Cat. 44

George Tooker
(American, 1920-2011)
The Subway, 1950
tempera on composition board
18½ × 36½ in.
Whitney Museum of American Art,
New York
Purchase, with funds from the Juliana
Force Purchase Award, 50.23
DIXON AND JOSLYN ONLY
Cat. 45

Kay Sage
(American, 1898-1963)
Unusual Thursday, 1951
oil on canvas
31¾ × 38¾ in.
New Britain Museum of American Art
Gift of Mrs. Naum Gabo, 1978.90
Cat. 27

Otto Kuhler
(American, born Germany, 1894-1977)
Work Train at Wagonmound, n.d.
oil on canvas
23⅝ × 29⅝ in.
Collection of the New Mexico
Museum of Art
Gift of Otto August Kuhler, 1976,
3648.23P
Cat. 9

Carroll Cloar
(American, 1913-1993)
The Red Caboose, 1964
Casein tempera on Masonite
22½ × 31½ in.
Private collection
Cat. 28

BIBLIOGRAPHY

Aldrich, Mark. "Combating the Collision Horror: The Interstate Commerce Commission and Automatic Train Control, 1900-1939." *Technology and Culture* 34, no. 1 (January 1993): 49-77.

Alex, Lynn M. *Iowa's Archaeological Past*. Iowa City: University of Iowa Press, 2000.

Arnesen, Eric. *Brotherhoods of Color: Black Railroad Workers and the Struggle for Equality*. Cambridge, MA: Harvard University Press, 2001.

Association of American Railroads. "Chronology of America's Freight Railroads." Accessed September 6, 2023. https://www.aar.org/chronology-of-americas-freight-railroads/.

Barrett, Ross. "Bursting the Bubble: John Quidor's Money Diggers and Land Speculation." *American Art* 30, no. 1 (Spring 2016).

Bedell, Rebecca. "Asher Durand's *Progress* Reconsidered." *Panorama: Journal of the Association of Historians of American Art* 5, no. 1 (Spring 2019). https://doi.org/10.24926/24716839.1688.

Bookbinder, Judith Arlene, and Sheila Gallagher, eds. *First Hand: Civil War Era Drawings from the Becker Collection*. Chestnut Hill, MA: McMullen Museum of Art at Boston College, 2009. Exhibition catalogue.

Bowes, John P. *Land Too Good for Indians: Northern Indian Removal*. Norman: University of Oklahoma Press, 2016.

Burns, Sarah. *Pastoral Inventions: Rural Life in Nineteenth-Century American Art and Culture*. Philadelphia: Temple University Press, 1989.

Carter, Ian. *Railways and Culture in Britain: The Epitome of Modernity*. Manchester: Manchester University Press, 2001.

The Centennial Exposition: Catalogue of the Exhibition of Paintings, Sculptures, Graphic Arts. Dallas: Dallas Museum of Fine Arts, 1936. Exhibition catalogue.

Cat. 13: Leon Kroll, *Terminal Yards* (detail), 1912-1913; Flint Institute of Arts, Flint, Michigan

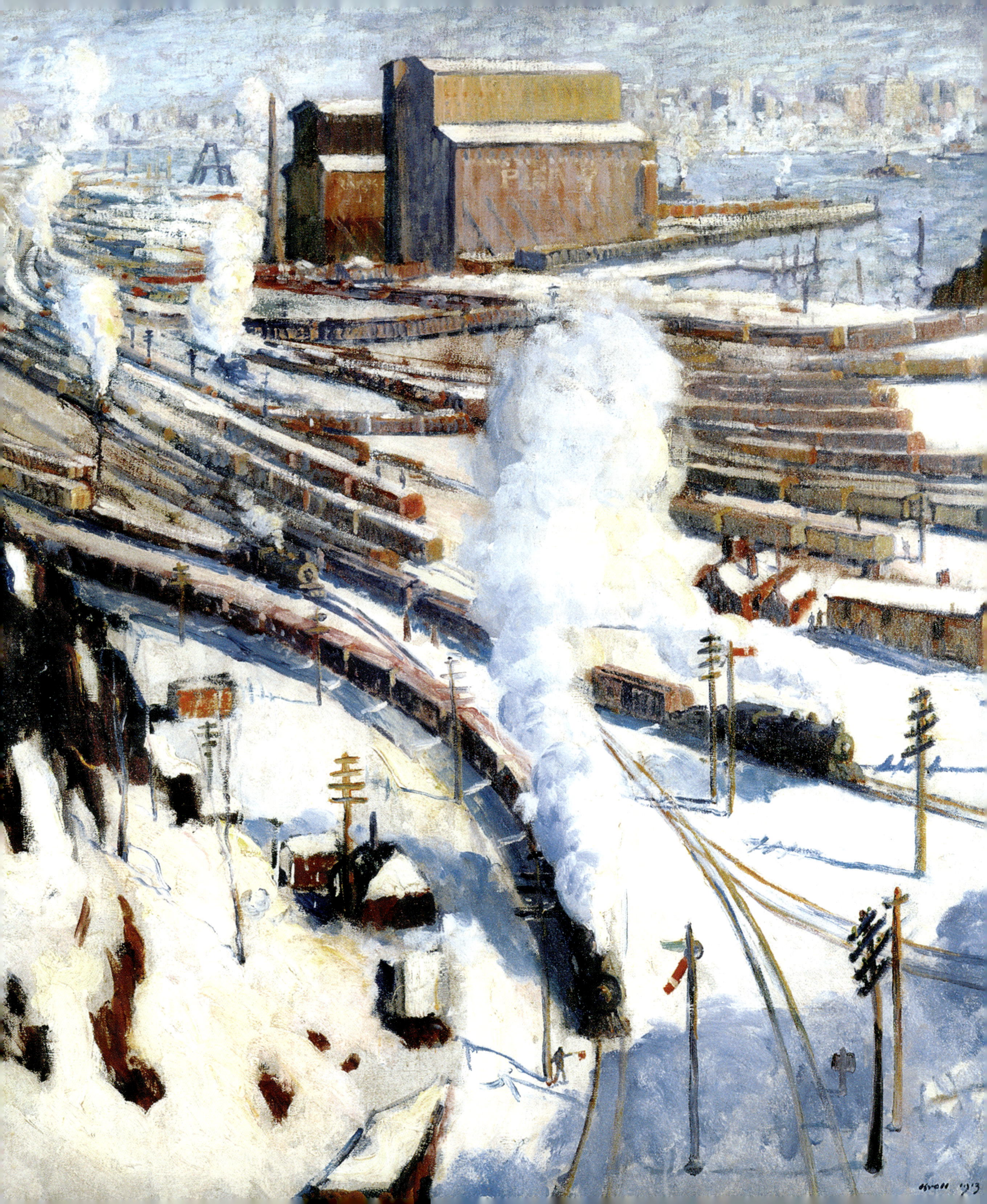
Kroll 1913

Chang, Gordon H. *Ghosts of Gold Mountain: The Epic Story of the Chinese Who Built the Transcontinental Railroad*. New York: Houghton Mifflin Harcourt, 2019.

Chang, Gordon H., and Shelley Fisher Fishkin, eds. *The Chinese and the Iron Road: Building the Transcontinental Railroad*. Redwood City, CA: Stanford University Press, 2019.

Chappell, Gordon. "American Diesel-Electric Locomotives." In *Steam over Scranton: The Locomotives of Steamtown*. Special History Study, Steamtown National Historic Site, Pennsylvania. Washington, DC: National Park Service, 1991. https://www.nps.gov/parkhistory/online_books/steamtown/shs.htm.

Coming Home: American Paintings, 1930-1950, from the Schoen Collection. Athens: Georgia Museum of Art, 2003. Exhibition catalogue.

Cowart, Jack, Juan Hamilton, and Sarah Greenough. *Georgia O'Keeffe: Art and Letters*. Washington, DC: National Gallery of Art, 1987.

Cuthbert, John A. *Early Art and Artists in West Virginia: An Introduction and Biographical Directory*. Morgantown: West Virginia University Press, 2000.

Daughton, J. P. *In the Forest of No Joy: The Congo-Océan Railroad and the Tragedy of French Colonialism*. New York: W. W. Norton & Company, 2021.

Dearinger, Ryan. *The Filth of Progress: Immigrants, Americans, and the Building of Canals and Railroads in the West*. Oakland: University of California Press, 2016.

Decker, Julio. "Lines in the Sand: Railways and the Archipelago of Colonial Territorialization in German Southwest Africa, 1897-1914." *Journal of Historical Geography* 70 (October 2020): 74-87.

Depew, Chauncey M. *My Memories of Eighty Years*. New York: C. Scribner & Sons, 1924.

Dippie, Brian W. *The Vanishing American: White Attitudes and U.S. Indian Policy*. Middletown, CT: reian University Press, 1982.

Doezema, Marianne. *George Bellows and Urban America*. New Haven, CT: Yale University Press, 1992.

Emotion Expressed through Precision: The Art of Charles Goeller. New York: Franklin Riehlman Fine Art, 2003. Exhibition catalogue.

Fine, Ruth E. *John Marin*. New York: Abbeville Press, 1990.

Francaviglia, Richard. *Go East, Young Man: Imagining the American West as the Orient*. Logan: Utah State University Press, 2011.

Gage, John. *Turner: Rain, Steam and Speed*. London: Allen Lane the Penguin Press, 1972.

Gottfried, Herbert. *Erie Railway Tourist, 1854-1886: Transporting Visual Culture*. Bethlehem, PA: Lehigh University Press, 2018.

Graff, Nancy Price, and E. Thomas Pierce, eds. *Charles Louis Heyde, Nineteenth Century Vermont Landscape Painter: With Catalogue Raisonné*. Burlington, VT: Robert Hull Fleming Museum, 2001.

Hughes, Langston. *The Weary Blues*. New York: Alfred A. Knopf, 1926.

Hughes, Langston. *Fine Clothes to the Jew*. Alfred A. Knopf, 1927.

Hughes, Langston. *The Big Sea: An Autobiography*. New York and London: Alfred A. Knopf, 1940.

Jensen, Kiersten M. *Industrial Sublime: Modernism and the Transformation of New York's Rivers, 1900-1940*. New York: Fordham University Press, 2013.

Kahn, Sonia. "What Goes Up Must Come Down: A Brief History of New York City's Elevated Rail and Subway Lines." *Worlds Revealed: Geography and Maps at the Library of Congress* (blog), Library of Congress, May 19, 2022. https://blogs.loc.gov/maps/2022/05/what-goes-up-must-come-down-a-brief-history-of-new-york-citys-elevated-rail-and-subway-lines.

Karuka, Manu. *Empire's Tracks: Indigenous Nations, Chinese Workers, and the Transcontinental Railroad*. Oakland: University of California Press, 2019.

Kennedy, Ian. "Crossing Continents: America and Beyond." In *The Railway: Art in the Age of Steam*, edited by Ian Kennedy and Julian Treuherz, 119-54. New Haven, CT: Yale University Press, 2008. Exhibition catalogue.

Kim, Kristine. *Henry Sugimoto: Painting and American Experience*. Los Angeles: Japanese American National Museum; Berkeley, CA: Heyday, 2001. Exhibition catalogue.

Knighton, Andrew Lyndon. *Idle Threats: Men and the Limits of Productivity in Nineteenth Century America*. New York: New York University Press, 2012.

Kornweibel, Theodore. *Railroads in the African American Experience: A Photographic Journey*. Baltimore: Johns Hopkins University Press, 2010.

Larsen, Lawrence H. *Upstream Metropolis: An Urban Biography of Omaha and Council Bluffs*. Lincoln: University of Nebraska Press, 2007.

Levin, Gail. *Edward Hopper: An Intimate Biography*. New York: Alfred A. Knopf, 1995.

Lewis, David L. *The Public Image of Henry Ford: An American Folk Hero and His Company*. Detroit: Wayne State University Press, 1976.

Lozowick, Louis. "The Americanization of Art." In *Machine-Age Exposition: Catalogue*, 18-19. New York, 1927. Exhibition catalogue.

Marx, Leo. *The Machine in the Garden: Technology and the Pastoral Ideal in America*. Oxford: Oxford University Press, 1964.

Maddox, Kenneth W. "Thomas Cole and the Railroad: Gentle Maledictions." *Archives of American Art Journal* 30, no. 1/4 (1990).

Mauldin, G. E. "South Carolina Canal and Railroad." *The Railway and Locomotive Historical Society Bulletin*, no. 17 (October 1928): 70-80.

Meyn, Susan L. *Henry Farny Paints the Far West*. Cincinnati: Cincinnati Art Museum, 2007. Exhibition catalogue.

Miller, Perry. *The Life of The Mind in America: From the Revolution to the Civil War*. New York: Harcourt, Brace & World, 1965.

Miller, Stephen Robeson, and Jonathan Stuhlman. *Double Solitaire: The Surreal Worlds of Kay Sage and Yves Tanguy*. Katonah, NY: Katonah Museum of Art; Charlotte: Mint Museum, 2011. Exhibition catalogue.

Morrissey, Charles T. "More Than Embers of Sentiment: Railroad Nostalgia and Oral History Memories of the 1920s and 1930s." *Public Historian* 15, no. 3 (Summer 1993): 29-35.

Mukhopadhyay, Aparajita. *Imperial Technology and "Native" Agency: A Social History of Railways in Colonial India, 1850-1920*. New York: Routledge, 2018.

National Park Service. "Andrew J. Russell." Golden Spike National Historical Park, Utah. Last updated July 9, 2021. https://www.nps.gov/gosp/learn/historyculture/a-moment-in-time.htm.

National World War II Museum. "All Aboard! National World War II Museum Opens New Train Exhibit." Press release, November 11, 2013. https://www.nationalww2museum.org/media/press-releases/all-aboard-national-wwii-museum-opens-new-train-exhibit.

Neff, Emily B. *The Modern West: American Landscapes, 1890-1950*. New Haven, CT: Yale University Press, 2006. Exhibition catalogue.

Nemerov, Alexander. *To Make a World: George Ault and 1940s America*. New Haven: Yale University Press, 2011. Exhibition catalogue.

Novak, Barbara. *Nature and Culture: American Landscape and Painting, 1825-1875*. New York: Oxford University Press, 1980.

Nye, David E. *American Technological Sublime*. Cambridge, MA: MIT Press, 1994.

Nye, David E. *America as Second Creation: Technology and Narratives of New Beginnings*. Cambridge, MA: MIT Press, 2003.

Ott, John. *Manufacturing the Modern Patron in Victorian California: Cultural Philanthropy, Industrial Capital, and Social Authority*. Burlington, VT: Ashgate, 2014.

Pennsylvania Railroad Company. *Catalogue of the Exhibit of the Pennsylvania Railroad Company at the World's Columbian Exposition*. Chicago: Pennsylvania Railroad Company, 1893.

Penny, H. Glenn. *Kindred by Choice: Germans and American Indians Since 1800*. Chapel Hill: University of North Carolina Press, 2013.

Porterfield, Nolan. *Jimmie Rodgers: The Life and Times of America's Blue Yodeler*. Urbana, Chicago, and London: University of Illinois Press, 1979.

Pullman Museum. "The Pullman Company." Pullman History Site. April 2020. https://www.pullman-museum.org/theCompany/.

Pyne, Peter. *The Panama Railroad*. Bloomington: Indiana University Press, 2021.

Roob, Alexander. "Thomas Nast and Theodor Kaufmann: Higher Forms of Hieroglyph." Melton Prior Institute. November 10, 2012. https://www.meltonpriorinstitut.org/content/en/thomas-nast-and-theodor-kaufmann-higher-forms-of-hieroglyph-alexander-roob.

Romanski, Fred J. "The Fast Mail: A History of the U.S. Railway Mail Service." *Prologue Magazine* 37, no. 3 (Fall 2005).

Salter, Darren. "Brotherhood of Sleeping Car Porters (1925-1978)." BlackPast.org. November 24, 2007. https://www.blackpast.org/african-american-history/brotherhood-sleeping-car-porters-1925-1978/.

Sander, Kathleen Waters. *John W. Garrett and the Baltimore and Ohio Railroad*. Baltimore: Johns Hopkins University Press, 2017.

Schivelbusch, Wolfgang. *The Railway Journey: The Industrialization of Time and Space in the 19th Century*. Berkeley: University of California Press, 1977.

Schulman, Vanessa Meikle. *Work Sights: The Visual Culture of Industry in Nineteenth-Century America*. Amherst: University of Massachusetts Press, 2015.

Spiers, Edward M. *Engines for Empire: The Victorian Army and Its Use of Railways*. Manchester: Manchester University Press, 2017.

Stebbins, Jr., Theodore E., and Norman Keyes, Jr. *Charles Sheeler, the Photographs*. Boston: Museum of Fine Arts, 1987. Exhibition catalogue.

Stilgoe, John R. *Metropolitan Corridor: Railroads and the American Scene*. New Haven, CT: Yale University Press, 1985.

Stilgoe, John R. "Smiling Scenes." In *Views and Visions: American Landscape before 1830*, edited by Edward J. Nygren with Bruce E. Robertson, 213-28. Washington, DC: Corcoran Gallery of Art, 1986. Exhibition catalogue.

Stowell, David O. *Streets, Railroads, and the Great Strike of 1877*. Chicago: University of Chicago Press, 1999.

Sweeney, J. Gray. "Racism, Nationalism, and Nostalgia." In *Race-ing Art History*, edited by Kymberly N. Pinder, 155-68. New York: Routledge, 2002.

Taft, Robert. "The Pictorial Record of the Old West: XI. The Leslie Excursions of 1869 and 1877—Joseph Becker, Harry Ogden and Walter Yeager." *Kansas Historical Quarterly* 18, no. 2 (May 1950): 113-39.

Tarbell, Roberta K. *Hugo Robus (1885-1964)*. Washington, DC: Published for the National Collection of Fine Arts by the Smithsonian Institution Press, 1980. Exhibition catalogue.

Thomas, Stanton. *The Crossroads of Memory: Carroll Cloar and the American South*. Little Rock: Arkansas Art Center, 2014. Exhibition catalogue.

Thompson, Slason. *A Short History of American Railways: Covering Ten Decades*. New York and London: D. Appleton & Company, 1925.

Truettner, William H. "Ideology and Image: Justifying Westward Expansion." In *The West as America: Reinterpreting Images of the Frontier, 1820-1920*, edited by William H. Truettner, 31-32. Washington, DC: Published for the National Museum of American Art by the Smithsonian Institution Press, 1991. Exhibition catalogue.

Tsujimoto, Karen. *Images of American Precisionist Painting and Modern Photography*. Seattle: Published for the San Francisco Museum of Modern Art by University of Washington Press, 1982. Exhibition catalogue.

Turner, Frederick Jackson. "The Significance of the Frontier in American History (1893)." In *The Frontier in American History*, edited by Frederick Jackson Turner, 1-38. New York: Henry Holt & Company, 1920.

Vong, Sam. "The Impact of the Transcontinental Railroad on Native Americans." *O Say Can You See? Stories from the Museum* (blog), National Museum of American History, June 3, 2019. https://americanhistory.si.edu/blog/TRR.

Waddell, J. A. L. *Memoirs and Addresses of Two Decades*. Easton, PA: Mack Printing Company, 1928.

Wagner, Ann Prentice. *1934: A New Deal for Artists*. Washington, DC: Smithsonian American Art Museum in association with D Giles Limited, 2009. Exhibition catalogue.

Waite, Thornton. *Attacking the Union Pacific: The Truth and the Legend behind the 1867 Cheyenne Indian Raid at Plum Creek, Nebraska*. David City, NE: South Platte Press, 2020.

Wallach, Alan. "Thomas Cole's *River in the Catskills* as Antipastoral." *Art Bulletin* 84, no. 2 (June 2002): 334-50.

Walther, Susan Danly. *The Railroad in the American Landscape: 1850-1950*. Wellesley, MA: Wellesley College Museum, 1981. Exhibition catalogue.

White, Richard. *Railroaded: The Transcontinentals and the Making of Modern America*. New York and London: W. W. Norton & Company, 2011.

Wigmore, Deedee. *Reginald Marsh (1898-1954): Urban Realist, Master of Many Media*. New York: D. Wigmore Fine Art, 2008.

Wilson, Richard Guy. *The Machine Age in America, 1918-1941*. New York: Harry N. Abrams, 1986.

RAILROAD CHRONOLOGY

Ellen Daugherty

1815

The first railroad charter in the United States is granted to Revolutionary War veteran and steam power pioneer John Stevens.

1823

March

Spurred by commercial rivalries between New York, Philadelphia, and Baltimore, the Pennsylvania State Legislature authorizes construction of the eighty-two-mile Philadelphia & Columbia Railway as part of the Main Line of Public Works of the State of Pennsylvania. The nickname "The Main Line" is still in use in suburban Philadelphia.

1825

The Erie Canal opens, joining the Hudson River with Lake Erie, thus providing a transportation route between New York City and the Midwest.

1826

John Stevens demonstrates the feasibility of steam locomotion on a circular track in Hoboken, New Jersey, three years before George Stephenson perfects a practical steam locomotive in England.

1827

February 28

The Baltimore & Ohio becomes the first US railway chartered for commercial transportation of freight and passengers. The B&O is intent on accessing the Midwest and provides Baltimore, America's second-largest city at the time, with the means to compete with New York and the Erie Canal.

1828

July 4

Construction begins on the B&O, which has fourteen miles of track by the end of 1830. The B&O relies on horsepower. Horse-drawn railways persist for many decades, including the Omaha Horse Railway, operational 1867-89.

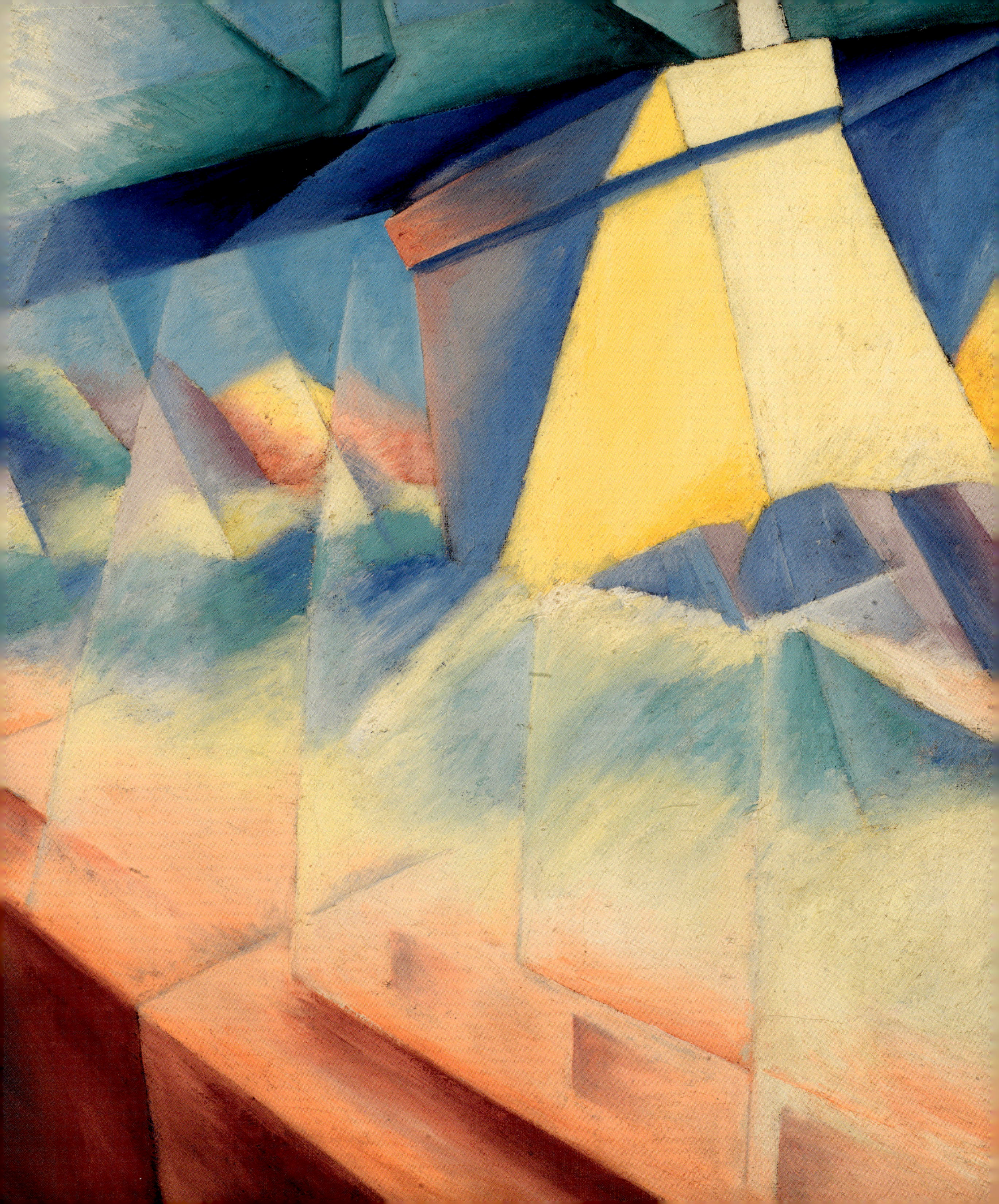

1830

The Camden and Amboy Railroad and Transportation Company is founded—one of many eastern railroad companies to incorporate in the 1830s, including the Boston and Providence Railroad (1831), the Bangor and Piscataquis Railroad (1832), and the Nashua and Lowell Railroad (1835).

Peter Cooper demonstrates that his "Tom Thumb" steam locomotive can pull a load of forty people at ten miles per hour.

1831

A steam locomotive of American manufacture is in service on the B&O.

1833

The South Carolina Canal and Rail Road Company's 136 miles of track comprises the longest steam railroad in the world.

1837

The Panic of 1837 and ensuing economic depression slow railroad construction.

1838

July 7

To strengthen postal service in the West, Congress declares that all railroads are post roads.

1830s–1860s

An extensive network of southern railroads is built primarily by enslaved labor. Men grade tracks while women and children move dirt, pick stones, and cook. Slaves with specialized skills, such as blacksmiths, work on construction crews. Southern railroad companies own or lease enslaved people, record their purchase and sale in balance sheets and account books, and annually report to stockholders on investments in human "property" and enslaved labor.

1841

March 19

William Lloyd Garrison publishes "Rebuke of the Eastern Railroad Company, for their Treatment of Colored Passengers" in the *Liberator*. Segregation on railroads, often remembered as a Jim Crow and Civil Rights Era issue, has a long history in the United States.

1843

The Western Railroad of Massachusetts is complete, reviving interest in the industry after the depression of the 1830s and 1840s.

1845

January

Asa Whitney, a New York merchant active in the China trade, petitions Congress for a charter and land grant to construct a railroad from Wisconsin across the Rocky Mountains to the Pacific. The chief opponent is Senator Thomas Hart Benton (D–MO) who argues for a route originating at St. Louis.

1846

The Pennsylvania Railroad, known as the PRR or the "Pennsy," is established with headquarters in Philadelphia. At its peak, the PRR is the largest corporation in the world.

1848

January 24

Gold is discovered at Sutter's Mill near Coloma, California.

February 2

The Treaty of Guadalupe Hidalgo, ending the Mexican-American War, cedes territory including all or part of what will become Arizona, California, Colorado, Kansas, Nevada, New Mexico, Oklahoma, Utah, and Wyoming—from Mexico to the United States. Territorial expansion concurrent with the gold rush increases interest in new railroad routes.

1850

Federal land is granted to the Illinois Central Railroad. Previously, funding sources for railroad construction had come mostly from private investment or indirectly from the government in the form of subsidies for route surveys by Army engineers.

1853

March

The Army Appropriation Act directs Secretary of War Jefferson Davis "to ascertain the most practicable and economical route for a railroad from the Mississippi River to the Pacific Ocean." The Army's Topographical Corps surveys four east-west routes roughly following specific latitude parallels, including between the 47th and 49th parallels, the 38th and 39th parallels (eventually moved to the 41st parallel due to fears of Native American attacks), the 35th parallel, and the 32nd parallel (the eventual path of the Southern Pacific Railroad). A fifth north-south survey assesses possible passes through the Sierra Nevadas and the California Coast Range.

1857

The Pennsylvania Railroad purchases the Philadelphia & Columbia Railway for $7.5 million. The PRR now has a continuous track from Philadelphia to Pittsburgh.

Late 1850s

Congress stalemates over the issue of where to build a transcontinental railroad due to sectional conflicts.

1862

May 20

Abraham Lincoln signs the Homestead Act allowing any loyal US citizen to claim 160 acres of western land, live on it and improve it for five years, then file for a deed of title at a local land office.

July 1

The Pacific Railway Act designates the 32nd parallel as the initial transcontinental route and provides government bonds and large land grants for rights of way. The legislation authorizes the Union Pacific and the Central Pacific to construct a railroad and telegraph line from the Missouri River to the Pacific Ocean and secures the use of that line for the government. Together with the Homestead Act, this law encourages increased settlement of the West.

1863

The Union Pacific Railroad employs more than eight thousand Irish, German, and Italian immigrants to build its rail line west from Omaha, while the Central Pacific Railroad's workforce, including as many as twenty thousand Chinese laborers, builds eastward from Sacramento.

1867

June

Chinese workers for the Central Pacific Railroad receive 30–50 percent lower wages and endure worse working conditions than white laborers. To protest, they hold an eight-day strike demanding $40 per month, no more than a ten-hour workday, and shorter shifts in dangerous tunnels. White railroad executives refuse to budge, and eventually most workers return to their jobs.

1869

April 1

George Westinghouse receives a patent for the air brake, substantially improving railroad safety by allowing the engineer to control braking instantly from the cab. Previously, brakemen went from car to car, often atop a moving train, to apply brakes manually. Hypothermia, loss of fingers, and death under the train's wheels were common fates.

May 10

The transcontinental railroad is completed at Promontory Summit, Utah, with the driving of a ceremonial 17.6-karat golden spike by railroad baron Leland Stanford. More than a thousand people attend the ceremony. Andrew J. Russell's photograph captures the Union Pacific's No. 119 engine and the Central Pacific's Jupiter nearly touching on their respective sections of track while workers and engineers celebrate with champagne and the railroads' chief engineers shake hands.

The completion of the transcontinental railroad impacts many Indigenous communities and changes their ways of life. Lakota peoples find their ability to move freely through the land following buffalo herds compromised while Pawnee men provide protection for railroad labor crews and gain access to wage labor.

1870s
"The Ballad of John Henry" possibly emerges out of actual events surrounding the construction of the Chesapeake & Ohio's Big Bend Tunnel in Talcott, West Virginia.

1877
July 16
The Great Railroad Strike begins in Martinsburg, West Virginia, after the B&O enacts a series of wage and job cuts, and quickly spreads throughout the country to other railroads, including the PRR, and to cities such as Pittsburgh, Buffalo, and Chicago. Although more than 100,000 workers participate, the strikes collapse because of lack of organization.

1878
The first reliable elevated train in New York opens. The "El" carries passengers from lower Manhattan to Harlem along Greenwich Street and 9th Avenue.

1887
The Interstate Commerce Act creates the Interstate Commerce Commission (ICC), making the railroads the first industry subject to federal regulation.

The Pullman Palace Car Company is chartered in Illinois. George Pullman and his former business partner Benjamin C. Field had been building sleeping cars since 1857. The Pullman Company becomes a foremost manufacturer of five classes of cars: hotel, parlor, reclining room, sleeper, and diner.

1890s
Railroad safety becomes a public preoccupation. Although standardized accident reporting does not yet exist, statistics in the *Railroad Gazette* indicate that 5,623 people were killed and 20,445 injured in railroad accidents between 1883 and 1892.

1890-1910
Boom in railway station building. Railway taxes triple during this period.

1893
March 2
The Railroad Safety Appliance Act requires mandatory use of air brakes and automatic couplers on all trains by 1900. Prior to automatic couplers, the "link and pin" method of connecting railroad cars was common, requiring workers to work between heavy cars and manually hook them together. Injuries incurred while manually coupling cars represented 44 percent of total railroad casualties.

May-October
The World's Columbian Exposition in Chicago is a showcase for the railroad industry. The PRR has its own exposition building filled with train technology, ephemera, and William Rau's photographs of operational and scenic views along all PRR lines. The Pullman Company displays a commemorative set of model railroad cars in its building. More than 27 million visitors could travel inside the fairgrounds on the Intramural Railway.

Cat. 15: Ernest Lawson, *Washington Bridge, Harlem River* (detail), ca. 1915; High Museum of Art, Atlanta

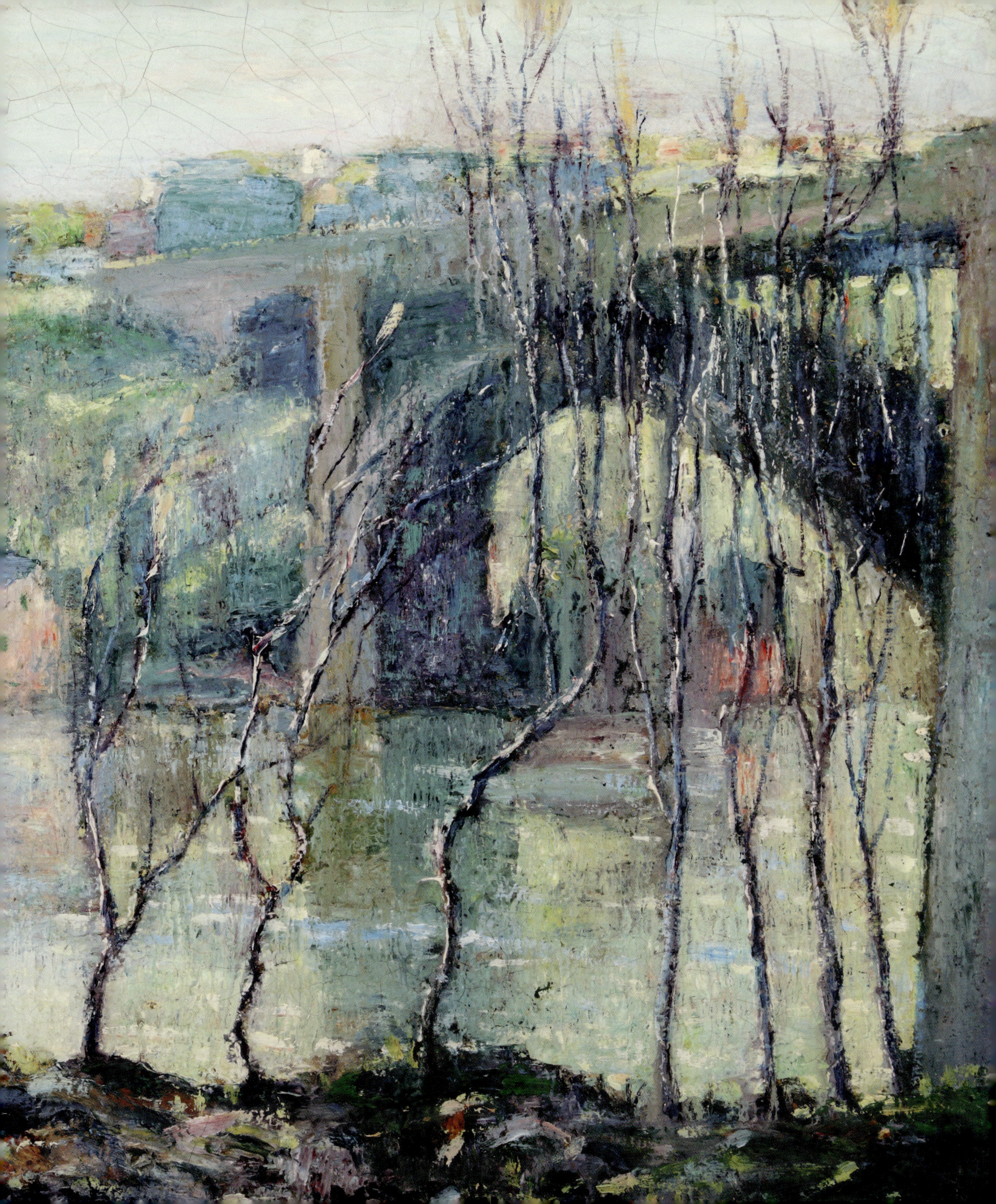

Ida B. Wells writes scathingly about segregation laws targeting railroad passengers in the booklet *The Reason Why the Colored American Is Not in the World's Columbian Exposition*.

1894

First publication of the song "I've Been Working on the Railroad." Like many folk songs, it is an amalgam of spirituals, blues, blackface minstrelsy, and Irish songs.

1903

February 19

The Elkins amendment to the Interstate Commerce Act strengthens the ICC's ability to forbid special rates or other means of offering preferential treatment to businesses that ship large quantities of goods.

Edwin S. Porter's silent film *The Great Train Robbery*, the story of a gang of outlaws who rob a train in the American West, is a commercial success.

1904

Construction begins on Pennsylvania Station in Manhattan. Covering two city blocks from 31st to 33rd Streets between 7th and 8th Avenues, the McKim, Mead & White design is one of the masterpieces of American Beaux-Arts architecture.

1905

The Office of Public Roads is created and offers advisory services on road construction to federal agencies. Nevertheless, there are only 161,000 miles of surfaced roads in the United States and rail networks dominate transportation.

1906

April 18

An earthquake and fire devastate San Francisco. The Southern Pacific Railroad evacuates upwards of 225,000 refugees, or more than 50 percent of the total population of the city.

June 29

The Hepburn Act gives the ICC the power to set maximum rates for both passengers and shippers using the railroad. The law is endorsed by President Theodore Roosevelt, who sees it as a compromise between unfettered competition that could lead to monopolies and government ownership of the railroads.

28 December

Alexander Cassatt, seventh president of the Pennsylvania Railroad and the brother of Mary Cassatt, dies. Alexander presided over the PRR during a period of massive expansion that included the projects to tunnel under the Hudson and East Rivers, bringing trains into Manhattan and the new Pennsylvania Station.

1907

The Panic of 1907 crushes railroad earnings. Recovery doesn't happen until 1910.

October 27

The first train arrives at Union Station Terminal in Washington, DC. Designed by architecture firm D. H. Burnham & Company, it is the only railroad station in the nation specifically authorized by Congress.

1910

The Mann–Elkins Act (Rail Rate Act of 1910) strengthens the ICC by giving it absolute authority over setting railroad rates.

May 6

The Accident Reports Act requires that railroad carriers file reports with the secretary of transportation on "all accidents and incidents resulting in injury or death to an individual or damage to equipment or a roadbed arising from the carrier's operations." Investigatory authority over accidents is eventually delegated to the Federal Railroad Administration after its creation in 1966.

September 8

Pennsylvania Station opens.

1911

June 4

Chicago and Northwestern Passenger Terminal opens, the second-largest train terminal in the US after Penn Station.

1913

February 2

Grand Central Terminal (commonly called Grand Central Station) opens at midnight. The station includes special "kissing galleries" where travelers can greet those who have come to meet them.

1916

September 2

To avoid a strike, Congress bows to labor demands and passes the Adamson Act, which makes an eight-hour workday and overtime pay standard for railroad workers.

1917

April 6

The United States enters World War I. The Railroad War Board is formed at the outset to support the war effort by running their lines in a coordinated manner.

December 28

President Woodrow Wilson forms the United States Railroad Administration, nationalizing the railroads for the duration of WWI.

1918

November 11

WWI ends.

United States Railroad Administration sets standards for locomotive and car design.

1920s

The hegemony of railroads is challenged by the Army Corps of Engineers, which improves rivers and canals, making barges more competitive with the rails again. Automobiles and buses change personal transportation patterns, and trucks compete for freight hauling. The US Postal service authorizes airmail contracts, cutting into another source of railroad profit.

Railroad enthusiasts emerge as a group. Lionel, American Flyer, and other manufacturers sell model trains.

1920

28 February

The Esch-Cummins Act (Transportation Act of 1920) returns railroads to private ownership.

The US railroad network is near its peak, with 253,000 miles of track operated by more than 1.5 million employees working for 1,000 railroad companies.

1921

The number of railroad passengers reaches an all-time high.

1922

July 1

The Great Railroad Strike (Railway Shopmen's Strike) begins as 400,000 shopmen and maintenance workers protest the Railroad Labor Board's wage cuts following the end of WWI. Violence escalates and ten men are killed before the railroad brotherhoods suffer a crushing defeat and are forced back to work on the railroads' terms.

Rising numbers of deadly train collisions cause Congress and the ICC to mandate that all railroads with high-speed passenger service over eighty miles per hour introduce Automatic Train Control, which safely stops trains should engineers miss signals.

1924

"The Wreck of the Old '97," a song telling the tale of the September 27, 1903, crash of the "Fast Mail" train running between Monroe, Virginia, and Spencer, North Carolina, is recorded by Vernon Dalhart. Although sales numbers are hard to verify, this record reputedly becomes country music's first million-selling hit.

1925

New Union Station in Chicago is dedicated.

A. Phillip Randolph and Milton P. Webster found the Brotherhood of Sleeping Car Porters, a labor union of 12,000 Black Pullman employees and an early civil rights organization.

October 20
The American Locomotive Company sells the first diesel–electric locomotive in the US. Other companies, including Baldwin Locomotive Works, Westinghouse Electric Company, and General Motors, also begin producing diesel locomotives, which are faster, more fuel efficient, and require less maintenance than steam locomotives.

Slason Thompson publishes *A Short History of American Railways* (D. Appleton & Company), one of several publications aimed at the growing number of railroad enthusiasts in the country.

There are now 521,000 miles of surfaced roads in the United States.

1926

May 20
The Railway Labor Act is the first federal law that guarantees the right of workers to unionize and elect representatives without employer interference.

Buster Keaton's silent film *The General*, about a loyal Confederate train engineer who tries to save his beloved locomotive after it is taken by Union spies, is a flop. Nevertheless, railroads become central to many other popular films, such as the *Perils of Pauline* series.

1927

Hudson 4-6-4 locomotives (characterized by four leading wheels, six coupled driving wheels, and four trailing wheels) built by the New York Central exemplify "big steam" of the 1920s.

Cleveland's Terminal Tower, a 52–story, 771–foot skyscraper serving as an office building atop the Cleveland Union Terminal, is completed and ready for tenants. Built during the skyscraper boom period, it is the tallest building in the US outside of New York until 1967.

Construction on Philadelphia's 30th Street Station begins.

1929

Cincinnati's Union Terminal, an Art Deco palace, is begun.

October 29
The stock market collapse known as "Black Friday" signals the start of the Great Depression. Railroad traffic drops immediately.

1930

Spring
Unemployment rises to nearly 4,000,000.

One in every five Americans owns an automobile.

1932

June
Unemployment reaches 12,000,000, the worst point in the Great Depression.

By the end of the year, net profits for railroads fall from $977 million in 1929 to $122 million in 1932. Railroads won't be profitable again until 1937. Railroad employment falls 42 percent.

1933/34

John and Alan Lomax record Huddie William "Lead Belly" Ledbetter's performance of "The Midnight Special" at Angola Prison in Louisiana. The song, about a passenger train on the Chicago & Alton Railroad that left St. Louis nightly at 11:30 p.m. and arrived the next morning in Chicago, is one of many train–themed African American work songs, blues, spirituals, and ballads.

1936

Intermodal transportation begins when the Chicago Great Western Railroad moves several hundred truck trailers on specially modified flatcars.

1941

"Chattanooga Choo Choo" by Mack Gordon and Harry Warren is among the popular train songs of the Swing Era. Others include "On the Atchison, Topeka, and the Santa Fe" by Harry Warren and Johnny Mercer, and Billy Strayhorn's "Take the A Train," made famous by Duke Ellington.

December 8

The United States enters World War II.

1941-45

During WWII, railroads enjoy a renaissance as they coordinate to move troops, military supplies, goods, and regular passengers. American railroads provide 44 million rides (or about three rides apiece) to 16 million service men and women during the war.

1945

September 2

WWII ends.

There are now 1,721,000 surfaced roads in the United States.

New York's Penn Station reaches its peak year for travel, with 109 million travelers passing through.

1948-49

The Chicago Railroad Fair, featuring *Wheels a-Rolling*, a daily musical production complete with vintage rolling stock, celebrates a century of railroading in the Windy City. The fair is one of the last of its kind.

1953

Junior Parker's hit "Mystery Train" is released. Elvis Presley's version appears in 1955.

1956

The Federal-Aid Highway Act creates the interstate highway system, furthering the decline of rail passenger service.

1960

With automobile and air travel on the rise, train travel declines to just 27 percent of all intercity traffic.

1963

October 28

The demolition of Penn Station terminal begins as part of a plan for the PRR to recoup income by razing its now largely empty terminal and renting its air space.

INDEX

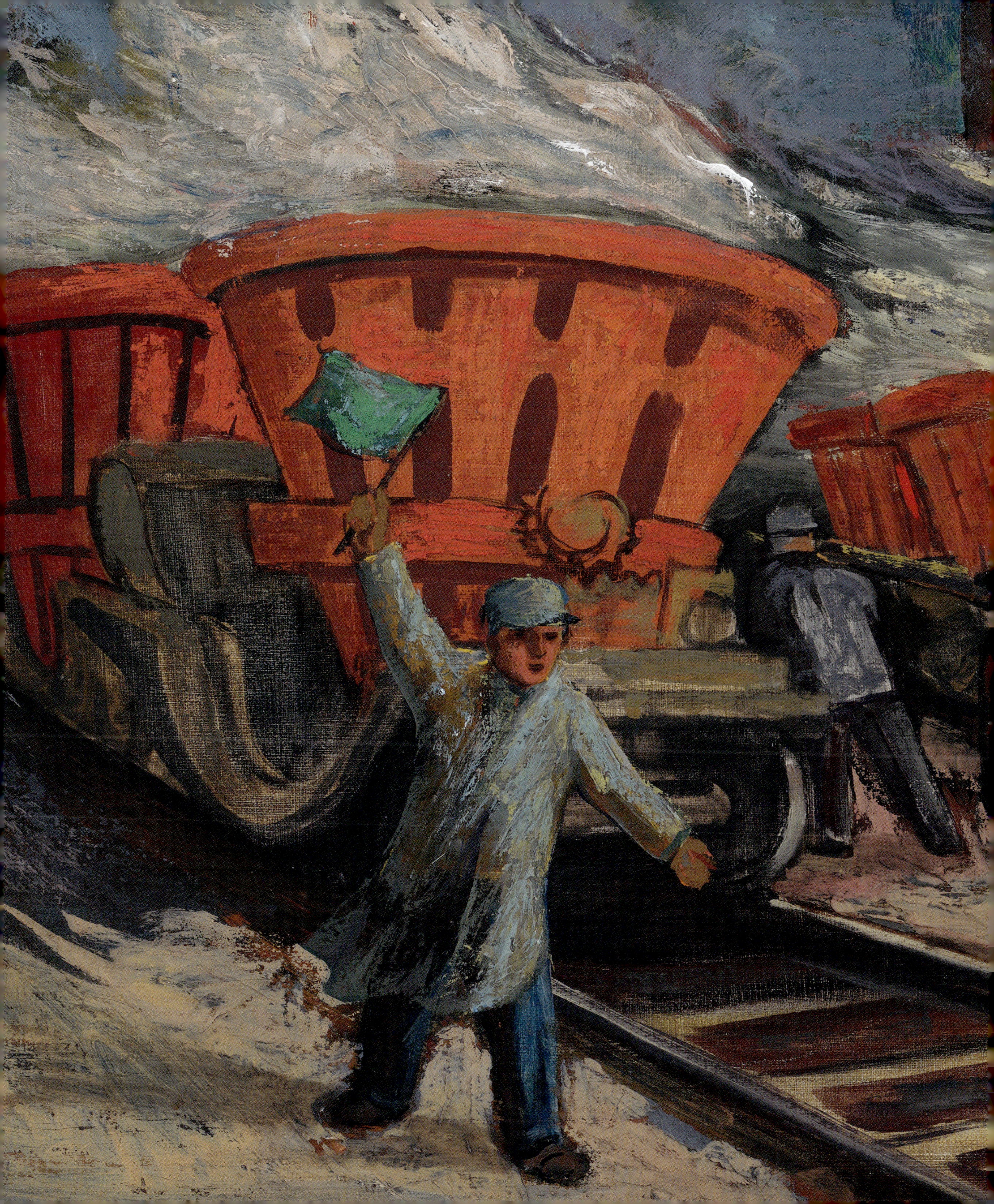

PHOTO CREDITS

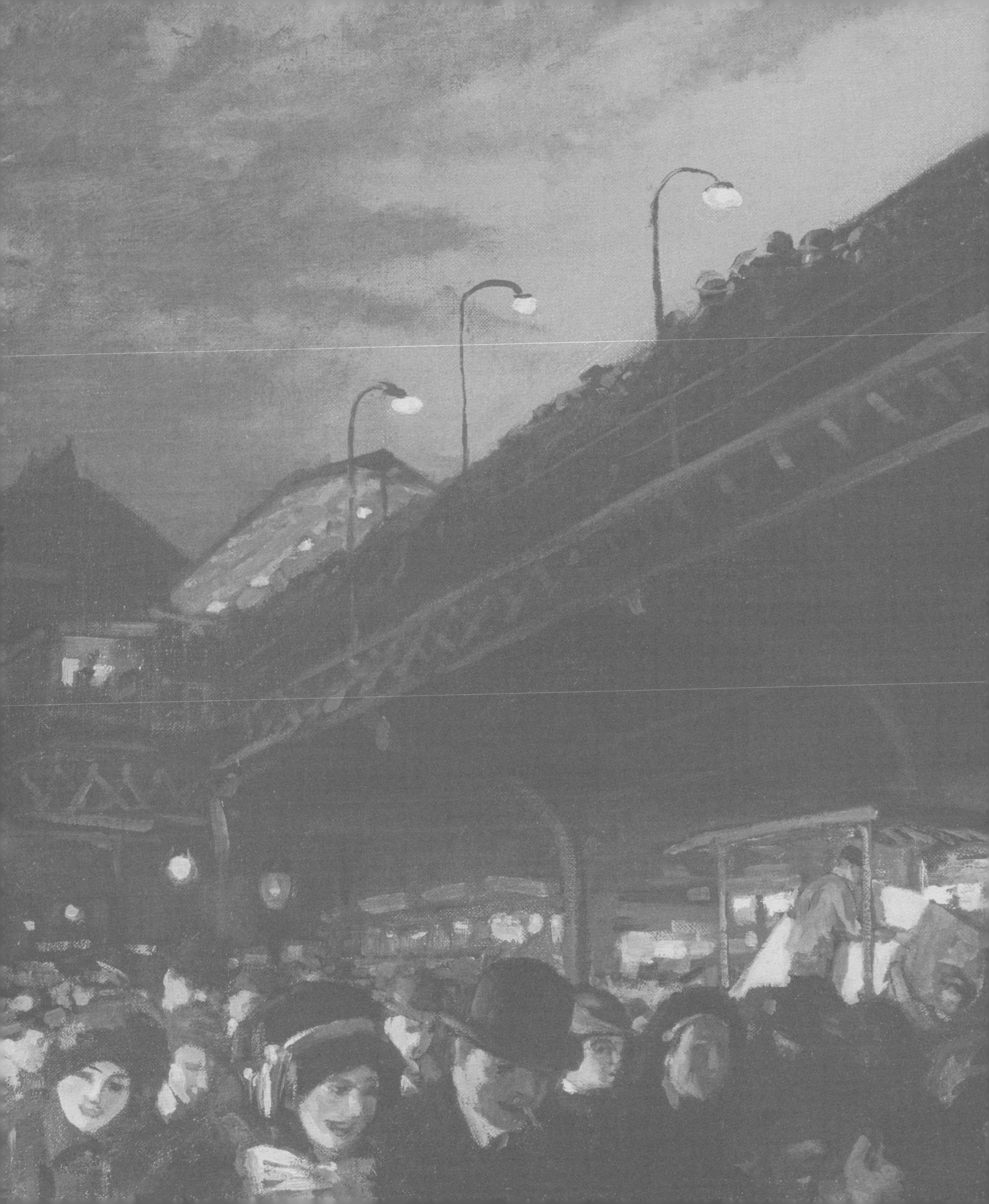